Organizational Culture - Cultural Change and Technology

Edited by Muddassar Sarfraz and Wasi Ul Hassan Shah

Published in London, United Kingdom

Organizational Culture - Cultural Change and Technology
http://dx.doi.org/10.5772/intechopen.111316
Edited by Muddassar Sarfraz and Wasi Ul Hassan Shah

Contributors
Tihana Babić, Matea Cvjetković, Dinko Herman Boikanyo, Jacek Grodzicki, Peter Paul Kithae, Kazuyuki Maeda, Ritu Mishra, Suruchi Pandey, Saumya Singh, Leonard Bright, Kivanc Bozkus, Barbara Mazur

First published in London, United Kingdom, 2024 by IntechOpen
IntechOpen is the global imprint of INTECHOPEN LIMITED, registered in England and Wales, registration number: 11086078, 5 Princes Gate Court, London, SW7 2QJ, United Kingdom
Printed in Croatia

British Library Cataloguing-in-Publication Data
A catalogue record for this book is available from the British Library

Additional hard and PDF copies can be obtained from orders@intechopen.com

Organizational Culture - Cultural Change and Technology
Edited by Muddassar Sarfraz and Wasi Ul Hassan Shah
p. cm.

This title is part of the Business, Management and Economics Book Series, Volume 16
Topic: Business and Management
Series Editor: Taufiq Choudhry
Topic Editors: Vito Bobek and Tatjana Horvat

Print ISBN 978-1-83769-318-4
Online ISBN 978-1-83769-319-1
eBook (PDF) ISBN 978-1-83769-320-7
ISSN 2753-894X

For EU product safety concerns:
IN TECH d.o.o., Prolaz Marije Krucifikse Kozulić 3, 51000 Rijeka, Croatia,
info@intechopen.com or visit our website at intechopen.com.

IntechOpen Book Series

Business, Management and Economics

Volume 16

Aims and Scope of the Series

This series will provide a comprehensive overview of recent research trends in business and management, economics, and marketing. Topics will include asset liability management, financial consequences of the financial crisis and covid-19, financial accounting, mergers and acquisitions, management accounting, SMEs, financial markets, corporate finance and governance, managerial technology and innovation, resource management and sustainable development, social entrepreneurship, corporate responsibility, ethics and accountability, microeconomics, labour economics, macroeconomics, public economics, financial economics, econometrics, direct marketing, creative marketing, internet marketing, market planning and forecasting, brand management, market segmentation and targeting and other topics under business and management. This book series will focus on various aspects of business and management whose in-depth understanding is critical for business and company management to function effectively during this uncertain time of financial crisis, Covid-19 pandemic, and military activity in Europe.

Meet the Series Editor

Prof. Choudhry holds a BSc degree in Economics from the University of Iowa, as well as a Masters and Ph.D. in Applied Economics from Clemson University, USA. In January 2006, he became a Professor of Finance at the University of Southampton Business School. He was previously a Professor of Finance at the University of Bradford Management School. He has over 80 articles published in international finance and economics journals. His research interests and specialties include financial econometrics, financial economics, international economics and finance, housing markets, financial markets, among others.

Meet the Volume Editors

Dr. Muddassar Sarfraz is an assistant professor at the School of Management, Zhejiang Shuren University, China. He is also a member of the Research Center for Engineering and Management at the Politehnica University of Timisoara, Romania. After completing a prestigious post-doctoral fellowship in business administration at Hohai University, China, he worked as a researcher and lecturer at various prominent institutions. Dr. Sarfraz has taught a diverse range of subjects, including business research methods, business management, corporate social responsibility, business strategy, and strategic management. His reputation as a keynote speaker at national and international conferences further highlights his expertise and influence in the academic community. With an impressive publication record, Dr. Sarfraz has contributed more than 150 papers to international academic journals and conferences, showcasing his dedication to advancing knowledge in his field. In addition to his scholarly contributions, he is an associate and guest editor for numerous journals, as well as an editorial board member for several others. Dr. Sarfraz's professional affiliations include memberships in the British Academy of Management, the Chinese Economists Society, the World Economic Association, and the American Economic Association. Furthermore, he represents Pakistan as an ambassador for the international MBA program at Chongqing University, China.

Dr. Wasi Ul Hassan Shah, an assistant professor and researcher at Zhejiang Shuren University, China, holds a Ph.D. from the Southwestern University of Finance and Economics, China, with a specialization in Management Science and Engineering. With a prolific research background, Dr. Shah has authored forty-seven journal papers on finance, economics, and management. His research spans performance evaluation and efficiency estimation, encompassing banking efficiency, environmental efficiency, energy efficiency, agricultural production efficiency, and water usage efficiency. Proficient in Data Envelopment Analysis (DEA), Dr. Shah applies this methodology across diverse sectors, including hospitals, agriculture, and manufacturing. Demonstrating a commitment to academic excellence, his impactful contributions enhance organizational efficiency and management practices, leaving a lasting mark on the academic landscape.

Contents

Preface

Today, the significance of cultural change within organizations is impossible to ignore. The organizational culture is the ultimate way of addressing a firm's problems. One reason for this is that organizations empowering change are presumably open to new ideas in every sphere. Changes in organizational culture are crucial for marginalizing a firm's activities. Organizational cultural change is a broad concept that elevates individuals' interest in firms' patterns, beliefs, values, and assumptions. Technology is the main driver of change within organizations. New technologies have helped firms advance in today's turbulent market through a wide cultural shift.

This edited volume, *Organizational Culture – Cultural Change and Technology*, is a collection of nine chapters that examine organizational cultural change from diverse perspectives. This book highlights the following topics:

- The strategic significance of organizational cultural change in today's world

- Opportunities and challenges of organizational change facilitated by technological implementation

- The role of individuals (i.e., organizations, employees, management, stakeholders) in organizational cultural change

- The outcomes of cultural change (i.e., innovation, competitiveness, performance, behavior, retention, employee satisfaction, etc.)

Chapter 1, "Organizational Culture Change and Technology: Navigating the Digital Transformation", highlights market demands to integrate new tools and techniques that are exceptional in bringing about change. This chapter is a well-written academic piece that explores the relationship between technology and organizational culture change in today's world.

Chapter 2, "Organizational Culture in Enterprises Applying the Humanistic and Economic Paradigm of Management", helps to understand how modern societies have altered the view of change as necessary. The need for change empowers employees to humanize the internal work environment. Under the humanistic approach, this topic determines the relationship between the management paradigm and the organizational culture's dependencies, references, and values.

Chapter 3, "The Impact of Technological Advances on Cultural Conflicts within Organizations", indicates how organizations have embraced technologies to influence their values and conventions. As technology affects a firm's behavior, norms, and performance, it shows that cultural heritage supported by digitalization leads to misunderstanding and hostilities.

Chapter 4, "Does Stress Type Matter? Clarifying the Relationships between Public Service Motivation, Work-Related Stress, and Employee Attitudes", highlights stress as the most common characteristic altering a firm's working environment. This chapter explores the relationship between public service motivation and environmental, organizational, and job stress, which has a direct effect on employee job satisfaction and turnover.

Chapter 5, "Organizational Culture as an Analytical Perspective on 'Organizational Failure'", suggests that the knowledge-based economy brings a major shift in the organizational models. This chapter shows that to function smoothly in a knowledgeable society, universities are required to function as organizations.

Chapter 6, "The Role of Organizational Climate in Cultural Transformation", explores the most common dimensions of the workplace climate and their influence on organizational culture. The employee's efficiency and productivity depend on the organization's climate. This chapter analyzes the employees' work duties and their effect on the organization's system and work culture.

Chapter 7, "The Role of Employee Behavior and Organizational Culture in Strategy Implementation and Performance in a VUCA World", examines how, today, organizations encountering numerous challenges need to adopt profound approaches that influence employee behavior and organizational culture. The cultural orientation enables firms to cope with market volatility, uncertainty, complexity, and ambiguities. This chapter emphasizes the need for effective strategy execution and employee behavior in achieving high performance in a world with volatility, uncertainty, complexity, and ambiguity (VUCA).

Chapter 8, "Interplay between Technology and Culture in Driving Change for Employee Satisfaction", expresses the synergetic relationship between technology, organizational culture, and employee satisfaction.

Chapter 9, "The Influence of Employer Brand Dimensions on the Affective Organizational Commitment of Employees in Small and Medium-Sized Enterprises", emphasizes building a healthy workplace by identifying the implements of employees' branding.

The volume includes the latest theoretical developments that are vital for driving organizational change. It highlights the concept that integrates new thinking, feelings, and intuitions needed for steering the change in the business culture. This book is a valuable guide for organizations, practitioners, writers, and professional audiences. The editor appreciates all those who contributed to the success of this book. We sincerely thank all the individuals who energetically supported us in this endeavor.

Muddassar Sarfraz and Wasi Ul Hassan Shah
School of Management,
Zhejiang Shuren University,
Hangzhou, PR China

Section 1

Global Perspectives on Digital Organizational Culture

Chapter 1

Organizational Culture Change and Technology: Navigating the Digital Transformation

Kivanc Bozkus

Abstract

The chapter investigates the critical relationship between technology and organizational culture change. It presents a framework that elucidates the interplay between technological adoption and the ensuing cultural shifts within organizations. The author delves into the various stages of the digital transformation process, examining the challenges and opportunities that organizations encounter as they integrate new technologies. By drawing on real-world examples and case studies, the chapter underscores the pivotal role that organizational leaders play in guiding their teams through these transitions, fostering a culture of adaptability, and promoting a growth mindset. The chapter also explores the importance of addressing the human element in digital transformation efforts, emphasizing the need to effectively manage change, overcome resistance, and bridge skill gaps to ensure a successful transition. Furthermore, the author discusses the ethical implications of adopting new technologies, advocating for a responsible and people-centric approach to innovation. In conclusion, the chapter offers a forward-looking perspective on the future of organizational culture in the digital era, anticipating emerging trends and novel technologies that will continue to shape the way organizations function. This informative chapter provides a valuable resource for understanding and navigating the complex interplay between organizational culture change and technology.

Keywords: organizational culture change, digital transformation, technological adoption, leadership and adaptability, ethical implications

1. Introduction

The digital age has brought about significant transformations in the way we live, work, and interact with one another. Technological advancements have allowed us to connect with people from all over the world, access vast stores of information at our fingertips, and automate a wide range of tasks. As these changes continue to unfold, it is increasingly apparent that technology is not only changing the way we live but also the way we work.

This chapter explores the interplay between organizational culture and technology in the digital era. I delve into the ways that technological advancements have influenced organizational culture and vice versa. I discuss how the adoption of new technologies has affected the way we communicate, collaborate, and make decisions within organizations. I also examine the ethical considerations associated with the use of technology in the workplace such as privacy and data security, job displacement, and environmental impact.

Furthermore, this chapter outlines the future of organizational culture in the digital era. I discuss how remote work arrangements and the increasing significance of diversity and inclusion are expected to impact corporate culture in the future. I also examine how the rapid development of automation and artificial intelligence technologies will continue to influence corporate culture, and the potential effects on employee well-being, work happiness, and mental health as they become more integrated into many facets of organizational life.

Ultimately, the dynamic interplay between organizational culture and technology is complex and multifaceted. As the rate of technological change quickens, businesses must continue to be watchful and proactive in spotting new trends and cutting-edge technologies that will influence organizational culture in the future. By doing this, organizations may foster a culture that is more adaptable, resilient, and inclusive, setting themselves up for long-term success in a setting that is dynamically unstable and uncertain.

2. The framework of the digital transformation

Numerous breakthroughs and technological advancements at the beginning of the digital age have changed how businesses function [1]. The interaction between technological adoption and subsequent cultural shifts inside businesses becomes an intriguing research topic as technology continues to advance at an exponential rate. Understanding the difficulties and opportunities brought on by these developments requires a framework that clarifies this interaction.

Organizations must first recognize the potential advantages of adopting new technologies before the adoption process can begin [2]. This understanding frequently results from a knowledge of the competitive environment and a desire to stay relevant in the face of upheaval [3]. The sheer use of technology, however, does not ensure success. To ensure the successful adoption and utilization of new technologies, corporate culture must undergo a fundamental transition [4].

Technology advances must be successfully implemented, and organizational culture, which is the shared values, assumptions, and beliefs that shape behavior within a company [5], is a key determinant. A positive cultural shift that embraces change is necessary to create an atmosphere in which people feel empowered to try new things, learn new things, and adapt to new ways of doing things [6]. Promoting a growth attitude, open communication, and teamwork are essential components in creating a culture that welcomes technology improvements [7].

It is crucial to take into account both the macro and micro-level factors that have an impact on this relationship in order to better understand how technological adoption and cultural changes interact. On a larger scale, firms are under a great deal of pressure to adapt due to the external environment, which is characterized by quick technological development, escalating competition, and altering customer preferences [8]. Due to this external pressure, businesses must assess their current procedures and consider using new technology in order to stay competitive [9].

Simultaneously, at the micro-level, individual attitudes and behaviors play a vital role in the successful integration of technology within organizations. Research has shown that individual resistance to change can hinder the successful implementation of technological innovations [10]. Thus, organizations must invest in training, skill development, and change management initiatives to ensure employees are equipped to navigate the dynamic landscape shaped by technology [11].

In conclusion, a framework that elucidates the interplay between technological adoption and the ensuing cultural shift within organizations recognizes the complex interdependencies between macro-level environmental factors and micro-level individual behaviors. By understanding this interplay, organizations can better anticipate and navigate the challenges and opportunities that arise from technological advancements, ultimately fostering a culture that supports innovation, adaptability, and growth.

3. Stages of the digital transformation process

The digital transformation process, a multifaceted endeavor, has piqued the interest of scholars and practitioners alike as it involves the integration of new technologies into the core of an organization's operations, fundamentally altering the way it creates and delivers value to customers [12]. As organizations embark on their digital transformation journeys, they encounter a myriad of challenges and opportunities at various stages of the process. A deeper understanding of these stages, in conjunction with the associated challenges and opportunities, is essential for organizations seeking to navigate the complexities of digital transformation.

The acknowledgment of the need for change by an organization and the following creation of a future vision are what define the initial stage of digital transformation [1]. At this stage, firms struggle to determine the most pertinent technology and create a comprehensive strategy that is in line with their main business goals [4]. However, if firms keep a strong emphasis on strategic planning and resource allocation, the chances for growth and greater competitiveness that result from integrating digital technologies can offset these initial hurdles [3].

Organizations must deal with the challenges of integrating new technologies into their existing processes and infrastructure as they go to the deployment stage [13]. Effective change management is essential at this level because firms must deal with potential resistance from staff members who are concerned about how new technologies may affect their jobs and duties [10]. Organizations must make targeted training and skill development investments to promote a culture of learning and flexibility in order to address these issues and seize the potential for increased productivity and efficiency [11].

Organizations refine their usage of new technology and change their processes during the optimization stage of digital transformation to get the most benefit possible from these advances [14]. Organizations at this stage struggle to strike a balance between utilizing the advantages of current technology and remaining adaptable in the face of ongoing technological breakthroughs [6]. Organizations in this stage have opportunities if they can use data and analytics to guide decision-making and promote continuous improvement [15].

The ability of an organization to fully integrate new technologies into its core business processes and culture defines the maturity stage of digital transformation. At this point, the organization has achieved a level of digital readiness that enables it to continuously adapt and innovate in response to changing market conditions [16]. Organizations must negotiate the difficulty of maintaining their innovative edge at this level to avoid becoming complacent and risking falling behind their rivals [9]. Organizations that have successfully traversed the previous phases of digital transformation are well-positioned to use their digital capabilities for sustained growth and competitiveness, thus the prospects in this stage are wide [12].

In conclusion, the process of digital transformation takes place over a number of stages, each of which presents its own set of opportunities and problems for companies. Organizations can more successfully navigate the challenges of digital transformation by understanding the nuances of these stages and the implications that go along with them. In doing so, they will ultimately realize the enormous potential of new technologies to spur growth and competitiveness in the digital age.

4. The role that organizational leaders play in guiding their teams through transitions

Organizational leaders are crucial in supporting their staff through changes, establishing an adaptable culture, and encouraging a growth mentality in the quickly changing digital landscape [6]. Understanding the duties and skills needed of leaders to successfully manage these changes is essential given the growing incidence of digital transformation programs [1].

Leaders must first present a clear vision and strategy that is in line with the larger corporate goals and explain the advantages of adopting new technology as firms undergo digital transformation [12]. By sharing this vision, executives may address team members' potential fears and uncertainties while also instilling a sense of urgency and direction for the organization [17]. Additionally, as the environment is constantly changing, leaders must be adaptable and flexible in order to make changes in reaction to new knowledge and market conditions [9].

The development of a culture that welcomes change and adaptability is essential to guiding teams through digital transformation [5]. Organizational leaders can influence this culture by exhibiting actions that show a willingness to try new things, learn from mistakes, and adapt [18]. Cultivating a culture of adaptation requires fostering open communication, teamwork, and a willingness to challenge the status quo [19].

Additionally, leaders must encourage their team members to adopt a growth mentality [7]. This way of thinking, which is defined by the conviction that skills and intellect can be acquired *via* work and education, has been associated with higher levels of motivation, adaptability, and performance [20]. Leaders may foster a culture where team members feel empowered to adopt novel technology and strategies by praising and rewarding effort, tenacity, and ongoing learning, ultimately spurring innovation and growth [21].

The techniques and tactics used by these leaders to effectively manage the complexity of digital transformation can be better understood by real-world examples and case studies. Microsoft's change under CEO Satya Nadella's direction is one noteworthy example. Nadella realized right once that the company needed a cultural change to encourage innovation and agility in response to the quickly evolving digital landscape [22]. He promoted a growth mindset, urging staff members to embrace a "learn it all" attitude rather than a "know it all" attitude [23]. Microsoft was able to revitalize its product line, enter new markets, and achieve tremendous growth by adopting this attitude [24].

The evolution of DBS Bank, a preeminent financial organization in Asia, is another intriguing case study. DBS Bank started a digital transformation journey under the direction of CEO Piyush Gupta [25]. Gupta promoted an organizational cultural shift by highlighting the value of cooperation, experimentation, and customer-centricity [26]. DBS Bank was able to successfully restructure its business model through these initiatives, utilizing digital technologies to optimize operations, enhance client experiences, and spur innovation [25].

Walmart is a shining example of a business adopting digital transformation to keep its competitive edge in the retail sector. Walmart has made significant investments in its e-commerce capabilities and introduced a number of digital initiatives targeted at improving the consumer experience, such as mobile apps and click-and-collect services, under the direction of CEO Doug McMillon [27]. A culture of innovation and adaptation has been fostered throughout the company thanks to McMillon's leadership, allowing Walmart to maintain its lead in the quickly changing retail sector [28].

These case studies show how essential organizational leaders are in assisting their teams as they undergo digital transformation. These executives have effectively navigated the opportunities and challenges given by the digital revolution by adopting a growth mentality, encouraging an environment of adaptation, and continuously emphasizing customer-centricity.

In summary, organizational leaders are crucial in supporting their teams, while they undergo digital transformation, creating an environment that is flexible, and encouraging a growth attitude. Leaders may successfully negotiate the intricacies of technology change and position their organizations for long-term success in the digital age by fostering four crucial qualities.

5. The human element in digital transformation efforts

For firms hoping to stay competitive in today's ever-changing business environment, digital transformation has become essential. While the successful implementation of new technology is an essential component of these efforts, the human element must also be taken into consideration [1].

Effective change management is essential for handling the human element of digital transformation [17]. This entails creating a distinct vision and strategy, outlining the advantages of change, and including staff members at every stage [12]. Organizational leaders may support the successful integration of new technology while also addressing possible worries and uncertainty among team members by encouraging a culture of adaptability and growth [19].

Overcoming this natural human predisposition to reject change is a major issue in efforts to implement digital transformation [29]. Engaging staff members in decision-making can help overcome this resistance by giving them a sense of ownership and influence over the changes being made [30]. Additionally, supplying continuing assistance, materials, and training can assist staff members in developing the abilities and self-assurance required to adopt new procedures and technology [31].

Another critical component of addressing the human factor in digital transformation is bridging skill gaps. Digital talents are increasingly in demand as businesses adopt new technologies. Organizations must make targeted training and development program investments to provide their personnel with the essential skills and abilities to solve this challenge [32]. Additionally, encouraging an environment of constant learning and development can assist firms in being flexible and adaptable in the face of ongoing technological progress [21].

In conclusion, successful initiatives to implement digital transformation must focus on the human factor. Organizational leaders can assure a smooth transition, utilize the advantages of digital technologies, and position their companies for long-term success in the digital age by skillfully managing change, overcoming resistance, and bridging skill gaps. The different aspects that affect an organization's workforce, such as change management, resistance to change, and the need to fill skill gaps, must be understood by organizational leaders. Leaders may foster a positive environment, where people can adapt, grow, and succeed despite the continuous digital transformation by being proactive and addressing these concerns. In turn, this enhances the organization's long-term success and competitiveness in the rapidly evolving digital landscape.

6. The ethical implications of adopting new technologies

The rapid adoption of new technologies has undeniably revolutionized the way we live and work, offering unprecedented opportunities for innovation, efficiency, and growth. However, the relentless pursuit of technological advancement also raises a number of ethical concerns, necessitating a responsible and people-centric approach to innovation [33].

One significant ethical concern associated with technological adoption is the potential impact on employment and income inequality [34]. As automation and artificial intelligence (AI) increasingly replace human labor in a variety of tasks, there are growing concerns about job displacement and the widening gap between the highly skilled and less-skilled workers [35]. To mitigate these negative consequences, organizations and policymakers must prioritize workforce retraining and skills development, ensuring that individuals have the necessary skills to adapt to the changing labor market [36].

Privacy and data security are also pressing ethical concerns in the digital age as organizations increasingly rely on the collection and analysis of vast amounts of personal data to drive decision-making [37]. The potential misuse of this data, as well as the risk of unauthorized access by malicious actors, raises important questions about the ethical boundaries of data collection and surveillance [38]. Organizations must, therefore, adopt rigorous privacy and security measures, while also being transparent about their data practices and ensuring that individuals have control over their personal information [39].

The environmental impact of technology adoption is another important ethical consideration. While new technologies have the potential to drive sustainability efforts and reduce our environmental footprint, they can also contribute to increased energy consumption and electronic waste [40]. Organizations must carefully consider the environmental implications of their technology choices and strive to minimize their ecological impact through responsible practices such as energy efficiency, recycling, and sustainable sourcing [41].

It is critical for organizational leaders, legislators, and society at large to have continual conversations about the implications of technological adoption in light of these ethical considerations. Stakeholders can collaborate to create frameworks and rules that strike a balance between the pursuit of innovation and the defense of human values, rights, and dignity by encouraging open discourse and ethical thought [42].

Organizations should also give ethical issues top priority when making strategic decisions, focusing on the interests and well-being of those who will be impacted by new technology and their communities [43]. To make sure that ethical issues are promptly addressed and incorporated into organizational procedures, this may entail putting in place ethical monitoring mechanisms, such as the usage of ethics committees or the employment of ethics officers [19].

In the end, overcoming the difficulty of managing the moral ramifications of technological adoption necessitates a team effort and a shared dedication to responsible innovation. Organizations, politicians, and society as a whole may work together to fully utilize the potential of new technologies while preserving the values and principles that define our humanity by acknowledging the significance of ethical considerations and taking a people-centric approach.

In conclusion, there are several ethical ramifications of implementing new technology, necessitating a responsible and human-centered approach to innovation. Organizations may choose the technologies they adopt more wisely by taking into account the social, economic, and environmental repercussions of their choices, helping to create a more egalitarian, secure, and sustainable future for all.

7. The future of organizational culture in the digital era

In reaction to new trends and cutting-edge technologies, organizational culture is about to go through considerable changes. The ongoing expansion of remote and flexible work arrangements is one trend that is anticipated to have a significant impact on corporate culture [44]. Since the COVID-19 epidemic has expedited the shift to remote work, firms must reconsider conventional ideas of collaboration, communication, and employee engagement as they adjust to this new reality [45]. It will be necessary to create new procedures and technologies to accommodate a more scattered workforce in addition to placing more focus on encouraging a sense of connectedness and shared purpose among all employees, regardless of where they are physically located [46].

The increasing significance of diversity and inclusion is another significant trend influencing organizational culture in the future [47]. Organizations in the digital age must work to foster a culture that values individuals with varied viewpoints, life experiences, and backgrounds because diverse teams are better able to spark creativity and address challenging issues [48]. This will need, in addition to the adoption of more inclusive hiring and retention procedures, a sincere dedication to developing a culture of decency, empathy, and belonging [49].

In the future, the rapid development of automation and artificial intelligence (AI) technologies will also continue to influence corporate culture [50]. Leaders will need to consider the moral ramifications of adopting these technologies, as well as their potential effects on employee well-being, work happiness, and mental health as they become more integrated into many facets of organizational life [33]. Organizations must establish a people-centric innovation strategy to overcome these obstacles, ensuring that the advantages of AI and automation are fairly distributed and that any potential hazards are sufficiently addressed [51].

Organizations must take into account the possible effects of emerging technologies such as blockchain, the Internet of Things (IoT), and virtual reality (VR) on their organizational culture as they look to the future [52, 53]. These innovations have the potential to completely change how workers engage with one another and the company as a whole in terms of communication, collaboration, and decision-making [54]. Organizations must invest in the necessary infrastructure, training, and support, as well as address any potential ethical issues and make sure that staff members can adjust to these new tools and ways of working, in order to fully realize the potential of these technologies [55].

In conclusion, rising technology, changing labor dynamics, and shifting societal norms and expectations will interact in an increasingly complex and dynamic way to define organizational culture in the digital era. Organizations may build a more resilient, adaptable, and inclusive culture that is well-suited to thriving in the digital era by proactively tackling these obstacles and embracing the opportunities given by new technological breakthroughs.

8. The interplay between organizational culture change and technology

As businesses from all industries struggle with the intricate interactions between organizational culture change and technology, the digital era has brought up a wide range of benefits and problems. Technology adoption is both influenced by and results from organizational culture [5]. Organizations frequently undergo significant cultural changes as they embrace and integrate new technologies into their daily operations. These cultural changes can have an impact on whether these technology projects are successful or unsuccessful [56]. For instance, the implementation of communication and collaboration technologies can result in a culture that is more transparent and open, which would increase employee engagement and collaboration [57]. On the other hand, the use of monitoring and surveillance technologies might foster a climate of distrust and apprehension that eventually works against the organization's goals [37].

It is important to incorporate knowledge from many disciplines in order to comprehend this dynamic interaction better. For instance, organizational behavior provides insightful viewpoints on how people and teams interact with and are influenced by technology [58]. The fundamental mechanisms that promote successful technology adoption and integration inside businesses can be uncovered by studies by looking at elements such as individual characteristics, motivation, and communication [59].

However, management studies emphasize the structural and strategic aspects of technology adoption, offering guidance to organizational leaders on how to deal with the opportunities and problems presented by new technologies [9]. Technology studies offer a critical lens for examining the broader social, economic, and ethical implications of technology adoption within organizations. This includes understanding the role of leadership in fostering a culture of adaptability and innovation, as well as the significance of aligning technology investments with the organization's broader strategic objectives [33, 60]. Examining the unintended effects of emerging technology and promoting more responsible, human-centered approaches to innovation are some examples of this [42].

It is crucial for executives to comprehend the connections between cultural transformation and technology adoption as firms continue to traverse the digital era and to make use of the wealth of knowledge offered by diverse academic disciplines. To manage change and get over opposition, this requires encouraging a culture of ongoing learning and flexibility among staff members, as well as a growth attitude [7].

Additionally, organizations need to carefully weigh embracing the advantages that come with new technologies with considering the ethical ramifications of doing so [55]. This entails making sure that the advantages of innovation are dispersed fairly, as well as taking into account the potential effects of technology on employee well-being, job happiness, and mental health [33].

Finally, as the rate of technological change quickens, companies must continue to be watchful and proactive in spotting new trends and cutting-edge technologies that will influence organizational culture in the future. By doing this, businesses may foster a culture that is more adaptable, resilient, and inclusive, setting themselves up for long-term success in a setting that is dynamically unstable and uncertain.

In conclusion, by combining knowledge from a variety of disciplines, including organizational behavior, management, and technology studies, it is possible to gain a greater understanding of the intricate interactions between organizational culture change and technology. Organizations may create more effective strategies for handling the potential and challenges of the digital era by incorporating these various viewpoints, ultimately creating a culture that is well-prepared to flourish in the face of constant change and unpredictability.

9. Organizational culture theories and models

The study of organizational behavior and management has long recognized the significance of organizational culture in shaping employee behavior, influencing operational procedures, and impacting overall productivity. To gain insights into the diverse nature of organizational cultures, researchers have developed frameworks and models that offer a multidimensional understanding of cultural characteristics and their implications. By exploring these frameworks and models, organizations can gain valuable insights into their own culture, identify areas for improvement, and foster a positive and productive work environment.

The competing values framework (CVF) suggests four cultural kinds based on the contrasts between internal and exterior focus and flexibility and stability [61]. Clan, adhocracy, hierarchy, and market are a few examples of cultural types that offer insights into the norms, beliefs, and behaviors that distinguish various organizational cultures. The competing values framework's multidimensional structure is based on several theoretical stances. To create the framework, [62] drew influence from several disciplines, including organizational theory, management, and sociology. For a thorough knowledge of organizational culture, the CVF combines ideas from systems theory, organizational effectiveness, and cultural aspects. According to the CVF, there are four main cultural kinds, each of which is distinguished by organizational practices, attitudes, and behaviors.

1. Clan culture: Employee engagement, teamwork, and collaboration are prioritized in clan cultures. Clan cultures encourage a sense of community and prioritize fostering ties within the organization [61].

2. Adhocracy culture: The innovation, entrepreneurship, and adaptability that define adhocracy culture. Adhocracy-based organizations promote experimenting, taking calculated risks, and using a flexible approach to problem-solving [61].

3. Hierarchy culture: In hierarchy cultures, defined procedures, stability, and structure are stressed. Efficiency, defined roles and duties, and obedience to policies are valued in hierarchical organizations [61].

4. Market culture: Market culture places a strong emphasis on achievement, competition, and methods that are results-driven. Customer satisfaction, objective achievement, and attention to external market dynamics are prioritized in organizations with a market culture [61].

The CVF has applications for managing and comprehending organizational culture. The framework's cultural types can have an impact on organizational effectiveness, leadership philosophies, and strategic decision-making [61]. The framework supports attempts to promote cultural transformation, identify cultural gaps, and evaluate the current company culture.

The validity and application of the CVF in various organizational situations have been investigated through empirical investigations. Research by [63] gives proof of the CVF's ability to predict organizational outcomes such as employee commitment, performance, and satisfaction. These studies show the framework's applicability in actual organizational settings and add to its empirical underpinnings.

The Denison model highlighted the four cultural characteristics of engagement, consistency, flexibility, and mission [64]. It investigates the link between these cultural characteristics and organizational efficiency, emphasizing the value of a solid and adaptable culture in obtaining excellent performance. To provide a thorough knowledge of organizational culture, the Denison model draws on a number of theoretical stances. To provide a comprehensive framework, [64] combines ideas from systems theory, social psychology, and organizational behavior. The model places a strong emphasis on four crucial traits that together lead to a good organization: mission, adaptability, involvement, and consistency.

Mission: The Denison model's mission component is concerned with the strategic alignment and coherence of an organization. Strong mission-driven organizations display a common sense of purpose, specific goals, and a well-defined vision [64].

Adaptability: The adaptability dimension looks at an organization's capacity to meet changes and challenges from the outside. It includes traits such as adaptability, creativity, and the ability to learn and grow under challenging circumstances [64].

Engagement, participation, and employee empowerment levels within the organization are all reflected in the involvement dimension. Organizations with a high level of employee involvement encourage collaboration, ownership, and dedication [64].

Consistency: The alignment of systems, processes, and behaviors within the organization is the emphasis of the consistency dimension. Consistent organizations have coherence, distinct values, and a robust culture that penetrates every aspect of their operations [64].

The Denison model has applications in managing and comprehending organizational culture. It offers a framework for evaluating an organization's current cultural strengths and shortcomings, pinpointing opportunities for development, and directing cultural change initiatives.

The three levels of culture described by [65] include artifacts and behaviors, professed values, and underlying presumptions. This approach places a strong emphasis on how shared presumptions and ideas influence company culture, and how it affects how employees behave and make decisions.

According to Schein's three levels of culture paradigm, culture may be seen in three different ways: through objects and actions, professed beliefs, and underlying presumptions. These levels engage in specific interactions that influence organizational culture [65].

Objects and behaviors: On the surface, artifacts and behaviors are how culture is expressed. They comprise the physical setting, signs, customs, language, and the outward behaviors of the group's members [65]. These components offer hints about the deeper facets of culture.

Espoused ideals: Individuals inside the organization's represent their declared ideas and values through their espoused values. They are the clear manifestations of the organization's values, including its mission, objectives, and ethical standards [65]. Embedded values direct behavior and decision-making.

Underlying assumptions: Unconscious or taken for granted, underlying assumptions are the foundation of organizational culture. They are the deeply ingrained attitudes, expectations, and beliefs that shape how members view and interpret the outside world [65]. These presumptions influence behavior and are hard to alter.

The three levels of culture paradigm developed by Schein offers useful applications for comprehending and controlling organizational culture. It offers a guide for evaluating the outwardly apparent behaviors and artifacts, understanding the values upheld, and discovering the underlying presumptions. Organizations may better communicate, establish a healthy work environment, and connect their culture with their strategic goals thanks to this understanding [66].

Clan, adhocracy, hierarchy, and market are the four main organizational culture types identified by the framework provided by the organizational culture assessment instrument (OCAI) created by [61]. This paradigm makes it easier to evaluate and quantify organizational culture, assisting in the discovery of cultural assets and opportunities for development.

The clan, adhocracy, hierarchy, and market organizational cultures are the four categories identified by the competing values framework (CVF), which serves as the foundation for the OCAI model [61]. According to the paradigm, every organization has a dominant culture type that influences its members' beliefs, actions, and practices.

The OCAI model provides useful insights for identifying and controlling organizational culture. It is a structured assessment tool that enables companies to determine the type of culture they currently have and contrast it with the culture they would like to have. This knowledge makes it possible to implement focused interventions that will promote employee engagement, harmonize culture with strategic goals, and boost organizational performance [61].

The adaptability and efficacy of the OCAI model in diverse organizational situations have been confirmed by empirical study. For instance, [67] looked at the connection between organizational culture and organizational success and discovered that there is a correlation between performance and culture congruence. These studies add to the empirical support for the OCAI model and demonstrate its value for comprehending and controlling corporate culture.

10. Technology acceptance models

For organizations and people to succeed in the current digital world, technology must be widely adopted and used effectively. Researchers and practitioners have created a variety of technology acceptance models to better understand and anticipate technology adoption and usage patterns. These models are designed to provide light on the variables affecting people's acceptance and adoption of new technology.

Models of technology adoption act as frameworks for describing people's intent to adopt and use technology. These models take into account a number of variables, such as user beliefs, perceptions, attitudes, and behavioral intentions, that affect the acceptance and adoption of technology.

Technology acceptance model (TAM): Davis' technology acceptance model (TAM) is one of the most popular technology acceptance models [68]. Perceived utility and perceived usability are crucial variables in determining users' attitudes and behavioral intentions toward adopting technology according to TAM.

The UTAUT, or unified theory of acceptance and use of technology [59] created the unified theory of acceptance and use of technology (UTAUT) to combine and expand on a number of earlier technology acceptance models. Performance expectancy, effort expectancy, social influence, and facilitating conditions are the four main factors identified by UTAUT as influencing the uptake of technology.

Extended technology acceptability model (TAM2): By including new elements that affect technology acceptance, the extended technology acceptance model (TAM2) builds on the original TAM. TAM2, which was proposed by [69], comprises elements, including subjective norm, image, job relevance, output quality, and outcome demonstrability.

The Theory of Reasoned Action (TRA), created by [70], is a comprehensive social psychology theory that has been used to explain how people embrace new technology. According to TRA, a person's attitude toward a behavior and subjective norms can have an impact on their decision to accept a technology.

To explain consumers' acceptance and adoption behaviors, technology acceptance models rely on a variety of theoretical pillars. These foundations include diffusion of innovation theory, social psychology, and cognitive psychology.

Cognitive psychology: To explain how people create beliefs and attitudes toward technology, technology acceptance models include cognitive psychology principles. These models place a strong emphasis on cognitive processes, including information processing and decision-making, as well as perceived usefulness and usability.

Social psychology: Models of technology acceptance use social psychology concepts as social impact and subjective norms. These ideas emphasize how social variables, societal norms, and interpersonal influence affect people's decisions to accept new technologies.

Technology adoption models frequently cite Rogers' diffusion of innovation theory when discussing the spread of new ideas [71]. This theory examines variables such as innovativeness, compatibility, complexity, trialability, and observability to explain how ideas spread and are embraced within a social system.

For both researchers and practitioners, the application of technology acceptance models has important implications. The design and execution of technology-based treatments can be influenced by these models, which offer a framework for comprehending users' technology adoption habits. Organizations can create strategies to encourage technology adoption, enhance user experiences, and improve organizational performance by recognizing key factors impacting technology acceptance.

Technology acceptance models are essential for comprehending and forecasting how people will accept and adopt new technology. Models, such as TAM, UTAUT, TAM2, and TRA, offer useful insights into the variables that affect the acceptance and adoption of technology. These models provide a thorough understanding of users' ideas, attitudes, and intentions toward the adoption of technology by merging cognitive psychology, social psychology, and diffusion of innovation theory. These models' useful applications help businesses create efficient technology adoption strategies, enhance user experiences, and promote successful technology implementations.

Organizations can modify their strategies to overcome certain hurdles and increase the chance of technology adoption by utilizing the information offered by technology acceptance models. For instance, firms can emphasize the technology's perceived utility and simplicity in order to allay users' worries and boost their intention to adopt. Additionally, fostering good social norms and encouraging peer influence can help promote technology acceptance. These methods can be informed by an understanding of the social influence and subjective norms that drive technology adoption.

In addition, the design of user-centered interfaces, simple user interfaces, and efficient training programs can be influenced by technology acceptance models. Organizations can reduce complexity, give crystal-clear benefits and demonstrations of the technology, and foster an environment that encourages technology adoption by taking into account the elements outlined in these models. This can then result in greater productivity, better judgment, and superior organizational performance.

In summary, technology acceptance models offer useful perceptions into the variables affecting people's acceptance and adoption of new technologies. These models help organizations create efficient plans for fostering technology acceptance and adoption by taking into account users' beliefs, attitudes, and behavioral intentions. The theoretical underpinnings of these models are strengthened by the incorporation of cognitive psychology, social psychology, and diffusion of innovation theory. The applications of technology acceptance models enable businesses to enhance user experiences, adopt technology more effectively, and lead successful digital transformations.

11. The impact of digital transformation on organizational culture

Digital transformation is a strategic requirement for enterprises in the modern era and it is defined as the integration of digital technologies into various organizational functions. While technology developments are frequently the center of attention in the context of digital transformation, organizational culture is also significantly impacted.

The common values, beliefs, customs, and behaviors that influence the workplace and direct employee behavior are referred to as organizational culture. Due to their significant impact on work processes, communication channels, decision-making, and employee roles and responsibilities, digital transformation efforts have the potential to disrupt and redefine corporate culture.

Within enterprises, digital transformation develops an innovative and adaptable culture. It urges staff members to try new things, take chances, and value lifelong learning [72]. Organizations can increase productivity, automate jobs, and streamline operations by implementing digital technologies. Organizations must foster a growth mentality, promote cooperation, and offer resources for continual learning and development in order to keep up with this trend toward innovation and agility.

A more empowered and collaborative workplace culture is frequently the result of digital transformation. Between teams and departments, smooth communication, knowledge exchange, and cooperation are made possible through digital tools and platforms [73]. This change calls for a culture revolution in which networked and decentralized decision-making processes replace hierarchical ones. Employee participation in cross-functional collaborations, sharing of ideas, and sharing of expertise are all encouraged, establishing an inclusive and empowered work environment.

In order to successfully implement digital transformation, organizations must be agile and responsive to ongoing change. It calls into question established working practices, needs a culture that welcomes change and ambiguity, and motivates staff to actively look for new opportunities. The promotion of a culture that encourages experimenting, learning from mistakes, and embracing change as a driver of progress is crucially dependent on organizational leaders.

There are difficulties associated with how digital transformation affects company culture. Organizations may encounter cultural inertia entrenched in conventional working methods, reluctance to change, and fear of job displacement [74]. Effective change management techniques, transparent communication, and employee engagement are required to overcome these obstacles. To provide employees the digital skills they need to succeed in the new workplace, organizations must engage in training and upskilling initiatives.

The effects of digital transformation on organizational culture have broad-ranging repercussions. A supportive and flexible culture can boost worker satisfaction, draw in and keep top talent, encourage creativity and innovation, and boost organizational performance. On the other hand, a mismatch between organizational culture and digital transformation initiatives can result in resistance, disengagement, and eventually the failure of transformation attempts. Therefore, to achieve congruence with their aims for digital transformation, organizations must actively manage cultural change.

Digital transformation has a big impact on company culture and goes beyond just being a technological activity. A cultural shift inside businesses is required to accommodate the shift toward innovation, empowerment, collaboration, adaptation, and flexibility. Organizations may traverse the difficulties and take advantage of the opportunities brought by the digital era by identifying and resolving the influence of digital transformation on organizational culture. To create a culture that supports successful digital transformation, it is essential to utilize effective change management techniques, involve employees, and invest in the development of digital skills.

12. Challenges and opportunities in adopting new technologies

Organizations constantly struggle with the problem of implementing new technology to stay competitive and foster creativity in today's quickly changing digital market. Adopting new technology comes with a number of difficulties:

1. Technological complexity: Because new technologies frequently have complicated features and functionalities, businesses must engage in learning about and mastering them [12]. With regard to technology selection, system integration,

and personnel training for the new technologies, this complexity can provide difficulties.

2. Employee resistance to change: The implementation of new technology can cause disruption to typical work processes and elicit resistance from staff members. Employees may worry about losing their jobs, encounter a learning curve, or be unsure about how new technologies will affect their roles and duties. Gaining employee buy-in and fostering a good culture of technology adoption requires strong change management tactics and transparent communication to address this opposition.

3. Cost factors: Adopting new technologies frequently entails high upfront expenses, such as infrastructure upgrades, technology acquisition, and training initiatives [75]. To justify the adoption of new technology, organizations must carefully consider the financial ramifications and prospective return on investment.

4. Integration obstacles: Adding new technology to current systems and procedures can be a difficult and time-consuming undertaking [12]. Organizations may encounter compatibility problems, data migration issues, and interoperability problems, necessitating the development of strong integration strategies and ensuring seamless system connectivity.

Adopting new technology also present substantial opportunity for development and transformation:

1. Increased productivity and efficiency: New technologies offer the potential to automate operations, streamline workflows, and boost operational effectiveness [76]. Organizations can improve resource utilization, lower manual errors, and boost productivity by implementing new technology, which will produce better business results.

2. Innovation and competitive advantage: Using new technologies, businesses can frequently innovate and set themselves apart from competitors [77]. They can provide a competitive edge by opening doors to new business models, product offers, and consumer experiences. Organizations that embrace technological improvements have the chance to lead in their respective marketplaces and pioneer industry disruptions.

3. Data-driven insights: Organizations now have access to priceless data and useful insights thanks to emerging technologies, such as artificial intelligence and data analytics [12]. These insights allow for the identification of fresh growth prospects, improved customer comprehension, and evidence-based decision-making.

4. Better customer experience: Making use of new technology can improve how customers are treated generally, which will increase customer loyalty and satisfaction [76]. Mobile applications, personalized marketing platforms, and customer relationship management systems are just a few examples of the technologies that help businesses meet changing customer expectations and provide tailored experiences.

A deliberate approach is necessary for the effective adoption of new technology, one that takes advantage of the potential and handles the problems. Organizations ought to:

1. Create a technology adoption strategy: Businesses should integrate technology adoption into their overall company strategy by outlining their objectives in detail and selecting the solutions that will best help them achieve them [75].

2. Invest in change management: Successful technology adoption requires overcoming opposition to change. In order to promote employee acceptance and excitement, organizations should invest in change management activities, which include effective communication, training programs, and incentives.

3. Promote an innovation culture: Businesses should establish an atmosphere that values innovation, reward experimentation, and promotes lifelong learning [77]. Fostering cross-functional cooperation, offering resources for skill-upskilling and training, and recognizing and applauding successful technology adoption projects can all help achieve this.

4. Perform a cost-benefit analysis: Businesses should carefully assess the financial ramifications of using new technologies, taking into account both immediate costs and future gains. A thorough cost-benefit analysis can be done to help justify investments and guarantee that the technologies chosen are in line with the organization's strategic goals [12].

5. Prioritize user experience: When adopting new technology, user experience should be taken into account in the main. To ensure seamless technology adoption and optimize user happiness, businesses should consult end customers during the decision-making process, solicit their comments, and offer user-friendly interfaces and intuitive designs [76].

Organizations have opportunities and problems as a result of the adoption of new technology. Organizations can take advantage of opportunities for increased efficiency, innovation, data-driven insights, and better customer experiences despite constraints, including technological complexity, reluctance to change, financial considerations, and integration issues that may occur. Organizations can overcome obstacles and seize opportunities to promote successful technology adoption and gain a sustainable competitive advantage by developing a strategic approach, investing in change management, fostering an innovation culture, conducting cost-benefit analyses, and placing a high priority on user experience.

13. Conclusion

In conclusion, the intricate relationship between organizational culture and technology adoption highlights the importance of understanding and addressing the multifaceted challenges and opportunities presented by the digital era. As businesses navigate this rapidly evolving landscape, embracing adaptability, continuous learning, and a people-centric approach will be crucial for long-term success.

Leaders play a pivotal role in fostering a culture that not only embraces innovation but also prioritizes ethical considerations, striking a delicate balance between leveraging new technologies and upholding human values. By doing so, organizations can create an environment that is not only resilient but also inclusive and supportive of all stakeholders.

The rapid expansion of remote work, the growing emphasis on diversity and inclusion, and the increasing integration of technologies such as AI, automation, and IoT present both challenges and opportunities for organizations. To thrive in this ever-changing environment, businesses must develop strategies that acknowledge and address the human factor in digital transformation, focusing on communication, change management, and skills development.

Moreover, recognizing the ethical implications of technology adoption is essential for organizations to ensure a responsible and sustainable approach to innovation. By engaging in open discourse and collaboration, businesses, policymakers, and society can work together to harness the full potential of emerging technologies while safeguarding the well-being of individuals and communities.

Finally, understanding the complex interplay between organizational culture change and technology adoption requires insights from various disciplines, enabling businesses to develop a comprehensive and proactive approach to managing change. By cultivating a culture of adaptability, curiosity, and growth, organizations can position themselves for success in an increasingly uncertain and dynamic world.

In summary, the digital era presents a unique set of challenges and opportunities for businesses. By adopting a people-centric approach to technology adoption, carefully weighing the ethical ramifications, and fostering a culture that promotes adaptability, inclusivity, and continuous learning, organizations can successfully navigate the complexities of the digital age and secure their place in the future.

Author details

Kivanc Bozkus
Artvin Coruh University, Artvin, Turkey

*Address all correspondence to: kbozkus@artvin.edu.tr

References

[1] Kane GC, Palmer D, Phillips AN, Kiron D, Buckley N. Strategy, Not Technology, Drives Digital Transformation. Deloitte: MIT Sloan Management Review and Deloitte University Press; 2015

[2] Rogers EM. Diffusion of Innovations. 5th ed. Glencoe: Free Press; 2003

[3] Christensen CM. The innovator's Dilemma: When New Technologies Cause Great Firms to Fail. Harvard: Harvard Business Review Press; 1997

[4] Bughin J, van Zeebroeck N. The best response to digital disruption. MIT Sloan Management Review. 2018;**59**(4):80-86

[5] Schein EH. Organizational Culture and Leadership. 4th ed. Hoboken, NJ: Jossey-Bass; 2010

[6] Birkinshaw J, Gupta K. Clarifying the distinctive contribution of ambidexterity to the field of organization studies. Academy of Management Perspectives. 2013;**27**(4):287-298

[7] Dweck CS. Mindset: The New Psychology of Success. London: Random House; 2006

[8] Porter ME. The five competitive forces that shape strategy. Harvard Business Review. 2008;**86**(1):78-93

[9] Teece DJ. Business models and dynamic capabilities. Long Range Planning. 2018;**51**(1):40-49

[10] Oreg S, Bartunek JM, Lee G, Do B. An affect-based model of recipients' responses to organizational change events. Academy of Management Review. 2018;**43**(1):65-86

[11] Agarwal R, Prasad J. The role of innovation characteristics and perceived voluntariness in the acceptance of information technologies. Decision Sciences. 1997;**28**(3):557-582

[12] Bharadwaj A, El Sawy OA, Pavlou PA, Venkatraman N. Digital business strategy: Toward a next generation of insights. MIS Quarterly. 2013;**37**(2):471-482

[13] Karimi J, Walter Z. The role of dynamic capabilities in responding to digital disruption: A factor-based study of the newspaper industry. Journal of Management Information Systems. 2015;**32**(1):39-81

[14] Westerman G, Calméjane C, Bonnet D, Ferraris P, McAfee A. Leading Digital: Turning Technology into Business Transformation. Harvard: Harvard Business Review Press; 2014

[15] Davenport TH. Big Data at Work: Dispelling the Myths, Uncovering the Opportunities. Harvard: Harvard Business Review Press; 2014

[16] Ross JW, Beath CM, Quaadgras A. You may not need big data after all. Harvard Business Review. 2016;**92**(12):90-98

[17] Kotter JP. Leading change: Why transformation efforts fail. Harvard Business Review. 1995;**73**(2):59-67

[18] Berson Y, Nemanich LA, Waldman DA, Galvin BM, Keller RT. Leadership and organizational learning: A multiple levels perspective. The Leadership Quarterly. 2008;**19**(1):19-38

[19] Edmondson AC. The Fearless Organization: Creating Psychological Safety in the Workplace for Learning, Innovation, and Growth. Hoboken, NJ: Wiley; 2019

[20] Yeager DS, Dweck CS. Mindsets that promote resilience: When students believe that personal characteristics can be developed. Educational Psychologist. 2012;**47**(4):302-314

[21] Heslin PA, Keating LA. In learning mode? The role of mindsets in derailing and enabling experiential leadership development. The Leadership Quarterly. 2017;**28**(3):367-384

[22] Copeland R. The Woman Who Transformed Microsoft's Culture from Cutthroat to Creative. Fast Company; 2017. Available from: https://www.fastcompany.com/40457458/the-woman-who-transformed-microsofts-culture-from-cutthroat-to-creative

[23] Nadella S. Hit Refresh: The Quest to Rediscover Microsoft's Soul and Imagine a better Future for Everyone. Harper Business; 2017

[24] Iansiti M, Lakhani KR. Managing our hub economy. Harvard Business Review. 2017;**95**(5):84-92

[25] Bose S, Henseler J, Sahoo S. DBS Bank: Leveraging digital technology for service excellence. Asian Journal of Management Cases. 2018;**15**(1):3-25

[26] Gupta P, Berzins J. How DBS Bank Became the Best Digital Bank in the World by Becoming Invisible. Strategy+Business; 2018. Available from: https://www.strategy-business.com/article/How-DBS-Bank-Became-the-Best-Digital-Bank-in-the-World-by-Becoming-Invisible

[27] Wahba P. Fortune Walmart CEOs plan to fight Amazon Win with stores Comments, Fortune, 16 October 2015. [Online]. Available from: https://fortune.com/2017/10/19/walmart-amazon-technology/

[28] Kaplan AM, Haenlein M. Higher education and the digital revolution: About MOOCs, SPOCs, social media, and the cookie monster. Business Horizons. 2016;**59**(4):441-450

[29] Oreg S, Vakola M, Armenakis A. Change recipients' reactions to organizational change: A 60-year review of quantitative studies. The Journal of Applied Behavioral Science. 2011;**47**(4):461-524

[30] Ford JD, Ford LW, D'Amelio A. Resistance to change: The rest of the story. Academy of Management Review. 2008;**33**(2):362-377

[31] Agarwal R, Angst CM, Magni M. The performance effects of coaching: A multilevel analysis using hierarchical linear modeling. The International Journal of Human Resource Management. 2010;**21**(10):1558-1575

[32] Pereira AM, Ferreira JJ, da Costa FA. Digital transformation: Identifying critical success factors. In: Proceedings of the European Conference on Information Systems (ECIS), Guimarães, Portugal. 2017

[33] Brynjolfsson E, McAfee A. The Second Machine Age: Work, Progress, and Prosperity in a Time of Brilliant Technologies. New York: W. W. Norton & Company; 2014

[34] Autor DH. Why are there still so many jobs? The history and future of workplace automation. Journal of Economic Perspectives. 2015;**29**(3):3-30

[35] Arntz M, Gregory T, Zierahn U. The risk of automation for jobs in OECD countries: A comparative analysis. In: OECD Social, Employment and Migration Working Papers, No. 189. 2016

[36] Kaplan A, Haenlein M. Siri, Siri, in my hand: Who's the fairest in the land? On the interpretations, illustrations, and

implications of artificial intelligence. Business Horizons. 2019;**62**(1):15-25

[37] Zuboff S. The Age of Surveillance Capitalism: The Fight for a Human Future at the New Frontier of Power. UK: Hachette; 2019

[38] Mittelstadt BD, Allo P, Taddeo M, Wachter S, Floridi L. The ethics of algorithms: Mapping the debate. Big Data & Society. 2016;**3**(2):1-21

[39] Cohen JE. The surveillance-innovation complex: The irony of the participatory turn. In: Haggerty KD, Gazso A, editors. Age of Surveillance Capitalism: The Fight for a Human Future at the New Frontier of Power. Toronto: University of Toronto Press; 2018. pp. 23-48

[40] Malmodin J, Lundén D. The energy and carbon footprint of the global ICT and E&M sectors 2010-2015. Sustainability. 2018;**10**(9):3027

[41] Park Y, Chertow M, Geyer R. The environmental implications of digitalization: Insights from the mining, automotive, and semiconductor industries. Resources, Conservation and Recycling. 2019;**142**:1-8

[42] Floridi L. The 4th Revolution: How the Infosphere Is Reshaping Human Reality. Oxford: Oxford University Press; 2014

[43] George G, Howard-Grenville J, Joshi A, Tihanyi L. Understanding and tackling societal grand challenges through management research. Academy of Management Journal. 2016;**59**(6):1880-1895

[44] Bloom N, Liang J, Roberts J, Ying ZJ. Does working from home work? Evidence from a Chinese experiment. The Quarterly Journal of Economics. 2015;**130**(1):165-218

[45] Gibson CB, Gibbs JL, Taylor SG. Navigating the digital shift: Multicollaborator research opportunities for organizational communication in the age of digital transformation. Journal of Management. 2019;**45**(1):153-175

[46] Raghuram S, Hill NS, Gibbs JL, Maruping LM. Virtual work: Bridging research clusters. Academy of Management Annals. 2019;**13**(1):308-341

[47] Nishii LH. The benefits of climate for inclusion for gender-diverse groups. Academy of Management Journal. 2013;**56**(6):1754-1774

[48] Hewlett SA, Marshall M, Sherbin L. How diversity can drive innovation. Harvard Business Review. 2013;**91**(12):30-30

[49] Mor, Barak ME. Managing Diversity: Toward a Globally Inclusive Workplace. Newbury Park: Sage Publications; 2017

[50] Daugherty PR, Wilson HJ. Human + Machine: Reimagining Work in the Age of AI. Harvard: Harvard Business Press; 2018

[51] Makridakis S. The forthcoming artificial intelligence (AI) revolution: Its impact on society and firms. Futures. 2017;**90**:46-60

[52] Iansiti M, Lakhani KR. The truth about blockchain. Harvard Business Review. 2017;**95**(1):118-127

[53] Huang MH, Rust RT, Maksimovic V. The feeling of VR presence: A multiple mediation analysis. Journal of Business Research. 2019;**100**:445-452

[54] Lee I, Lee K. The internet of things (IoT): Applications, investments, and challenges for enterprises. Business Horizons. 2015;**58**(4):431-440

[55] Bélanger F, Crossler RE. Privacy in the digital age: A review of information

privacy research in information systems. MIS Quarterly. 2011;**35**(4):1017-1041

[56] Battilana J, Casciaro T. Change agents, networks, and institutions: A contingency theory of organizational change. Academy of Management Journal. 2012;**55**(2):381-398

[57] Leonardi PM, Huysman M, Steinfield C. Enterprise social media: Definition, history, and prospects for the study of social technologies in organizations. Journal of Computer-Mediated Communication. 2013;**19**(1):1-19

[58] Robbins SP, Judge TA. Organizational Behavior. New York: Pearson; 2017

[59] Venkatesh V, Morris MG, Davis GB, Davis FD. User acceptance of information technology: Toward a unified view. MIS Quarterly. 2003;**27**(3):425-478

[60] Bijker WE, Hughes TP, Pinch T. The Social Construction of Technological Systems: New Directions in the Sociology and History of Technology. Cambridge: MIT Press; 2012

[61] Cameron KS, Quinn RE. Diagnosing and Changing Organizational Culture: Based on the Competing Values Framework. Hoboken, NJ: John Wiley & Sons; 2011

[62] Quinn RE, Rohrbaugh J. A spatial model of effectiveness criteria: Towards a competing values approach to organizational analysis. Management Science. 1983;**29**(3):363-377

[63] Ehrhart MG, Schneider B, Macey WH. Organizational Climate and Culture: An Introduction to Theory, Research, and Practice. Oxfordshire: Routledge; 2014

[64] Denison DR. Corporate Culture and Organizational Effectiveness. Hoboken, NJ: John Wiley & Sons; 1990

[65] Schein EH. Organizational Culture and Leadership: A Dynamic View. Hoboken, NJ: John Wiley & Sons; 1985

[66] Schein EH. Organizational Culture and Leadership. Hoboken, NJ: John Wiley & Sons; 2010

[67] Denison DR, Mishra AK. Toward a theory of organizational culture and effectiveness. Organization Science. 1995;**6**(2):204-223

[68] Davis FD. Perceived usefulness, perceived ease of use, and user acceptance of information technology. MIS Quarterly. 1989;**13**(3):319-340

[69] Venkatesh V, Davis FD. A theoretical extension of the technology acceptance model: Four longitudinal field studies. Management Science. 2000;**46**(2):186-204

[70] Fishbein M, Ajzen I. Belief, Attitude, Intention, and Behavior: An Introduction to Theory and Research. Boston: Addison-Wesley; 1975

[71] Rogers EM. Diffusion of Innovations. Glencoe: Free Press; 1995

[72] Ransbotham S, Kiron D, Gerbert P, Reeves M. Reshaping Business with Artificial Intelligence: Closing the Gap between Ambition and Action. Cambridge: MIT Sloan Management Review and Boston Consulting Group; 2019

[73] Fuchs C, Prandelli E, Schreier M. The psychological effects of empowerment strategies on consumers' product demand. Journal of Marketing. 2018;**82**(1):119-137

[74] Bughin J, Hazan E, Ramaswamy S, Chui M, Allas T, Dahlström P, et al. Skill Shift: Automation and the Future of the Workforce. New York: McKinsey Global Institute; 2018

[75] Melville NP, Kraemer KL, Gurbaxani V. Review: Information technology and organizational performance: An integrative model of IT business value. MIS Quarterly. 2004;**28**(2):283-322

[76] Yoo Y, Henfridsson O, Lyytinen K. The new organizing logic of digital innovation: An agenda for information systems research. Information Systems Research. 2012;**23**(4):724-735

[77] Lacity MC, Willcocks LP, Feeny DF. Business process outsourcing and dynamic innovation. MIT Sloan Management Review. 2010;**52**(2):35-42

Chapter 2

Organizational Culture in Enterprises Applying the Humanistic and Economic Paradigm of Management

Barbara Mazur

Abstract

The issue of organizational culture has recently become particularly important. One of the reasons for that is the increasing empowerment of employees, which requires changes in organizational culture. The need for change stems from the belief that management and culture should stand in harmony. The aim of this chapter is to examine the relationship between management paradigms and the orientations of organizational cultures. To accomplish that, a literature review was carried out on both paradigms of management (economic and humanistic) and groups of vales (terminal and instrumental), as well as on the types of organizational culture (task-oriented and human-oriented). The research problem focuses on determining the orientation of organizational culture and its dominant values through the lens of the management paradigm. Reflections on the relationship between management paradigm, values, and the orientation of organizational culture are theoretical, revisional, and conceptual. On the basis of the literature analyses, a model of the relationship between the paradigms applicable in the management and the type of organizational culture resulting from their application was created. In the model, the economic paradigm was assigned a task-oriented type of organizational culture, unlike the humanistic paradigm, which was assigned a human-oriented type of culture.

Keywords: economic paradigm of management, humanistic paradigm of management, task-oriented organizational culture, human-oriented organizational culture, terminal and instrumental values

1. Introduction

In recent years, the internal work environment has become increasingly important. Researchers prove that nowadays, it is not the technological changes that are the most significant in the company, but rather a new approach to employees. This new approach means that an employee is perceived not as an economically understood capital, but primarily as a human being—each has his/hers unique potential and investments in him/her are unlimitedly developing. This humanistic approach assumes that man develops throughout all their life, and this is a crucial feature of human nature. Under the humanistic management, the employee shall strive to develop his/her personality, competences, and skills. There are no predictable limits to this development. The human-focused approach is more and more emphasized but still rarely applied. It contrasts the economic approach that prevails in the business world. Both approaches make different assumptions about human nature and refer to different values in management. The adopted values determine the shape of the organizational culture of the companies applying them. Thanks to organizational culture, the enterprise becomes a psychological environment with social dimensions.

The issue of organizational culture is not new in management literature, and the belief in its growing importance does not raise doubt among researchers. However, although the very concept is considered crucial in management sciences, it is also viewed as an ambiguous notion. Despite this ambiguity, it has been successfully adopted in management theory and is frequently used in interpreting the behavior of employees. Culture is attributed with many functions that can be performed in relation to both the internal and external environment of an organization. It is widely accepted that it is culture that decides whether a given organization is able not only to survive on the market but also to develop successfully. And although in every organization so much depends on it, there are still questions that have not found comprehensive answers in previous studies. One of such questions should examine the nature of the relationship between management system used in a given company and type of organizational culture. The present considerations attempt to fill this research gap. They fall within the broader context of the dependence of organizational culture on individual subsystems of organizations. The study of its relationship with those subsystems, for instance, with the management system, is possible thanks to recognizing organizational culture as part of the organizational system. In this article, the main research problem is to determine the linkage between the subsystem (management and its relevant paradigms) and the organizational culture orientation.

Investigating and explaining the relationship between the economic and humanistic paradigm of management and the orientation of organizational culture focused on tasks and social relations is the main axis of this research. In order to explain this dependence, reference was made to M. Rokeach's Test of Values and the types of final and instrumental values contained therein, which were grouped into categories of interpersonal, intrapersonal, competence, and moral values. A model approach to these relationships was presented after prior analysis of the literature concerning both management paradigms and specific types of values and orientations of organizational cultures.

The article consists of four parts preceded by an introduction and crowned with conclusion. They are devoted to presenting the basic assumptions of the economic and humanistic management paradigm, explaining the concept of organizational culture by defining the place of values and the typology of values in organizational culture, presenting orientation in organizational culture, and linking orientation with management paradigms.

2. Humanistic and economic paradigms in management

The humanistic and economic paradigms coexist in contemporary management theory. They differ, however, with regard to their understanding of a human being, its needs, and motivation to take action [1, 2].

The economic paradigm assumes that business activity aims at profit maximization and interpersonal relations are perceived as short-term transactions [3, 4]. With disregard to moral considerations, the mechanism of utility and self-interest prevails [2, 5, 6]. Hence, a man is conceived mainly as a *homo economicus*—he or she is searching for the quickest gratification of undertaken actions, often acting opportunistically for the sake of own gain. Therefore, people are creatures seeking to increase the material usefulness of the broadly understood benefit. It is appropriate to favor individual benefit rather than the social, collective one [3]. Supporters of the economic orientation in management tend to assume that the main goal of an enterprise is profit maximization, and the primary and only duty of managers is to earn money for the shareholders [7].

However, in recent years, a humanistic paradigm has emerged and is now being more and more heard of [7–9]. The basic concept of this approach is the one where a man is conceived as a *zoon politicon* and has the right to unconditional respect for dignity [10]. Unlike the economic paradigm, the humanistic one assumes that human nature is not given once and forever and can be improved through continuous education [11, 12]. Humanistic management flourishes as an almost natural response to management models where the main search for financial returns damages the well-being of people, both inside and outside the company. It is an alternative proposal to the management of the companies where the well-being of people is prioritized above the achievement of merely financial goals [12].

What mostly distinguishes the two views is the ethical component. It remains a central category in the humanistic approach as it attributes the inalienable right to respect for one's own dignity, independent of ethnicity, nationality, social status, or gender to every human being [8, 13]. Human is identified as a rational being who realizes his/her right to freedom in social interactions based on values.

Humanistic management creates and runs a business using three interrelated principles. All three have ethical connotations and require the use of:

1. Unconditional respect for the dignity of every human being that underpins all interpersonal relationships, including business relationships;

2. Ethical reflection, an integral part of all business decisions;

3. Seeking normative legitimacy for corporate actions that is critical to establishing corporate accountability [4].

Applied together, these three principles contribute to the development of humanism through economic activities that bring values to all mankind. The need to respect the human dignity as a goal of humanistic management results in economic and social impacts [2]. In this approach, management involves assuming responsibility for ethical issues in business decisions. Shifting from the one-dimensional goal of profit maximization to the multidimensional and value-based understanding of organizational success is a fundamental principle.

3. The concept of organizational culture

The term culture, which originally referred to the cultivation of fields, quickly gained a wider meaning. Since the times of Cicero, who wrote about the "cultivation of the human soul," it has been used in a metaphorical sense, referring to other spheres. In the broadest sense, culture encompasses all that is the aftermath of collective activity in the behavior of human societies. If one refers culture to an organization, it is the result of a joint action of managers and subordinates, aimed at achieving the set objective. It determines the manner of its implementation, resulting from the values professed in a given organization. Culture is about shared views, ideologies, values, beliefs, expectations, and norms [14]. By studying the organizational culture of a company, one learns about the way of thinking of its employees and the principles and norms they follow. With this knowledge, it is possible to choose effective methods of influencing their behaviors [15].

The adaptation of cultural analysis to business practice resulted in creating an organizational cultures elements canon. It includes cultural values, basic assumptions, social and organizational norms, ways of communication, stories, narratives, myths, metaphors, rituals, symbols, customs, organizational heroes, taboos, cultural patterns, cultural artifacts, and subcultures [16, 17]. Organizational culture is therefore a set of values manifested, among others, in such areas of behavior as the way employees are treated. It is a set of norms on how managers relate to their subordinates and how these subordinates relate to their subordinates [18].

The concept of organizational culture is broad-based, ambiguous, and abstract. Being a complex phenomenon, it is uneasy to analyze. The difficulties are caused by many reasons, one of which seems to be utterly important. It is the fact that organizational culture is not isolated from other elements of the whole organizational system. Multidirectional relationships with other subsystems (strategy, structure, human resource management, etc.) make culture arduous to study. Many elements and relationships between them are invisible, often unconscious, and thus difficult to observe and measure [19]. Despite that, researchers persistently strive to get to know organizational culture better because of the functions it performs. It sets boundaries, provides employees with a sense of identity, and facilitates their engagement not only in their own interest but in the interest of the entire organization. It is a social binder that serves to maintain the integrity of the organization thanks to standards that define what employees should do and how they should do it and what values should guide their behaviors. It also serves as an explanatory and control mechanism, shaping the attitudes and behaviors of employees [20]. The recognition of organizational culture as part of the organizational system makes it possible to study its relationship with other subsystems, for example, with the management system. In this work, the research problem was the interdependence between one of the organizational subsystems, that is, management and organizational culture. This issue has not received much attention so far. The article is an attempt to fill the existing gap in this field.

3.1 The place of values in organizational culture

The study of values is recognized as an appropriate and necessary part of the research on culture. "If we shy away from considering values, we cease to deal with something that is most important both within individual cultures and in human culture seen as a whole (...). When we eliminate values, we are left with a barren list of cultural elements or events, and there is a constant temptation to revive it by introducing the values we have just discarded, or by camouflaging the introduction of values derived from our culture" [21]. Benedict in "Patterns of Culture" [22] argues that the difference between cultures is not determined by the presence or absence of important values, but by the extent to which opposing values cooperate, that is, whether they are more or less synergistic in nature. If Benedict only analyzed values without paying attention to the relationships between them, she would not be able to understand the subtleties and power of culture. Referring to her concept of synergy as transcending the dichotomy of values, Trompenaars and Hampden-Turner [23] formulated the definition of culture, assuming that it is a scheme by which a group habitually mediates in the case of differences between values—for example, between rules and exceptions, technology and people, conflict, and consensus. Cultures can learn to reconcile such values at ever higher levels, so learning the many exceptions leads to better rules. Such reconciliation brings health, wealth, and wisdom. On the other hand, cultures in which one pole of values dominates and combats the other are a source of stress and plunge into stagnation.

American anthropologists Kluckhon and Strodbeck [24] argue that each culture emphasizes a limited number of values (called cultural values) that concern solving basic human problems. According to the dictionary, "values are culturally conditioned, established and transmitted views on what is desirable, beneficial and valuable in a given social reality: these views enter into mutual relations according to a hierarchy, creating a system of values and norms within a specific culture" [25].

The determination of individual cultures' typical values has long been used in the descriptions of cultures made by anthropologists or historians. In the most valuable characteristics or synthetic analyses presented by researchers such as Malinowski et al. an extraction of value determinations can be observed. "In this way, the description brings characteristics of the actual physiognomy of culture. Such a characteristic is important both in the internal aspect of its own coherence and non-contradiction, and in the external aspect – by formulating an implicit or explicit comparison with other described cultures" [21]. Values, like any other manifestation of culture, are part of nature and therefore fall within the field of science interest.

The concept of value derives from German words *Wert* and *Wuerde*, which mean honor, dignity, and seriousness. Values in an organization are a set of common features that determine the actions of people and thus constitute the criteria for making decisions. Some authors define values as the unique DNA of an organization that allows it to maintain its continuity and contributes to the consolidation of its market success. A value system assures that when making choices, everyone throughout the organization follows the same principles.

Numerous research of organizational culture emphasize that values are its key component. Ł. Sułkowski, who defines it as a "learned product of group experience based on values, norms, and resulting cultural patterns," perceives values as the core element. This view is consistent with the method of defining adopted by Schein et al. [17].

Ł. Sułkowski states that organizational culture contains four elements, the first of which—the most central—includes both terminal and instrumental values. The second element, forming another cultural circle, includes patterns, norms, and cultural rules, as well as rituals, myths, symbols, and taboos. These elements of culture are directly related to personal and environmental values and influence organizational behaviors (third element), constituting their basis. By embracing the behaviors of employees—intentional (conscious) and habitual (unconscious)—they shape the structure of communication and power in the organization. The last element, artifacts, is related to external, material aspects, such as the layout of space [26]. They are secondary to values, norms, and basic cultural assumptions. The system of elements established by Ł. Sułkowski is presented in **Figure 1**.

Assuming that values in an organization are centrally located, the study of organizational culture consists in the search for these values. It is easiest to observe the

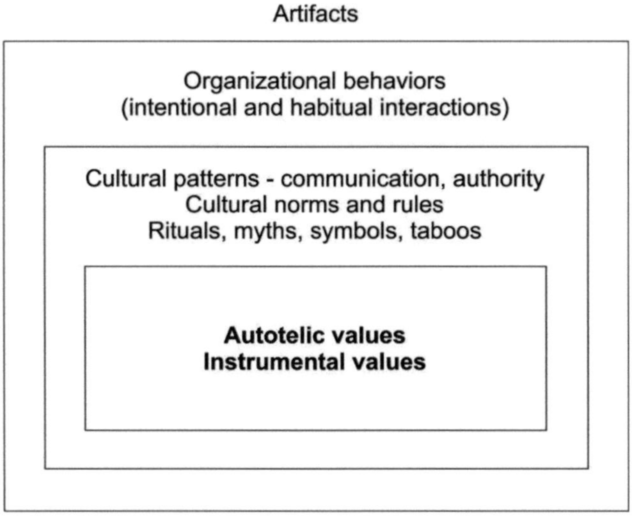

Figure 1.
Axiological model of organizational culture. Source: Sułkowski, 2002.

"outer" layer of culture, including artifacts and behaviors [27]. By examining the external symptoms of culture, one can indirectly look for basic, internal elements. A study in search for different value configurations in organizations should include an analysis of all presented spheres leading to the identification of key values. Such a study—indirectly also through the study of "external" symptoms of culture—makes it achievable to reach the internal key elements. However, it is also possible to take a different path, omitting external elements, consisting in reaching the values directly. Such a straight way gives a greater chance of reaching all the values present in the organizational culture, allowing for its better recognition.

3.2 Typology of values in organizational culture

Often used in research and treated as a universal tool for the study of values (thus used to study the organizational culture) is the M. Rokeach Value Test. M. Rokeach is the creator of the well-known and widely used classifications dividing values into two types: terminal and instrumental values.[1] Terminal values (safety, material well-being, social maturity, perfection, love, environmental protection, passionate life, beauty, self-esteem, friendship, pleasure, family, equality, inner peace, life success, happiness, social recognition, freedom, salvation, health, and human life) relate to behavior; instrumental values (ambitious, pure, intellectual, loving, logical, independent, responsible, courageous, cheerful, helpful, obedient, hardworking, tolerant, creative, honest, kind, talented, faithful, forgiving, and balanced) deal with the extreme (terminal) states of existence. Terminal values embrace moral categories (e.g., honesty) and competence categories (e.g., intelligence). They can also be classified into one of two groups: intrapersonal values—focused on the individual (such as prosperity, exciting life, social recognition, dignity, freedom, and prosperous life) or interpersonal values—focused on society (such as mature love, friendship, wisdom, equality, and sense of accomplishment).

[1] There are at least five versions of the M. Rokeach test, four of which show 18 final and instrumental values.

Instrumental values are described either as personal (the final way of describing oneself) or as social (the final way of describing society). Among personal values, there are moral values (e.g., honest, responsible, forgiving, and obedient) and competence values of cognitive and intellectual nature (e.g., ambitious, independent, courageous, intellectual, and gifted). Social values related to interpersonal relationships include such instrumental elements as helpful, tolerant, and courteous.

The usefulness of the M. Rokeach Value Test for management practice was confirmed by the research on professional groups [28, 29] and on ethnic and religious groups in the organization [17, 30] conducted in the 1980s, 1990s, and at the beginning of the twenty-first century.

4. Orientations of organizational cultures

Organizational culture has many theoretical models, typologies, and classifications. They are often cited in management literature and repeatedly used in empirical research undertaken by authors from many countries. Their most cited creators are E. Schein, G. Hofstede, F. Trompenaars and Ch. Hampden-Turner, and Ch. Handy. The issue of organizational culture orientations in terms of prevailing values has attracted less attention than models and classifications of cultures. However, a certain number of research do exist, the earliest of which was a study conducted at Ohio State University in the 1940s, when two fundamental values of behavioral traits were discovered: the structure of initiation (task orientation) and consideration (relationship orientation) [31]. Another research that yielded similar results is a University of Michigan study that presented two analogous types of behavioral traits: production-focused and worker-focused [32].

Also in later literature, it is noted that organizational culture, which is shaped by external and internal factors, can in practice adopt one of two orientations—task orientation or interpersonal relationships orientation. Each of them points to a different purpose and to those aspects of everyday life that are considered the most important in a given organization. Many analysts (despite the fact that not everyone uses the same terminology) consider these two orientations of organizational culture to be crucial [17, 33, 34].

Several researchers [19, 35, 36] deeply discussed task and relationship orientations and considered them to be the most important in organizational culture. They perceived them as valuable for studying as they bring forth the most general aspects in social groups in organizations. The two are also useful when investigating leadership, group processes, and conflict management [37]. Task orientation refers to the focus on the very work and goals of the organization. Relationship orientation refers to the human side and how interrelations are valued [34].

In literature, a diverse nomenclature is used in relation to the abovementioned orientations of organizational cultures. Harrison [36] proposes to use the term of task culture and person culture, arguing that the concept of task culture encompasses the goals of an organization that are relevant to all its activities and that members of the organization are expected to support. On the other hand, he refers to the concept of an organizational culture oriented at a person based on harmonious interpersonal relationships.

Cameron and Quinn [38] use different terms, namely, goal orientation and support orientation. The content of these terms remains coincident with the terms used by Schein [19] who distinguished task-oriented and relationship-oriented organizational culture. These two are also referred to by him as as aimed at "being" and "doing".

Task orientation reflects the degree to which members of an organization are willing to pursue common goals. In this case, achieving the goal is the greatest value [36]. The most important thing is to perform the task, so the focus is put on the achievements of employees, rewards, and competing.

Relationship orientation emphasizes the importance of belonging to a group—employees are actively involved in solving work-related problems. In this case, the aim of an organization is primarily to meet the needs of employees [19]. What this orientation reflects is the concern for employees, emphasizing the importance of bonding, participation, and cooperation. At the core of any organizational culture lies the assumption about proper interpersonal relationships, thanks to which a group can feel safe and efficient at work [19].

5. Bridging cultural orientations with management paradigms

Based on the terminal/instrumental division of values, it is possible to link the dominant values with the organizational culture orientation. Among terminal values, the intrapersonal ones—focusing on the individual (e.g., prosperity, exciting life, social recognition, dignity, freedom, and prosperous life)—will foster the emergence of task orientation, while interpersonal values—focusing on society (e.g., mature love, friendship, wisdom, equality, and sense of accomplishment)—will create favorable conditions for the relational orientation. Among the instrumental values, the relational orientation will be favored by moral values (e.g., honest, responsible, forgiving, and obedient), while task orientation will be supported by competence values, especially cognitive and intellectual, having a more personal character (e.g., self-acceptance—ambitious, independent, courageous, intellectual, and talented).

In task-oriented organizational cultures, intrapersonal values belonging to the group of terminal values will dominate, and as for the group of instrumental values, competence, cognitive, and intellectual values will be the most prevailing.

In the interpersonal relations oriented organizational cultures, interpersonal (focusing on society) and moral values will dominate from the group of ultimate values.

Referring the two orientations to management paradigms, it can be assumed that when a humanistic paradigm is present in management, an organizational culture concentrated on human relations is created, while when an enterprise is managed in accordance with the economic paradigm, a task-oriented culture emerges. This conclusion results from a comparative analysis of the values dominant in the organizational culture with the assumptions underlying in the studied management paradigms. The relationship between the discussed paradigms and the orientation of organizational culture is shown in **Figure 2**.

The conclusions drawn from the analysis allow to state that it is, as a consequence, the management system based on the dominant paradigm (economic or humanistic) that determines the basic values in the organization and thus affects the organizational culture orientation. The presence of certain values results from the assumptions adopted in a given management paradigm. The management system based on the economic paradigm emphasizes the importance of terminal values belonging to the group of intrapersonal values and instrumental values representing the competence group. The management system referring to the humanistic paradigm, in contrast, considers interpersonal and instrumental values (among moral ones) as the most important.

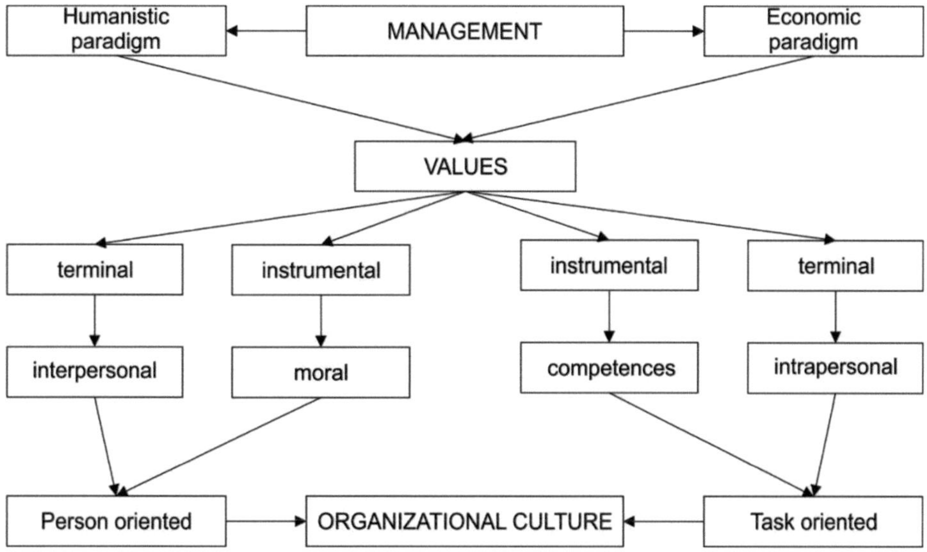

Figure 2.
The model of dependence between management paradigms and organizational culture orientations. Source: Own elaboration.

6. Discussion and conclusion

The subject of the article is the organizational culture under the influence of the management paradigm used in the enterprise. It presents two orientations of organizational culture, one of which—orientation on interpersonal relations and the values associated with them—is determined by the application of the humanistic paradigm, while the other—orientation on tasks—is more closely related to the economic paradigm and its basic values.

Usually, organizations are designed to achieve certain goals, and therefore, the organizational task must be known and highly accepted by all organizational members. Relationship-oriented and task-oriented behaviors are not seen as mutually exclusive and can be combined [39]. It should be recognized that aside from duties, the mutual relations are crucial. Therefore, on the one hand, it is necessary to know how important the organizational task is for its members and, on the other hand, how important mutual relations are.

When considering learning organizations and their cultures, Schein concluded that task and relational orientation are equally important [19]. It should therefore be assumed that both orientations determine the organizational culture. Effectiveness of the organization depends on the willingness of its members to accept the goals and tasks, together with the sense of community. Schein believed that in a stable environment, it is safer to be task-oriented, while in a complex and dynamic environment, there is a greater need for a relationship orientation. This is due to the necessity of mutual trust and the need for efficient communication between employees. The communication is necessary to solve numerous problems arising in the changing environment [19].

In contrast, Harrison [36] recognizes that the strongest side of task-oriented organizational culture is coping in a changing environment, but he also believes that human-orientation is not inappropriate in such conditions. He highlights the growing pressure on organizations to create a relational culture. This pressure stems from the changing environment in which organizations operate in. What is required is a greater emphasis on interpersonal relationships involving both employees and customers, business partners, shareholders, and representatives of various interest groups [32].

In the light of the discussion on the benefits of alternative use of particular paradigms in specific market situations, a complementary approach should be considered appropriate. Economic management is recommended in engineering companies with a project structure in which deadlines, rules, and the hierarchy of performed activities are important. However, in service companies, operating on the basis of employees' creativity and common values, better results in relation to teamwork and greater involvement of employees can be obtained by applying humanistic management. The alternative use of paradigms in management is also supported by cultural conditions affecting the orientation of the organizational culture of enterprises operating in a specific cultural and social environment.

Recently, as a result of organizational culture research on Vietnamese enterprises, a division of interpersonal orientation into two sub-orientations has appeared in literature [40]. The relationship orientation has been divided into status orientation and unity orientation. Status orientation reflects the distance between organizations/leaders and employees. It makes it easier to deal with bureaucratic systems that prevent local workers from competing fairly. Conversely, the unity orientation emphasizes the sense of community. Working in a group is perceived as efficient and harmless, even if it is inconsistent with the instructions received from superiors.

Increasingly numerous studies prove the cultural conditioning of organizational culture orientation. The orientation toward unity reflects the collectivist Confucian values [41]. This proves that organizational culture is influenced not only by management paradigms but also by other factors, such as the impact of cultural values. A need for further research into the determinants of organizational culture orientation is indicated. This need is also evidenced by the results of the comparative research on the value of organizational cultures of social and commercial enterprises in Poland operating in the dairy, trade, and insurance industries [42]. A comparative study of management reports relating to language artifacts constituting one of the elements of organizational culture confirmed the existence of differences in the orientation of the organizational culture of the surveyed enterprises. Organizational cultures of social enterprises turned out to be more oriented toward social relations than toward commercial enterprises, while organizational cultures of commercial enterprises were more often task-oriented. The study found that corporations often require employees to conform to predetermined values, while social enterprises build organizational culture to a large extent based on the values and needs of its members.

Values are a key component of organizational culture. The creation of a relevant value system in an organization contributes to improving the effects of its activities and consolidates its favorable image. In order to develop the appropriate organizational culture (fulfilling assigned functions), the knowledge of its relationship with other subsystems is needed. The article addressed the issue of the linkage of the organizational culture orientation with the adopted management paradigm. After analyzing the existing literature, the thesis was made that in humanistically managed enterprises, an organizational culture based on interpersonal relations is created, while in enterprises managed in accordance with the economic paradigm, a task-oriented culture prevails. This thesis was supported by referring to values and their model approach by M. Rokeach. The basis was the assumption that the management paradigm determines the values that consequently determine the orientation of the organizational culture. As a result of the undertaken analysis, a model of dependence of the organizational culture orientation on the management paradigm was created, indicating the final and instrumental values that generate and justify this dependence. This model can serve as a research framework in empirical research on the determinants of organizational cultures and value systems in organizations.

Conflict of interest

The author declares no conflict of interest.

Author details

Barbara Mazur
Lublin University of Technology, Lublin, Poland

*Address all correspondence to: b.mazur@pollub.pl

References

[1] Pirson MA, Lawrence PR. Humanism in business – Towards a paradigm shift? Journal of Business Ethics. 2010;**93**:553-565. DOI: 10.1007/s10551-009-0239-1

[2] Dierksmeier C. Reorienting management education: From the homo economicus to human dignity. Humanistic Management Network, Research paper series No. 13-05. 21 Feb 2011. DOI: 10.2139/ssrn.1766183. Available from: https://ssrn.com/abstract=1766183

[3] Pirson M. Humanistic Management: Protecting Dignity and Promoting Well-Being. Cambridge, United Kingdom: Cambridge University Press; 2017

[4] Pirson M, Kimakowitz E. Towards a human-centered theory and practice of the firm: Presenting the humanistic paradigm of business and management. Journal of Management. 2014;**2**:17-48. DOI: 10.13185/JM2014.02101

[5] Melé D. The challenge of humanistic management. Journal of Business Ethics. 2003;**44**:77-88

[6] Mazur B, Mazur-Malek M. Work, profit and dignity: Towards an integrative HRM paradigm. Journal of Business Management. 2021;**19**:5-19. DOI: 10.32025/JBM19001

[7] Mazur B. Diversity in the perspective of economic and humanistic management. Przedsiębiorczość i Zarządzanie. 2017;**18**:9-19

[8] Melé D. Antecedents and current situation of humanistic management. African Journal of Business Ethics. 2013;7:52-61. DOI: 10.4103/1817-7417.123079

[9] Zimnoch K, Mazur B. The cooperative and commercial business model on the polish market. Marketing i Rynek. 2022:14-24. DOI: 10.33226/1231-7853.2022.6.2

[10] Gintis H, van Schaik C, Boehm C. Zoon politikon: The evolutionary origins of human socio-political systems. Behavioural Processes. 2019;**161**:17-30. DOI: 10.1016/j.beproc.2018.01.007

[11] Pirson, M.A.; Kimakowitz, E. Von. Towards a human-centered theory and practice of the firm: Presenting the humanistic paradigm of business and management. Journal of Management 2014, 2, 1-7, doi:10.13185/JM2014.02101

[12] Arandia O, de La Torre G, Consuelo. Humanistic Management: A History of a Management Paradigm from the Human Dignity. Humanistic Management in Latin America, First Published. London, New York: Routledge Taylor & Francis Group; 2021. pp. 1-20

[13] Melé D. Ética en dirección de empresas: Calidad humana para una buena gestión. Madrid, (España): Primera edición; Pearson Educación; 2016

[14] Cameron KS, Quinn RE. Kultura organizacyjna. Diagnoza i zmiana.; Oficyna Ekonomiczna: Kraków; 2006

[15] Czerska M. Zmiana kulturowa w organizacji: Wyzwanie dla współczesnego menedżera. Difin: Warszawa; 2003

[16] Sułkowski Ł. Elementy kultur organizacyjnych przedsiębiorstw rodzinnych w Polsce. Przedsiębiorczość i Zarządzanie. 2013;**XIV**:13-20

[17] Mazur B. Kultura organizacyjna w zróżnicowanym wyznaniowo otoczeniu.

Białystok: Oficyna Wydawnicza Politechniki Białostockiej; 2012

[18] Armstrong M. Jak być lepszym menedżerem. Dom Wydawniczy ABC: Warszawa; 1999

[19] Schein EH. Organizational Culture and Leadership: 2nd Ed. 3rd ed. San Francisco: Jossey-Bass; 2004

[20] Legięć J. Wpływ kultury organizacyjnej na zarządzanie pracą człowieka. Perspektywy kultury/ Perspectives on culture. 2018;**21**:69-87

[21] Kroeber AL, Kultury I. Wyd. 3. Wydawnictwo Naukowe PWN: Warszawa. 2002:175

[22] Benedict R. Patterns of Culture. London: Reprinted.; Routledge & Kegan Paul; 1980

[23] Trompenaars A, Hampden-Turner C. Zarządzanie personelem w organizacjach zróżnicowanych kulturowo. Oficyna Ekonomiczna: Kraków; 2005

[24] Kluckhohn FR, Strodtbeck FL. Variations in Value Orientations; Row, Peterson. New York: Evanston; 1961

[25] Olechnicki K, Załęcki P. Słownik socjologiczny. Graffiti BC: Toruń; 2004

[26] Sułkowski Ł. Procesy kulturowe w organizacjach: Koncepcja, badania i typologia kultur organizacyjnych; TNOiK - Towarzystwo Naukowe Organizacji i Kierownictwa "Dom Organizatora": Toruń. Łódź. 2002. p. 225

[27] Rousseau M. Assessing organizational culture: The case for multiple methods. In: Schneider B, editor. Organizational Climate and Culture. San Francisco, Calif.: Jossey-Bass; 2010. pp. 153-193

[28] Kościuch J. Koncepcja wartości Miltona Rokeacha. Studia Philosophiae Christianae. 1983;**19**:83-96

[29] Czerniawski J, Czerniawska M. Rola zawodowa a system wartości. Test. 1994;**4**:133-139

[30] Czerniawska M. Narodność jako czynnik determinający kody etyczne - analýza comparativcza studentów polskich i rosyjskich. In: Tomczonek Z, editor. Filozoficzno-kulturowe i prawno-gospodarcze aspekty procesów integracyjnych w Europie Środkowo-Wschodniej. Oficyna Wydawnicza Politechniki Białostockiej: Białytok; 2007. pp. 81-90

[31] Oaklander H, Fleishman E. Patterns of leadership related to organizational stress In hospital settings. Nursing Research. 1964;**13**:363. DOI: 10.1097/00006199-196413040-00067

[32] Schermerhorn JR, Hunt JG, Osborn R, Uhl-Bien M. Organizational Behavior. 11th ed. New York: Wiley & Sons; 2010

[33] Mazur B. Organizational Culture under Religious Influence. A Closer Look at Organizational Culture in Action. London, UK: InTech; 2021

[34] Hämmal G, Vadi M. Diagnosing organizational culture through metaphors and task and relationship orientations. University of Tartu Faculty of Economics and Business Administration. 26 Mar 2010;**68**. DOI: 10.2139/ssrn.1578902. Available from: https://ssrn.com/abstract=1578902

[35] Schultz M. On Studying Organizational Cultures: Diagnosis and Understanding. Berlin: Walter de Gruyter; 1995

[36] Harrison R. The Collected Papers of Roger Harrison. 1st ed. 1. print: Jossey-Bass: San Francisco; 1995

[37] Vadi M, Allik J, Realo A. Collectivism and its consequences for organizational culture. Faculty of Economics and

Business Administration, University of Tartu (Estonia). 2002. pp. 1-41

[38] Cameron KS, Quinn RE. Diagnosing and Changing Organizational Culture: Based on the Competing Values Framework: 3rd Ed. 3rd ed. San Francisco, CA: Jossey-Bass; 2011

[39] Mujtaba BG, Khanfar NM, Khanfar SM. Leadership tendencies of government employees in Oman: A study of task and relationship based on age and gender. Public Organization Review. 2010;**10**:173-190. DOI: 10.1007/s11115-009-0103-x

[40] Tran QHN, Jaakson K, Vadi M. Universal task and two faces of relationship orientation: A novel scale to measure organizational culture in Vietnam. Asia Pacific Business Review. 2023. DOI: 10.1080/13602381.2022.2152675

[41] Edwards V, Phan A. 2013 Managers and Management in Vietnam 25Years of Economic Renovation (Doi Moi). New York: Routlege; 2013

[42] Mazur B, Zimnoch K. Kultura organizacyjna przedsiębiorstw społecznych. Przegląd Organizacji. 2022;**8**:14-21

Chapter 3

The Impact of Technological Advances on Cultural Conflicts within Organizations

Ritu Mishra, Saumya Singh and Suruchi Pandey

Abstract

Although some beliefs and norms may not change, as few hold the opinion "culture reflects the heritage of society" rapid pace of digitization and pressures of global competitiveness have accelerated the organizational changing processes and employees behavior patterns. When people from various cultures get together, it might lead to misunderstandings and hostilities. Recent decades have seen significant shifts in cultural norms and values as a direct result of technological advancements. These shifts are happening faster than ever before, and they are causing tension between different cultures which is negatively impacting their Performance. This chapter will examine how technological advancements have influenced culture, and the impact of organizational culture on employee performance and behavior. And contain broad introspective musings on Cultural Shifts and historical contemporary roles of digital technologies; defining traits that encode in our minds and support positive behavior. Rest sections focus on flawed human characteristics with the concept of culture and how it is defined to examine the ways in which technology can lead to cultural change in Employees and the potential for conflict that might come from these changes. The last section will discuss the societal consequences of technologically-induced cultural shifts and techniques to cope with them.

Keywords: norms, digitalization, cyber culture, technology, performance

1. Introduction

1.1 Organizational culture

In today's world, technology is so pervasive that at first, people reacted strangely to it and thought something must be wrong. However, by passing of time they began to adapt these technologies, and eventually, technology began to take inspiration from the way individuals, groups, and societies conceived of the world [1]. The importance of an organization's culture in fostering peak performance cannot be overstated as involvement of modern techniques had changed the human behavior by making things easy and time saving, which is improving their performance at all levels [2]. In the modern world, a thorough understanding of organizational behavior—including its subsets of culture, values, and norms—is essential before attempting to broaden an organization's cultural standards. According to Stephen P. Robinns' Perspective on Organizational behavior is the study of how an organization's structure, culture, and policies influence employee actions and decisions for the benefit of enhancing that organization's efficiency. Culture gives the vitality essential to optimal functioning, much like a healthy cardiovascular system ensures that all of the organs receive sufficient blood flow [3]. Numerous studies have shown introspective looks into the ways in which digital technology has altered modern western civilizations in boosting human organizational performance. The rules, beliefs, customs, and culture of an organization are the glue that holds its myriad individuals, groups, and structures together [4]. What make a country's culture trendy are kinds of things that foreigners do there, such as eating, drinking, and socializing. When it comes to cultural shifts, technology has always acted as a barrier. There is a risk of conflict as new technologies arise and pose threats to established norms and values. Culture is a broad and intricate subject with many facets. The views, values, and customs held in common by a community. People's thoughts, emotions, and actions are molded by the beliefs, values, and norms they were raised with [5]. They also have an impact on interpersonal dynamics. Cultures refers to the deep structure of organization which is rooted in the value, belief, and assumptions held by organizational members. Also Members' perceptions of themselves, their inner workings, their relationships with the outside world, and their hopes for the future are all manifestations of the organization's culture. According to The Business Dictionary, culture is based on shared attitudes, beliefs, customs, and written and unwritten rules that have evolved over time and are considered valid [6].

There are eight mainstays that support a thriving company culture influencing Performance and behavior of employees. The Openness, Confrontation, Trust, Authenticity, Proactively, Autonomy, Collaboration, and Experimentation (OCTAPACE)" profile was created by U. Park. Research into the OCTAPACE culture of any organization lends credence to the importance of training staff members to keep the workplace healthy and productive. Later, T.V. Rao proposed the OCTAPACE culture as a forward-thinking, beneficial method of constructing businesses.

In this way, an organization's culture serves as the social glue that binds its members together by outlining acceptable norms for communication and behavior. Finally, organizational culture functions as a control and meaning-making system that influences employee dispositions and actions. There appears to be a growing recognition of the power of company culture in shaping employee actions in the modern workplace. Technology now plays a central role in shaping every aspect of our lives, and the modern workplace is no exception [7]. The unexpected Covid-19 outbreak accelerated the speed of technology-driven businesses as many employees worked from home, changing societal attitudes about the importance of technology in the workplace. Despite the fact that an organization's culture provides a common language and framework for understanding one another, there is still room for improvement in this area [8]. Culture can have a significant impact on an employee's performance if it fails to adequately support these roles. So, the members of a culture have a common set of values and other ideas, concepts, or notions. A company's culture is something that Culture shapes how people behave, how they see the world around them and what are the changes occurred in their behavior with the changing Technological Culture.

1.2 Types of organization culture

A strong company culture is essential to the success of any business [9]. A company's culture consists of the norms that employees follow when interacting with one another and with those outside the company. There have been many helpful attempts to identify and quantify different types of organizational culture, which can help you learn more about the prevalent corporate culture at your company. Two business professors at the University of Michigan, created the Organizational Culture Assessment Instrument (OCAI) to measure company culture. Based on their analysis of over 12,000 businesses, they identified four distinct corporate cultures: clan, adhocracy, market, and hierarchy. While some cultures are more pervasive than others within an organization, every company has its own distinct blend of the four major cultural dimensions [10]. Below is a breakdown of the Competing Values Framework's 39 indicators and 2 dimensions:-.

Hierarchy Culture: Characterized by a strict organizational structure; What people do is governed by formal rules, processes, and policies; Bureaucracy implies a value for consistency, predictability, and effectiveness [11]. Procedure and process are valued more in hierarchical societies. Leaders make sure workers stick to the company way — the methods that have been shown to be effective in the past. This society has a strong preference for doing things right [12]. Following the laws and guidelines helps businesses cut money and avoid making many mistakes. The military units I served with often emphasized rank and authority. NASA, Exxon Mobil, and General Electric are three other companies that could have a hierarchical culture.

Market Culture: Goal-oriented and competitive in dealings with the outside world. A market culture is one in which people value efficiency and productivity above all else. Competition is commonplace, even among coworkers [13]. The market culture places a premium on steadiness while maintaining an outward gaze. This culture has a strong preference for getting the job done. The primary focus of these businesses is to maximize profits and expand their market share. Amazon and, historically, Ford Motor Company under Henry Ford are two examples of companies that may have a market culture.

Clan Culture: Friendly and cooperative, clan cultures are like one big happy family or clan where everyone knows each other and works together. In this way of life, people enjoy doing things together [14]. The clan's culture encourages adaptability and inward concentration. Members of these groups have common values and are bound together by a sense of loyalty and tradition. Companies such as Ben & Jerry's, Pixar, and Love's Travel Stops may have clan cultures. Organizational structure modeled after a family; Characterized by mutual respect, care, and support; Emphasizing the cultivation of a compassionate workplace.

Adhocracy Culture: Fundamental to this way of life is the idea of ad hoc. Leaders in an adhocracy are often viewed as inspirational innovators who are willing to challenge assumptions and take risks, and employees in such an environment are not afraid to take risks themselves [14]. Organizations are in the business of creating novel products and services (* ad hoc: temporarily, specialized), making them the most responsive to the hyper volatile business conditions. In an adhocracy, they value adaptability and keeping an eye on the outside world. These people take pride in being the ones that do it first. Culture places a premium on adaptability and novelty. Companies like Tesla and Door Dash may have an adhocracy culture.

1.3 Cultural components influencing employees performance

Several factors can be identified that influence employee behavior and performance at work place, Cultural components always have unique personal characteristics which periodically put a dramatic influence on both individual behavior and the behavior of those around us [15]. Any leadership position may be attained with the proper skills and abilities to adjust changes with the culture if required. Few components affecting culture are as follows.

1.4 Norms

Norms are the unspoken standards of conduct that serve as informal guidance for social interaction. People are told by norms what they should be wearing, talking, and believing. They are never put into writing because that would be considered a policy or practise. They spread by word of mouth and behavior, and are upheld by the consequences people face when norms are broken [16]. Because of these responses, they are able to exert considerable control over the behaviors of those around them. The adage "work hard, play hard," "show early, stay late," that "consistently appear busy or relaxed" are frequently used in the workplace are few excellent examples of norms.

1.5 Artifacts

Organizational artifacts are the things people can see, touch, hear, and read about the business. Artifacts can include anything from the physical layout of an office to the wording of memos and letters to the greetings exchanged during meetings and phone calls to the receptionists' responses to visitors and outside calls. Artifacts have the potential to disclose a lot of information.

1.6 Leadership

The "first step in improving an organization's culture is for its leaders to take an honest inventory of how things currently stand [17]. Everyone must ascertain wherever our culture lags low about the employees and normal people have envisioned and whether there are areas that can be enhanced. Leaders who can inspire this kind of introspection must be approachable and sympathetic. By exhibiting these traits, leadership can assess the culture and win the respect of those who work for them.. Trust in leadership, management, and coworkers, as well as trust that the company will deliver on its promises, are essential to fostering a healthy culture inside any organization. They must acquire Qualities to:

- Possess sound communication and listening abilities, and be approachable, genuine, open, and transparent.
- Make two-way communication a priority by paying attention to your staff and allowing for open, frank discussion
- Reinforce the organization's goals, objectives, and values on a regular basis in both your words and your deeds.

1.7 Purpose and values

Organizational values are the core convictions about what is right and beneficial for the business. An organization is said to be value-driven if its 'value set' is known and understood by all its employees, rather than just the management. The more the value, the greater its impact on one's actions [18]. This is true regardless of whether or not they have been stated. Unlike professed ideals that are idealistic and not expressed in the action of the management, the influence of "couched morals rooted down in organization and are toughened by behavioral attitude that can be substantial. Performance, proficiency, competition, and teamwork are all terms that can be implied or stated directly.

The stated goal and core values of the corporation should match its declared objectives and ways of operation. Any discrepancy between an employer's words and deeds will be swiftly pointed out by their staff. Employees who adhere to the organization's goal are more committed to its success, more inclined to work there for a long time, and better equipped to contribute to that success. Organizations need to do the following to foster a purpose-driven culture that strengthens workers' ties to their work:

- Adopt a framework for introducing their purpose or mission to life through action and conduct (values).

- Clearly communicate the purpose, mission, and values; and

- frequently exhibit concrete examples of employees' contributions to the success of the organization.

1.8 Employee empowerment

Workers wish making difference and contribute to the team. What they really want from their employers is the freedom to do their jobs when, where, and how they see fit. When companies give their workers more freedom, responsibility, and appreciation, they foster a more positive work environment. Workers who have more autonomy in their work get better results. As a result, the company culture has become more robust. A culture of empowerment can be fostered in a company by:

- "Providing flexible work arrangements, including location flexibility (e.g., remote, hybrid and work from anywhere) and schedule flexibility (e.g., flextime, compressed work week, shifted start-stop times, part-time schedules, job sharing and more)

- Demonstrating appreciation for employee contributions through rewards, recognition, compensation and benefits

- Encouraging managers and peers to provide employees with frequent and meaningful feedback"

1.9 Holistic and inclusive well-being

Employers have a significant role to play in reviving their exhausted staff members. In particular, employers should prioritize the health and happiness of underrepresented employee groups, who are disproportionately affected by discrimination and stress in the workplace. The following are some ways in which businesses can make holistic and inclusive well-being central to their mission and values:

- "Investing in resources and tools that support employees' physical, emotional and mental health

- Reinforcing business norms that promote healthy culture, including regular business hours, meeting-free days, recommended daily breaks, PTO usage and ideas for connecting informally with colleagues

- Evaluating diversity, equity and inclusion programs to assess whether all employees feel supported to be their authentic selves at work regardless of whether they work on-site, remotely or a combination of the two

- Ensuring equity and inclusion is not just touted in hiring practices, but is also ingrained throughout all business practices and reflected in the culture

1.10 Professional development and growth opportunities"

When workers do not see room for advancement in their careers, they generally look elsewhere for employment. Employees are more inclined to stay with a company if they can see a clear route for professional growth and promotion. Employees in a company with a growth culture are more likely to innovate because they are more open to trying new things, taking calculated risks, and looking beyond the status quo for answers.

Organizations can foster a culture of growth by:

- Activating professional development frameworks that include financial support and time allocations

- Offering coaching and internal advancement programs

- Intentionally developing young talent by encouraging mentorship connections and strong on boarding programs

- Rethinking how they create growth and connection opportunities in today's hybrid and remote work environments, especially for young talent who may need more hands-on mentorship."

1.11 Communication

A healthy company culture is built on solid communication. The other five factors of organizational culture outlined in this article are only as effective as the level of employee engagement, awareness of the employee experience, and implementation of new programmes and products that are communicated to the workforce. Employers can gain employees' trust by open communication. When companies are able to effectively convey information to their staff, it helps them feel more included and invested in their work. Organizations can build a trusting and healthy culture with communication by:

- Having an internal communication strategy aligned to the organization's purpose and values

- Investing in communication training for leaders and managers and identifying employee influencers capable of championing the culture and values

- Listening to employees by asking them questions, providing space for employee input, and taking time to reflect on what they have to say

- Adopting the tools and channels necessary to frequently reach out, listen to and engage all employees, regardless of when, where and how they work.

Today's" businesses encounter intricate problems. Despite the ever-shifting landscape, one constant remains: a company's success or failure hinges on its ability to attract and retain the best individuals available. These six aspects of company culture they directly or indirectly effects employees are essential to the success of every business. In the normal context of constant development and competition, the alternative cannot survive for very long in lack of any of these components.

2. Cultural change

The HRD environment and culture of an organization originates in the values of its leadership and is further shaped by the HRD system and its associated practices [19]. Cultural transitions were previously seen as highly idiosyncratic or only tenuously linked to other social movements, making their research the purview of historians and political scientists [20]. "Changes in the ideas, norms, and behaviors of a group of people (or shifts in the contents or themes of their products reflecting such shifts) over time, typically on the scale of decades or centuries, are difficult to study and understand, but recent theoretical and methodological advances have led to the emergence of more systematic and rigorous approaches in psychology". In Strong organization culture, employee feels appreciated and hence have gained great decision making ability which ultimately leads to better performance [21]. They do not feel helpless at work; they at least have some influence over it whether via working from home or selecting their own endeavors, or even in new job orientation. An organization's culture consists of the unspoken norms, customs, and underlying values that shape employee behavior and ultimately, productivity [22]. As the nature of global competition shifts and the demand on businesses increases, companies are increasingly prioritizing and putting more emphasis on their cultures. This is due to the paradoxical fact that strong organizational cultures foster both continuity and change. Consensus on a common set of values acts as a stabilizing force inside an organization. The psychological insights gained from studying cultural shifts in relation to the reliability of different tests of mental operations can be quite novel [23]. Many studies of cultural shift have assumed that persistent cultural ideas like individualism/collectivism, social capital, and gender disparity have constant characteristics throughout history. It's an empirical question, though, whether the psychological import of such ideas holds steady or shifts over time [24]. The term culture change or transformation refers to a transition that can affect an entire company or just one division. To achieve the desired culture, it is necessary to alter the attitudes, beliefs, and abilities of the workforce. It all starts with a person's conviction (heart) to alter their ways. Then, individuals need the knowledge (thought) and ability (skills) to implement the changes in behavior that are necessary.

However, organizational culture is a major stumbling block to change; the requirement for cultural change is often overlooked in transformation initiatives, which is known to contribute to the high rates of transformation project failures [25]. The culture of an organization and its strategic direction tend to converge over time and reinforce one another. The challenge arises when top management makes a strategic shift that calls for a sea change in employee mindset and behavior [26]. While in theory a new strategy can be adopted instantly, in practice it often takes much longer and requires much more effort to do so, especially if the status quo of old attitudes and behavior patterns persists. Our world is characterized by two main types of cultural shift:

2.1 Employee level cultural change

People have a natural inclination to resist change; a comprehensive strategy that takes into account both personnel and the organizational processes that shape their actions and behaviors on the job is necessary to overcome this resistance and achieve lasting improvements in the company's culture. There must be two steps involved at the employee level. First, all employees should be updated on the company's new business plan or other changes in a way that takes into account their individual learning styles and interests. Second, employees should be actively engaged through team meetings, staff workshops, or other venues in adapting the new strategy or goals to their specific areas of responsibility. Taking a two-pronged approach like this can assist foster new norms that will drive the behaviors needed to get there.

2.2 Organizational level culture change

However, attempts at the individual level are insufficient to foster long-term cultural change since culture eventually becomes institutionalized and engrained in the very fabric of the organization, creating its structure and systems and reinforcing these in turn. In specifically, seven change shaping levers that support organizational culture can be identified; these levers need to be realigned with a new strategy to encourage good cultural changes.

3. Developing organizational climate

The term organizational climate refers to the degree to which a company encourages its workers to express their unique personalities and ideas on the job. An organization's mood, or organizational climate, as some call it, can evolve slowly over time and fluctuate often depending on how much attention is paid to it [27]. The climate of an organization can be gauged with the help of questionnaires and other instruments. The health of an organization's culture can be gauged by measuring employee satisfaction on a variety of factors. A company may, for instance, find out through its staff that, while its constraint system is robust, its decision-making procedures are in effect [1]. Several variables impact the atmosphere in an organization. The culture of an organization can be improved with the help of incentives like annual bonuses, parties, and presents. When employees are trusted, valued, heard, and given opportunities to contribute, it's a sign of a positive work environment. When companies invest in their employees' personal and professional development, they boost morale and productivity [28]. The morale and output of workers can be affected by the atmosphere of the workplace. However, in order to achieve these desirable outcomes, a company must make substantial investments in a number of critical areas. The following are domains where the influence of organizational climate can be seen.

3.1 Constraints

The importance of setting limits and limits in the workplace cannot be overstated. When workers have clear goals and responsibilities but are also encouraged to think beyond the box, they tend to excel. However, it is important for businesses to avoid placing too many restrictions on their employees, as this can have a negative impact on morale and output.

3.2 Communication

Organizational climate is enhanced when employees feel they receive constructive, fair, and regular feedback from their leaders [29]. They also appreciate the opportunity to be heard on issues that matter to them and their daily work. In other words, communication works best when all parties have a fairly equal amount of time to share their thoughts.

3.3 Decision-making

Buy-in is a powerful motivator. That is why it is good for an organization to seek their employees' input on important decisions, especially when it comes to individual and departmental goals. If employees feel involved with business efforts from beginning to end, they are more likely to feel a stronger sense of ownership and accountability.

3.4 Policies and procedures

Employees can be a valuable resource in developing better policies and procedures for their work units and even companywide. By being on the front lines and experiencing processes firsthand, they can help root out inefficiencies, errors, and discriminatory practices. As a result, organizational climate improves.

3.5 Infrastructure

Organizational climate is also affected by infrastructure, which includes facilities, equipment, technologies, and other tools that help employees do their work. Though some innovations in infrastructure may be more challenging to a workforce at first (e.g., getting new computers), a forward-thinking, responsive organizational climate usually appeals to employees. Organizational climate is important for many reasons. It establishes constraint systems so employees know appropriate boundaries. It also drives how organizations communicate, make decisions, establish policies and procedures, and contribute innovatively to their fields.

3.6 Classification of organizational climate

All organizations are unique, which means each one differs in organizational climate from one another sharing peoples of different mindset and behavior. As cultural climate are the recurring patterns of behavior, attitudes and feelings that characterize life in the organization, while an organization culture tends to be deep and stable [30]. However, they can often be categorized under some common organizational climate types, four of which are explained.

1. **People-Oriented Climate** The organizational culture that includes a core set of values and puts its onus on care and concern for the employees' results in people-oriented climate.

2. **Rule-Oriented Climate** The organizational culture that provides for featured benefits and puts its burden on attention to details by all the members' result in rule-oriented climate.

3. **Innovation-Oriented Climate** The organizational culture that introduces new ways and processes to develop new and innovative things results in innovation-oriented climate.

4. **Result-Oriented Climate** The organizational culture that gives preference to values and puts its onus on refining every detail of the processes to refine and achieve results is known as result-oriented climate.

3.7 Technological impact on cultural norms

In recent years, technology has had a profound effect on culture, causing shifts in norms and priorities. These shifts will become more obvious as technology advances, increasing the potential for cultural friction. In this paper, we'll look at how technological advancements have influenced culture, how those shifts have affected values and conventions, and how that might lead to friction between groups with different worldviews. "*Technology is available in the market for a price. But what is not available in the market for a price are Values, which translates to – Culture, Empathy, Ethics, Transparency, and Trust.*" (Arundhati Ashoka, 23). In recent decades, technological advancements have fueled a wide range of cultural shifts. The emergence of social media has been one of the most transformative factors since it has radically affected people's habits of sharing information and interacting with one another. The advent of social media has made it easier for people to communicate with one another across geographic and cultural boundaries. Because of this, individuals are more open to discussing their beliefs and ideals with one another, which has altered their perspectives on life [31]. The expansion of online shopping is another example of how technology has influenced cultural shifts. The advent of online marketplaces has revolutionized the way commodities are bought and sold, making it simpler than ever to gain access to a global market. As a result, people's perspectives on consumption and the worth of material goods have shifted. The proliferation of mobile devices has also contributed significantly to the shift in values. Thanks to smart phones and other mobile devices, we can now get our hands on news, music, and movies whenever and wherever we choose. The result is a shift in how we value social interaction and how we spend our free time [32]. The idea of technology is similarly intricate and varied. It's the methods employed to resolve issues or accomplish objectives. Technology has the potential to better people's lives, but it also has the potential to cause them harm [33]. There are numerous ways in which technological advancements may alter cultural norms. It has the potential to alter people's modes of expression, education, employment, and socialization. People's perspectives on themselves and the world can also be altered by technological advancements [34]. Technology-driven cultural transformation has the potential to spark serious conflicts [35]. Emergence of new technology might pose a threat to established norms and values. People with contrasting norms and beliefs may find themselves at odds as a result. Technology can influence cultures in a number of different ways. Introducing novel concepts and ideals is one approach. For instance, the proliferation of online communication has facilitated the exchange of ideas and ideals among people from different parts of the world. Traditional patterns of living can also be altered as a result of technological advancements. People's ways of working and living have shifted as a result of the advent of automation and the resulting displacement of some workers. Altering social structures is another way in which technology contributes to cultural shifts.

For instance, [36] the proliferation of social media has given rise to brand new online communities, which have the potential to profoundly affect individuals' attitudes and actions.

- Technology-driven cultural transformation has the potential to spark serious conflicts. Emergence of new technology might pose a threat to established norms and values. People with contrasting norms and beliefs may find themselves at odds as a result.

- For instance, the proliferation of social media has contributed to wider societal divisions. This is because social media users can choose to exclusively interact with other users who share their views, creating a kind of echo chamber. Because of this, there is a higher potential for confusion and strife. The rise of automation is another example of the potential for conflict that might arise as a result of technology-driven cultural change. Displacement of workers due to automation is a potential source of friction between employees and their employers.

There is no denying the profound effect that technological advancements have had on our culture [37]. Rapid technological progress has facilitated widespread cultural corruption through materialism, edging us ever closer to an unhealthy lifestyle's nonexistence. One positive effect of technology is that it has allowed society to increase production, provide services to a wider population, and enjoy more prosperity. It has also had a significant cultural impact and impacted daily life. Language, art, movement, education, and faith are just few of the cultural spheres that have been profoundly influenced by technological advancements [38]. The global dissemination of knowledge made possible by digital technology has altered the ways in which different societies perceive and engage with one another. Cultures are influenced by and can mingle with one another thanks to technological advances. It has had an impact on every facet of society, including medicine, transportation, and even power. However, there are many who worry that technology is replacing humans' intellectual success with mindless conveniences. The good and the bad effects of technology on culture are equally significant. While it has improved areas like education, healthcare, and research, it has also altered cultural norms and practices in profound ways. The overemphasis on technology is to blame for unemployment and cultural backwardness [39], as well as the resulting lack of trust among the general public.

- There have been both beneficial and negative impacts of technology on culture.

- Causes of addiction include reliance on others, mass-produced culture.

4. Organizational culture transformation

Industry's repeated failures at Change Management gave rise to Cultural Transformation, a pumped-up procedural and behavioral paradigm [40]. In the early 21st century, as we re-engineered businesses and procedures, we learned that people were not like machines or processes and therefore could not be re-engineered [41]. As a result, Endeavor employs an array of methods for bringing about the cultural and individual shifts that are necessary for every business to function at its highest potential [42]. To make any kind of lasting change at a firm in the modern day, we must first acknowledge that individuals must condition their attitudes, values, beliefs, and priorities in order to alter their behavior and, by extension, the company's culture. Intentional leadership behavior, leadership actions, and employee inputs are required to successfully design an organization-wide transformation beyond.

4.1 Three M's of cultural transformation

Organizational culture always a hot topic within human resources departments as it effects impact all aspects of a company's operations and Functioning. Recent [36]. Psychological Researches has uncovered three leading elements of Cultural Transformation [43].

4.2 Measure

This is the first essential step in any cultural change initiative – finding out where you are starting from by taking the time to learn the core values of your valued employees. By determining what is important to people at levels within your organization, you can align your culture effectively. And Baumgartner says not to be surprised that values can differ by level, function and, if your company has multiple offices, by location as well.

4.3 Manage

Once you have a list of your employees' core values, simplify them as best you can and narrow them down to 1–3 values so that you can methodically adjust your organization's recruitment, engagement and retention around a manageable list. Focusing on these main values, apply them to your organization's:

- Communication: values to reinforce those ideals in every written and spoken communication. In the end, this will result in the development of a language exclusive to your company's culture. Integrate your company's beliefs into the way you evaluate applicants for employment and the recruiting process. Standardize the criteria through which you assess applicants' values. Establish culture gatekeepers and refrain from recruiting candidates who do not strongly fit the culture.

- Employee Engagement / Development: Establish a road map for success beneath your organization by letting your fundamental values dictate how you engage and develop your staff. For instance, if your staff members desire to Encourage everyone to be challenged by your company's principles by assigning them to tasks that will push and broaden their horizons. Give them benefits that will help them achieve a better work-life balance if they want one. Play to your staff's strengths and honor your company's basic beliefs.

4.4 Monitor

It is essential to establish metrics by which your progress may be monitored. According to Baumgartner, in order to effect lasting cultural shifts, you must provide concrete evidence that people's lives are improving as a result of your efforts. Think about and evaluate: Are individuals more involved and content than before? Is there an increase in output? What kind of progress have we made in terms of memory retention? Is there greater nuance in the hiring process? How well do new hires mesh with the existing team dynamic?

Supporting your organization in achieving its goals is no easy task, but by keeping these three Ms. in mind and addressing them, you can help it succeed. Once it happens, good things will start happening across the board for your business.

4.5 Cultural values and its dimensions

The IBM Values Survey was conducted from 1967 to 1973. (Geert [44]) Factor analysis on the findings of a global survey provided Geert Hofstede with the foundation for his first model. It's been improved upon since then. Using a framework borrowed from factor analysis, he explains how a culture shapes individuals' values and how those values influence their actions. Cultural values were intended to be analyzed along four dimensions in the original theory: The cultural dimensions theory given by Hofstede are as under;

1. "Power Distance Index (PDI),

2. Individualism vs. Collectivism (IDV),

3. Uncertainty Avoidance Index (UAI),

4. Masculinity vs. Femininity (MAS)

5. Long-term Orientation vs. Short-term Orientation (LTO)

6. Indulgence vs. Restraint (IND)".

The Power Distance Index (PDI) measures how much less powerful members of institutions and organizations (such as families) acknowledge and anticipate that power is not allocated fairly. In this dimension, followers at the lower level sense inequity and authority. A higher Index degree means that hierarchy is undeniably created and followed in society, without hesitation or justification. A lower Index score indicates that individuals challenge authority and want to share power.

Collectivism vs. Individualism (IDV): This indicator investigates the degree of social integration of individuals. Individualistic cultures tend to have weak relationships that frequently only connect a person to his or her immediate family. "I versus the We" is emphasized. Collectivism, which is its antithesis, Imagine a world where extended families and other in-groups are connected through tightly-integrated ties. These in-groups have an undeniable bond of loyalty and stand by one another when there is an issue with another in-group.

Index of Uncertainty Avoidance (UAI): The Uncertainty Avoidance Index measures a society's propensity to welcome or avoid an occurrence that is unexpected, uncharted, or inconsistent with the status quo. An index with a lower value indicates that more people accept different viewpoints. The environment is more free-flowing, ambiguity is more common, and society tends to put less restrictions.

Masculinity vs. Femininity (MAS): Masculinity refers to the inclination in society for success, bravery, aggressiveness, and monetary benefits. Its opposite stands for a preference for harmony, modesty, helping the weak, and high quality of life. Women tend to exhibit distinct ideals in their respective communities. Equally with males, feminine civilizations value modesty and compassion. Women are more competitive and emphatic in civilizations where men are more dominant, although they are noticeably less emphatic than men. They nevertheless acknowledge the discrepancy in values between men and women. In communities that are predominately masculine, this component is typically seen as forbidden.

IND: Indulgence vs. Restraint Whether or not the basic delights are realized, this dimension ultimately serves as a gauge of happiness. A civilization that permits the relatively unrestricted satisfaction of fundamental and natural needs is considered indulgent to human needs.

4.6 Changes in values and norms

There have been substantial shifts in values and conventions as a result of technological advancements. Popularity of social media is only one factor that has pushed individuals to put more effort into marketing themselves. The ideals, customs, and practices of a society are all manifestations of its culture [45]. A culture can learn about itself through its members by examining how they think, act, and share knowledge and technology. Language, art, movement, education, and religion are just few of the essential facets of human civilization that have been profoundly influenced by technological advancements. A community's culture provides a benchmark against which technological innovations are evaluated, and assessed. Technology has an impact on every facet of culture; it ultimately dictates the course of Cultural Revolution [46]. If technology is not in tune then will be conflict between the advancement of technology and the preservation of cultural norms depending on the social and cultural circumstances of the community. When reason and emotion are in balance, freedom of speech in the technical world transcends boundaries of race, age, and educational attainment. The lack of limits, regulations, and repercussions could lead to a cultural decline if people exploit it to live out their wildest ambitions [47]. Culture can be seen in the ways in which people think and act. Culture is observed by people as a mirror reflecting their own ideas, behaviors, values, and acquired knowledge. Technology has had profound effects on fundamental facets of human culture, including language, education, mobility, art, and religion [48]. The cultural norms of a society are used as a yardstick by which technological innovations evaluate. The development of culture is ultimately shaped by technology since it has an influence on all facets of culture. Technology must be in sync with community social and cultural contexts if it is to occupy the larger cultural dimension. If it is not, there will be tension between technological progress and the maintenance of cultural norms".

It increasingly common for people to construct identities based on how they appear online. Because of this, people's views on privacy and authenticity have shifted [49]. Values and customs have shifted as a result of the expansion of online shopping. Nowadays, ease of use and availability are prioritized by consumers over product perfection. Our standardized way of life has erased traces of our heritage. Inevitably, technology has had a profound effect on our customs and values, and this influence may be broken down into subcategories based on how they manifest in modern society. The language was developed so that younger generations may communicate with their elders and gain wisdom from their experiences. They created tools for farming, structures for living in, and weapons for both offense and defense [50]. Technology advances in tandem with the expanding human population. Because of scientific and technological progress, the average human lifespan has risen. The advent of the printing press paved way for more people to gain access to education, literature, and information. When the technical world kept in check, people of various ages, backgrounds, and levels of expertise are able to openly express their ideas and opinions. We rely on current techniques to fulfill our dreams letting true, and if no restrictions are there on rules, regulations, or consequences, humanity could suffer [28]. Every facet of human life is being affected by the rapid development of technology. Benefits of cutting-edge digital methods are having far-reaching effects on our societies. However, the process of cultural change management is one of the most important business problems, not the devices, software, or solutions themselves.

5. Cultural conflicts and conflict resolution

Because wars are fought between people, cultures are always present. The naming, framing, blaming, and taming of conflicts are all influenced by cultural norms. The existence or nonexistence of a conflict is a matter of perspective [51]. Culture is always a factor in conflict, regardless it has a significant impact or a minor one [27, 52]. Any argument that has an impact on us where it counts—where we create meaning and uphold our identities—always has a cultural component.. Disputes that refuse to be resolved, such as the Israeli-Palestinian conflict or the dispute between India and Pakistan over Kashmir, involve more than just questions of territory, boundaries, and sovereignty; they also involve the recognition, expression, and legitimization of distinctive identities and methods of existence and meaning-making [53].

Generational culture shapes teen-parent problems, while gender culture shapes marital or partnership disagreements [54]. Conflicts between different disciplinary cultures in the workplace can lead to misunderstandings and miscommunication among coworkers. Culture is always present in war, whether it surges ahead with overwhelming force or creeps along undetected until it is almost tripped over by the unaware. A Brief Discussion. The following are the levels at which conflicts can be found:

5.1 Level 1 – Individual level conflict

All people have internal conflict, which management should be aware of. When a person's desires and motivations are suppressed or when he is presented with opposing roles and objectives and is forced to make choices, conflict develops inside them. Unacceptability, Incomparability, and Uncertainty are other causes of interpersonal conflict.

Types of conflict at individual level are:

a. Frustration: An individual feels irritated when they fail to achieve their goals. The highest level of discontent is frustration, which leads to conflict in the individual. The four major categories for the protective mechanism, result, or response to frustration are as follows: [55]

(i) Aggression (ii) Withdrawal (iii) Fixation and (iv) Compromise

b. Goal Conflict: When two or more issues compete with one another, goal conflict arises. Conflict arises when an individual cannot decide which objective should be pursued because it has both good and bad aspects or because there are two or more goals that are in competition with one another. The following aim conflicts have been discovered in this context.

c. On the Basis of Individual Cultural identity Conflict are then sub categories as:-

5.2 Approach-approach conflict

In this sort of conflict, one person will have two intense, positively valenced desires. Consider the following scenario: A person is faced with two tempting employment offers and must select one of them. Tension results. Such conflicts are less destructive after choosing a side. The other one instantly becomes less significant to him or diminishes. But in some circumstances, choosing will be exceedingly challenging. For instance, a lady must decide between choosing her parents or a lover for an intercaste marriage. These situations are similar to "you can't have your cake and eat it, too."

5.3 Avoidance-avoidance conflict

There are two negative ends at stake here. There are times when a person must pick between two undesirable outcomes. Both outcomes are undesirable in a dispute of this nature, but he cannot remain neutral. A woman, for instance, is forced to choose between working a job she despises and staying unemployed. The person is hemmed in by two antagonistic dangers, anxieties, or circumstances. If she is stuck between the two options, she can always leave the field. However, the escape could have negative repercussions. A person who is unable to persuade his or her mother or spouse could, for instance, turn to harmful behaviors like excessive alcohol usage or suicide.

When trapped in such situations with no way out, some people may resort to 'amnesia' or other defense mechanisms like regression or fantasy to alleviate their stress.

5.4 Approach-Avoidance conflict

This is also a very tough and complex conflict to resolve. For the simple reason that in this kind of struggle, the target of one's desires serves as both an attraction and a repulsion. In this case, the target item will be emotionally charged in two ways. The pleasant valence first draws the guy in, but the negative valence pushes him away. Frustration and stress result from being drawn to the target but unable to approach it. An individual may be torn between accepting a job offer because the pay is good and turning it down because it's too dangerous. Aman wants to get married and start a family, but he has little interest in taking on parental obligations.

5.5 Multiple-Approach-Avoidance conflict

Multiple positive and negative valences will be at play in some of life's events. Let us say a woman has accepted a marriage proposal [54]. For her, marriage represents a number of good things—namely, the chance to spend the rest of her life with someone she adores. However, if she feels she will lose out in the marriage because she will no longer be able to maintain her current level of financial and social status, she may become resentful of the union. The cumulative value of both valences will determine the outcome of this conflict. If positive valence wins out, she'll leave her career and pursue marriage; if negative valence wins out, she might turn down marriage and keep working.

5.6 Level-2 Interpersonal conflict

Interpersonal conflict is the most common and readily apparent sort of "conflict, and it happens when two or more people disagree. All conflicts may be boiled down to interpersonal tensions since the majority of disputes result from tensions between members of the same organization or group and members of other companies or groups (2001).

According to Researcher Wherten and Cameron, there are four sources of interpersonal conflict.

1. Personal Disparities: Personal disparities can be a key cause of interpersonal conflict. The upbringing, cultural and familial customs, family background, educational experiences, and values of each person vary.

2. Information Deficiency: Information deficiencies can sometimes lead to disputes between people. This kind of dispute frequently comes from a breakdown in organizational communication.

3. Role incompatibility is yet another potential cause of interpersonal conflict. Many managers work in cross-functional organizations nowadays, where their particular positions may not be compatible due to interrelated duties and functions.

4. Environmental Stress: Environmental stress may also be the cause of the interpersonal conflict. Environment-related stress is brought on by dwindling or scarce resources, downsizing, pressure from the marketplace, and a high level of uncertainty.

5.7 Level3- Group level conflict

Most of the group is made up of two or more people who interact with one another, possess distinct roles and status relationships, and adhere to certain principles and standards of conduct to ensure efficient operation. Groups have an influence on other organizations as a whole in addition to the conduct of its individual members. Two different sorts of conflict arise during this contact process:

a. **Intra Group Conflict**: Intra group conflict is visual when group conflict may arise in three ways [56].

Intra group conflict is like the interpersonal conflict with the difference that the persons involved in the conflict episode belong to a common group. The causes are similar to those of interpersonal conflicts.

i. An all new issue arises.

ii. When new values are imported from the social environment into the group and

iii. When a person's extra group role comes into conflict with his intra group role.

b. **Inter Group Conflict:** Conflicts between different groups in the organization are known as inter-group conflicts [57]. Organizational conflict is another way to describe inter-group conflict. Intergroup conflict factors can be categorized under the following four headings:

1. No joint decision-making.

2. Disparate objectives.

3. Differences in objectives and perceptions and.

Organizational conflict may be categorized structurally into four categories:

a. Hierarchical Conflict: This is the conflict that arises between several organizational levels. For instance, the top or lower level management may disagree with the intermediate level management.

b. Functional Conflict: Conflict that arises inside an organization's multiple functional divisions is referred to as functional conflict. Because the marketing department and the manufacturing department could clash

c. Line-Staff Discord: One may say that line staff conflict is the conflict between members of the queue and staff: Conflict between members of the queue and staff may also be referred to as line-staff conflict. Conflict arises when staff personnel have little control over those in queue because of this. d) Formal-Informal Conflict: This type of conflict occurs when formal and informal organizations are involved.

5.8 Level 4-Organizational level conflict

De Dreu and Weingart [58] the term stress brought on by the surroundings. Resources are becoming increasingly scarce, which causes environmental stress. Conflict at the organizational scale might arise between the buyer and seller organizations, between a union and the organizations that employ its members, or between the organizations that are regulated by the government and those that are impacted by it.

5.9 Process of conflict

Conflict is a dynamic process consisting of a chain of events which tend to unfold in a particular sequence There are 5 stages of a conflict episode as described below.

1. **Latent Conflict:** Conflict episode begins with latent conflict. Important sources of organizational conflict include competition for scarce resources, drive for autonomy, divergence of sub-unit goals, competition for organizational positions and even role conflict.

2. **Perceived Conflict:** In few situations Conflict perceive even if, no conditions latent conflict exists and latent conflict circumstances present might be in a relationship with out of the participant perceiving conflict. Perceived Conflict results due to the misunderstanding of each other's true position.

3. **Felt Conflict**: It is at the felt level that college of employees becomes sensitively mixed up in a conflict and face anxiety, tension, frustration, or hostility. There is an important distinction conflict. Between perceiving conflict and already Perceived conflict results due to feeling conflict, Because a conflict is perceived does not mean that it is — personalized. The Cognition and personalization are two distinct stages.

4. **Manifest conflict:** Conflict behavior that is really manifested can take many different forms, including open anger, physical and verbal violence, sabotage, indifference, retreat, and so on Parties act in ways that cause reactions from one another.

5. **Aftermath Conflict**: Depending on how the dispute is resolved, the consequences of conflict-related behaviors can either be beneficial or harmful for the parties involved.

5.10 Models of conflict resolution management

Conflict Management by M P Follet M P Follett highlighted prime issues rise by conflicting environment. She makes the case in her essay "Constructive Conflict" that conflict should be seen as a typical organizational process [59]. She believed it to be no wasteful outbreak of incompatibilities, in spite regular methods through which socially valuable differences register themselves for the enrichment of all concerned [60]. For the constructively working on conflict. Follett says there are 4 ways of resolving conflict:

1. Dominance is the triumph of one side over the other: This is the quickest approach to resolve a dispute, but it rarely works in the long run.

2. Making a compromise is the second technique to resolve a dispute. In this, each party makes a small concession in order to achieve peace, or, to put it another way, in order to resume the activity that the war has halted. The cornerstone of trade union strategies is compromise.

3. Situational manipulation by one party is what manipulation is all about.

4. Integration seeks an outcome in which neither party is required to make any concessions and where the goals of both parties are satisfied. Only integration, she said, actually stabilizes.

Conflict Mode of Thomas-Kilmann [61] on the Instrument Behavioral scientists Kenneth Thomas and Ralph Kilmann devised the Thomas-Kilmann Conflict Mode responding to right or wrong, although one or more styles might be avoidance, and accommodation. This is another form of conflict resolution. Conflict resolution methods that are improper for the circumstances at hand, such as competitiveness, cooperation, and compromise, have the affect of making the situation quickly get out of hand.

- **Competing (Goal: I win, you lose)**

A competitive personality comes off as forceful, dictatorial, confrontational, and threatening in others. A competitive style is an effort to exert pressure and achieve authority at the expense of the opposing party. When you need to execute an unpopular choice, make a speedy decision, the decision is crucial in a crisis, or it's critical to let people know how important an issue is to you standing up for your rights, using a competitive style of conflict management may be acceptable. The major drawback of utilizing this approach is that relationships may be irreparably damaged, which may inspire other parties to utilize subversive tactics to further their interests.

People have become nothing more than if you are not with me, you.

- **Accommodating (Goal: I lose, you win)**

In accommodating, we put other people's wants ahead of your own because you want to maintain harmony. Maintaining the connection is of utmost importance. Smoothing or harmonizing can produce emotions in a person that vary from rage to joy and can lead to a false solution to a problem: The role of the martyr or complainer may be played by accommodating people because they lack confidence and are cooperative. However, because it maintains relationships, accommodation may be advantageous when one is mistaken or when one wants to minimize losses when they are going to lose anyhow. It may become competitive — I'm nicer than you are — if you use it all the time, which may lead to a lack of originality in dispute resolution and worsened power disparities.

- **Avoiding (Goal: I lose, you lose)**

Avoidance is the purposeful avoidance or withdrawal from a disagreement rather than its confrontation. This approach could come off as indifference to one's own problems or those of others. Those who ignore a situation do so in the hopes that it will go away, solve itself without their assistance, or that someone else will step up to the plate. There are times when it is wise to avoid conflict, such as when you need more time to consider your options, pressing deadlines require a delay, conflict would damage a working relationship, or your requirements are unlikely to be met. Avoidance, meanwhile, can backfire if the other person thinks you do not care enough to interact. This approach permits the avoidance of conflict by ignoring it.

- **Compromising (Goal: I win some, you win some)**

The compromise approach shows that you are prepared to put up some of your aims in exchange for other people's agreement to give up some of theirs. Resolutions may entail dividing the disagreement or looking for a middle ground, but compromising keeps the partnership intact and can go more quickly than collaborating. Compromise has the drawback of sometimes being a quick fix and limiting fresh creative possibilities. It can lead to game-playing and less-than-ideal results if you consistently straddle the line or split the difference.

- **Collaborating (Coal: I win, you win)**

Conflicts are seen as issues to be solved in the collaborative approach, and innovative solutions that address the needs of all parties are sought for. You examine the situation in order to discover the underlying issues, challenge your own beliefs, and comprehend other people's points of view without sacrificing your own self-interest. Collaboration takes time, consequently it might not be worthwhile constructing a win-win solution if the relationship between the parties is not significant. However, cooperation promotes connections, respect, and trust. Address the dispute immediately and in a way that shows willingness for all parties to obtain what they need in order to foster a more collaborative atmosphere.

6. Conclusion

Potential for conflict that can arise from technology-driven cultural change is significant. Undoubtfully technology is changing every aspect of our lives. And the benefits provided by new digital approaches are showing a huge improved impact on our societies. However, one of the greatest business challenges is not about the devices, software or solutions – it is about how we positively manage the process of cultural change. It's important to remember that technology is not inherently bad as Technology and culture directly influence each other. As cultures change, so does the technology it innovates Structure. Much of this is for the greater good. It can be used to improve the quality of life and living Standards, but it can also be used to harm people. So it's important to be aware of the potential for conflict that can arise from technology-driven cultural change, so that we can take steps to mitigate this conflict.

One way to mitigate the conflict that can arise from technology-driven cultural change is through education and sharing knowledge about not only our customs, traditions and norms but also to respect each and every culture in the same way as we do ours. It is important to educate people about the potential impact of new technologies; so that they can make informed decisions about how to use these technologies. Another way to mitigate the conflict that can arise from technology-driven cultural change is through dialog. It is important to create spaces where people can come together to discuss the impact of new technologies, and to find ways to bridge the gaps between people who hold different values and norms. Through taking these corrective measures we can help to create a more all-encompassing and harmonious societal face of technology-driven cultural change.

Author details

Ritu Mishra[1*], Saumya Singh[2] and Suruchi Pandey[3]

1 Amity University, Patna, India

2 Sam Higginbottom University of Agriculture, Technology and Sciences, India

3 Symbiosis Institute of Management Studies, Symbiosis International University, Pune, India

*Address all correspondence to: mishraritu590@gmail.com

References

[1] Zohuri B, Mossavar-Rahmani F. The impact of technology on human behavior. 2019:353-402. DOI: 10.1201/9781003000662-9

[2] Tyna Yunita A, Sasmoko B, Agustinus Bandur C, Firdaus AD. Technological capacity and organizational culture: The importance of organizational ambidexterity in the banking sector. 2023:1-18. DOI: 10.26668/businessreview/2023.v8i5.1479

[3] Zhang M, Tansuhaj P. Organizational culture, information technology capability, and performance: The case of born global firms. Multinational Business Review. 2007;**15**. DOI: 10.1108/1525383X200700012.pp.1-15

[4] Auge M. The Future. New York: Verso Book; 2015

[5] Puri V. The Future of SaaS: Emerging Trends for a Dynamic Industry. (NASSCOM); 2023. pp. 1-3

[6] Fatima S. A Study of Organisational Culture: "OCTAPACE" Profile (December 4, 2020). e-journal – First Pan IIT International Management Conference – 2018. 2020. Available from: https://ssrn.com/abstract=3742977 10.2139/ssrn.3742977

[7] Limone P, Toto GA. Psychological and emotional effects of digital technology on children in COVID-19 pandemic. Brain Sciences. 2021;**11**(9):1126. DOI: 10.3390/brainsci11091126

[8] Trikha M. Organization Culture "Octapace". International Journal of Science and Research (IJSR). 2018;**8**:665-659

[9] Pasiechnik J. Out with the old, and in with the new: book review of 'Modernity at Large: Cultural Dimensions of Globalization1996. pp. 229-240

[10] Gerlach P, Eriksson K. Measuring cultural dimensions: External validity and internal consistency of Hofstede's VSM 2013 scales. Frontiers in Psychology. 2021;**12**

[11] Siocon G. Hierarchy Culture: An Informative Guide for HR. Academy to Innovative HR; 2015. pp. 1-6

[12] Michelle Chin Chin Lee. Hierarchical culture as a cross-level moderator of the relationship between transformational leadership. Performance Feedback, and Employee Job Performance, MPDI. 2023;**2023**:504-520. DOI: 10.3390/merits3030030

[13] Gallagher S, Brown C, Brown L. A strong market culture drives organizational performance and success. Employment Relations Today. 2008;**35**:25-31. DOI: 10.1002/ert.20185

[14] Hung Y-C, Su T-C, Lou K-R. Impact of organizational culture on individual work performance with national culture of cross-strait enterprises as a moderator. Sustainability. 2022;**14**:6897, 1-6899. DOI: 10.3390/su14116897

[15] Mohsen A, Neyazi N, Ebtekar S. The Impact of Organizational Culture on Employees Performance: An overview. International Journal of Management. 2020;**11**:879-888. DOI: 10.34218/IJM.11.8.2020.079

[16] Wilson AM. Understanding organisational culture and the implications for corporate marketing. European Journal of Marketing. 2001;**35**(3/4):353-367. DOI: 10.1108/03090560110382066

[17] Ozturk I, Ozcan O. Impact of organizational culture and leadership styles on employee performance: A research study on the banking industry. Research Journal of Business and Management. 2020;7(1):45-55. DOI: 10.17261/Pressacademia.2020.1187

[18] Nur D, Supriyanto A, Maharani V. Factor influencing employee performance: The role of organizational culture. Journal of Asian Finance Economics and Business. 2021;**8**:545-553. DOI: 10.13106/jafeb.2021.vol8.no2.0545

[19] Tannoury J. The impact of culture on employees' performance: The case of Lebanese Companies. European Journal of Business and Management Research. 2022;**7**(5):160-168. DOI: 10.24018/ejbmr.2022.7.5.1636

[20] Marsick VJ, Watkins KE. Demonstrating the value of an organization's learning culture: The dimensions of the learning organization questionnaire. Advances in Developing Human Resources. 2003;**5**(2):132-151

[21] Julia C, Naranjo-Valencia DJ-J, Sanz-Valle R. Studying the links between organizational culture, innovation, and performance in Spanish companies. Revista Latinoamericana de Psicología. 2016;**48**(1):30-41

[22] Pacey A. Technology: Practice and culture. Ethics and Emerging Technologies. 2013;**2013**:27

[23] Raisch S, Birkinshaw J, Probst G, Tushman ML. Organizational ambidexterity: Balancing exploitation and exploration for sustained performance. Organization Science. 2009;**20**(4):685-695. DOI: 10.1287/orsc.1090.0428

[24] Jørgensen MS, Jørgensen U, Clausen C. The social shaping approach to technology foresight. Futures. 2009;**41**(2):80-86

[25] García-Morales VJ, Ruiz-Moreno A, Llorens-Montes FJ. Effects of technology absorptive capacity and technology proactivity on organizational learning, innovation and performance: An empirical examination. Technology Analysis and Strategic Management. 2007;**19**(4):527-558. DOI: 10.1080/09537320701403540

[26] Miles RE, Snow CC. Organizational Strategy, Structure, and Process. New York: McGraw-Hill; 1978

[27] du Gay P, Hall S, Janes L, Mackay H, Negus K. Doing Cultural Studies: The Story of the Sony Walkman. Sage Publications (in association with the Open University); 1997

[28] Combi M. The imagery, the computer, artificial intelligence: A cultural anthropological approach. AI & Society: The Journal of Human-Centred Systems and Machine Intelligence. 1992;**6**(1):41-49

[29] Prensky M. Digital natives, digital immigrants. Horizon. 2001;**9**(5):1-6

[30] Schulz AW. Enhancing thoughts: Culture, technology, and the evolution of human cognitive uniqueness. Mind and Language. 2022;**37**(3):465-484. DOI: 10.1111/mila.12320

[31] Graham Spickett-Jone J, Kitchen PJ, Reast JD. Social facts and ethical hardware: Ethics in the value proposition. Journal of Communication Management. 2003;**8**(1):68-82. DOI: 10.1108/13632540410807556

[32] Hartl E. A Characterization of Culture Change in the Context of Digital Transformation. 2019. pp. 1-10

[33] Hooper SS. Generational change and the military dictatorship in Brazil: The debate on the "AI-5 generation". Creative Education. 2016;7:2338-2351. DOI: 10.4236/ce.2016.715226

[34] Hang M, Tansuhaj PS. Organizational culture, information technology capability, and performance: The case of born global firms. Multinational Business Review. 2007;**15**(3):43-78. DOI: 10.1108/1525383X200700012

[35] Babaeian JM, Yiu KTW. Evaluation of relationship quality in construction cases using a process model of conflict and disputes in project management. 2012

[36] Uzkurt C, Kumar R, Kimzan HS, Eminoğlu G. Role of innovation in the rc culture and firm performance: A study of the banking sector in Turkey. European Journal of Innovation Management. 2013;**16**(1):92-117. DOI: 10.1108/14601061311292878

[37] Villena-Manzanares F, García-Segura T, Pellicer E. Organizational factors that drive to bim effectiveness: Technological learning, collaborative culture, and senior management support. Applied Sciences. Switzerland. 2021;**11**(1):1-16. DOI: 10.3390/app11010199

[38] Vinding AL. Absorptive capacity and innovative performance: A human capital approach. Economic Innovation New Technology. 2006;**15**(45):507-517

[39] Shahzad F. Impact of organizational culture on employees' job performance: An empirical study of software houses in Pakistan. International Journal of Commerce and Management. 2014;**24**(3):219-227. DOI: 10.1108/IJCoMA-07-2012-0046

[40] Melo T. Determinants of corporate social performance: The influence of organizational culture, management tenure and financial performance. Social Responsibility Journal. 2011;**8**:33-47

[41] Ipiñazar A, Zarrabeitia E, Rio-Belver R, Mancisidor I. Organizational culture transformation model: Towards a high performance organization. Journal of Industrial Engineering and Management. 2021;**14**:25. DOI: 10.3926/jiem.3288

[42] Suhariadi F. Organizational Culture Change Effectiveness. 1st International Conference on Psychology 2013 in Health, Educational, Social and Organizational Settings (ICP-HESOS 2013)2013. pp. 1-9

[43] Canato A et al. SMEs performance in Malaysia: The role of contextual ambidexterity in innovation culture and performance. Sustainability (Switzerland). 2022;**14**(3):1-18. DOI: 10.3390/su14031679

[44] Hofstede G. Dimensionalizing cultures: The Hofstede model in context. Readings in Psychology and Culture. 2011;**2**(1):1-26. DOI: 10.9707/2307-0919.101

[45] Salehipour A, Ahmand A. The impact of organizational culture and performance work system on employees' performance. International Business Research. 2018;**11**(6):199. DOI: 10.5539/ibr.v11n6p199

[46] Yildiz E. A study on the relationship between organizational culture and organizational performance and a model Suggestion. International Journal of Research in Business and Social Science. 2014;**3**(4):52-67. DOI: 10.20525/ijrbs.v3i4.117

[47] Uddin MJ, Luva RH, Hossain SMM. Impact of organizational culture on employee performance and productivity: A case study of telecommunication

sector in Bangladesh. International Journal of Business and Management. 2012;**8**(2):1-11. DOI: 10.5539/ijbm.v8n2p63

[48] Azanza G, Moriano JA. Authentic leadership and organizational culture as drivers of employees' job satisfaction. Journal of Work and Organizational Psychology. 2013;**2013**:45-50. DOI: 10.5539/ibr.v11n6p199

[49] Combi M. Cultures and technology: An analysis of some of the changes in Progress—Digital. Global and Local Culture. 2016;**2016**:3-15. DOI: 10.1007/978-3-319-29544-2_1

[50] Du Gay P. Doing cultural studies: The story of the Sony Walkman (Sage Duff, W. M., & Johnson, C. A. 2002. Accidentally found on purpose: Information seeking behavior of historians in archives). The Library Quarterly. 1997;**1997**:472-496

[51] Liu Y, Luo M, Wei X. The effects of cultural diversity, conflict and conflict management on performance in global virtual teams. In: 2008 International conference on wireless communications, Networking and Mobile Computing, WiCOM. 2008. pp. 1-4. DOI: 10.1109/WiCom.2008.1721

[52] Guetzkow H, Gyr J. An analysis of conflict in decision making groups. Human Relations. 1954;7:367-381

[53] Quaddus MA, Tung LL. Explaining cultural differences indecision conferencing. Communications of the ACM. 2002;**45**:93-98

[54] Jehn KA. A multi method examination of the benefits and detriments of intra group conflict. Administrative Science Quarterly. 1995;**40**:256-286

[55] Paul I, Samarah P, Seetharaman P, Mykytyn P. An empirical investigation of collaborative conflict management style in group support system-based global virtual teams. Journal of Management Information Systems. 2004-5;**21**:185-222

[56] Jehn KA, Northcraft GB, Neale MA. The dynamic nature of conflict: a longitudinal study of intra group conflict and group performance. Academy of Management Journal. 2001;**44**:238-251

[57] Kankanhalli BC, Tan Y, Wei K. Conflict and performance in global virtual teams. Journal of Management Information Systems. 2006;**23**:237-274

[58] De Dreu CKW, Weingart LR. Task versus relationship conflict, team performance and team member satisfaction: A meta-analysis. Journal of Applied Psychology. 2003;**88**:741-749

[59] Mortensen M, Hinds PJ. Conflict and shared identity in geographically distributed teams. International Journal of Conflict Management. 2001;**12**:212-238

[60] Morris MW, Williams KY, Leung K, Larrick R, Mendoza MT, Bhatnagar D, et al. Conflict management style: Accounting for cross-national differences. Journal of International Business Studies. 1998;**29**:729-747

[61] Thomas KW. Conflict and negotiation processes in organizations. In: Dunnette MD, Hough LM, editors. Handbook of Industrial and Organizational Psychology. Palo Alto, CA: Consulting Psychologists Press; 1992. pp. 651-717

Chapter 4

Does Stress Type Matter? Clarifying the Relationships between Public Service Motivation, Work-Related Stress, and Employee Attitudes

Leonard Bright

Abstract

This study explored the relationship that public service motivation (PSM) has to environmental, organizational, and job stressors, as well as the relationships that those stressors have to job satisfaction and turnover intentions. Based on a sample of frontline federal employees working as airport baggage and security screeners for the Transportation Security Administration (TSA) in the state of Oregon, the findings of this study revealed a complex pattern of relationships. PSM was found to be positively related to the environmental stressors, negatively related to the organizational stressors, and not directly related to the job stressors. The primary path through which PSM impacts turnover intentions and job satisfaction was found to exist through its relationship with the organizational stressors. The respondents with high levels of PSM reported significantly lower organizational stress, which increased their job satisfaction, which then lowered their turnover intentions. While PSM had no direct relationship to the job stressors, it was found to be indirectly related through organizational stress. That is, high levels of PSM were related with lower organizational stress, which lowered the salience of the job stressors, which then increased job satisfaction. The implications of this study are discussed.

Keywords: public management, public service motivation, stress, satisfaction, turnover

1. Introduction

Stress is a common characteristic of most work environments, and in our fast-changing society, the number of highly stressed employees is on the rise. According to a recent poll, two-thirds of professional employees have reported that they are more stressed than they were five years ago [1]. Understanding the causes and consequences of stress should be a top concern for public managers and scholars alike. Stress has been linked to a variety of physical and psychological disorders [2].

Alleviating stress in the workplace is likely to improve job satisfaction, which has been found to be negatively associated with turnover [3–6].

Scholars have also explored work stress in the public sector. Recent polls have suggested that government workplaces are among the most stressful workplaces, when compared to private and nonprofit workplaces [7]. This fact may dampen the already strained public sector recruitment efforts. One potential solution to this conundrum is public service motivation (PSM), which is an altruistic need that attracts individuals to contribute to the well-being of their communities and to public service work. There is a large body of research that have explored the benefits of PSM on individual behavior in work organizations. This research has confirmed that PSM has both direct and indirect influences on a range of work outcomes such as job satisfaction [8, 9], performance [10, 11], and well-being [12] among public employees. However, one area of the literature that is still unresolved is the extent to which PSM reduces or increases stress in public sector workplaces. Some have theorized that high levels of PSM may cause individuals to be more resilient to the stress that is associated with public service [13]. However, empirical research has not confirmed this hypothesis. PSM has been found to be positively related to work stress [14–16].

There is a need for more research on this topic for at least two reasons. For one, there is a need to better understand the process whereby PSM impacts a wider range of stressors. Many existing studies in this area of research have used global unidimensional measures of work stress that conceal its more specialized and diverse sources. As Jiang et al. [17] have stated, the field has "*failed to deeply explore or classify the sources of work-related stress as well as the mechanisms that influence it*". This is important given the fact that the distinguishing aspects of work stress in the public sector stress come not only from the difficulty of the formal job tasks but also from the environmental of large impersonal bureaucracies and the scrutiny that public organizations routinely receive from the public. Exploring the connections that PSM has on a wider range of stressors will help the field build a deeper understanding of the extent to which PSM is a detrimental or beneficial predictor of stress.

More research is also needed to explore the connections between the stressors that are related to PSM and work outcomes. Scholars have argued that the positive association that PSM has to work stress is an example of the dark side of PSM [14, 15]. However, empirical research is needed that connects the stress that is positively associated with PSM to the attitudes and behaviors of employees. Given the diverse sources of stress, do all the stressors that are associated with PSM lead to lower job satisfaction and higher turnover among public employees? Addressing this question would boost the importance of fostering strategies (i.e., person-organizational fit) that have been shown to help mitigate the negative effects of stress [14, 18], and it will help pinpoint which stressors and related work outcomes need to be addressed.

Therefore, the purpose of this study is to investigate the relationship that PSM has to a range of work-related stressors and their impact on the job satisfaction and turnover intentions of a sample of federal employees. This paper is organized into several parts. First, this paper will explore research on work stress and various sources of stress in the public sector workplace. Second, the hypotheses that this study will test will be presented. Third, the methodology used to test this study's hypotheses will be explored. Lastly, this paper will conclude with a discussion of the findings and implications of research to the research and practice in public administration.

2. Work stress and strain

Work-related stress is one of the most researched areas in general literature. While there is no universally agreed upon definition of stress, there are several widely used definitions and concepts [19]. One of the most widely used definitions of stress was given by Folkman and Lazarus [20] who defined it as a "*relationship between the person and the environment that is appraised by the person as taxing or exceeding his or her resources and endangering his or her well-being*". Others have conceptualized stress as a function of the level of control, resources, and/or support that are available to an individual to address the job demands [21, 22]. Still more have framed stress as a misfit between the characteristics of individuals and the demands of their environment [23, 24]. In most models and conceptualizations, stress by itself does not automatically lead to aversive outcomes. Stress will become aversive when it leads to a strain, which is a condition that occurs when stress surpasses the available resources, coping strategies, and control available to manage it. The consequences of stress and/or strain on the physical and psychological health of employees, as well as their performance, commitment, and satisfaction, are well-documented [25, 26].

2.1 Sources of stress and public sector work environments

The public sector is home to many of the most stressful occupations, such as corrections and policing, nursing, firefighting, and other government occupations [27–33], even though the findings are mix in terms of whether public sector workplaces are more stressful than other sectors [34, 35]. The source and type of stress in the public sector varies greatly. There is a plethora of scale and typologies of stress that can be used to understand stressors in the public sector [28, 36–38]. Most of the typologies of stress can be organized into at least three levels: job, organizational, and environment characteristics.

For one, job level stressors stem from the formal job responsibilities of employees. Job responsibilities vary in terms of the exposure that employees have to emotional demands, co-worker relationships, and work role conflicts, and overload. Jobs that expose employees to high emotional demands, poor co-worker relationships, and tasks that are difficult to address are associated with higher stress [27, 30, 32, 33, 39–41]. Next, organizational-level stress stems from the internal characteristics of the organizations, such as goal ambiguity, climate, participative opportunities, and reward/compensation strategies. For example, there are scholars that suggest that public organizations are unique in terms of the ambiguity of their goals [42, 43], even though some have challenged this assertion [44]. Nevertheless, goal clarity has important consequences on the attitudes and behaviors of employees, such as stress [45, 46]. Work environments that contain ambiguous goals, few participative opportunities, and unfair reward strategies are associated with higher stress [30, 32, 39, 41].

Finally, environmental stress stems from the characteristics of an organization's environment, such as media coverage and citizen perceptions/support. The mass media is a powerful institution that has shaped the behavior of organizations, governmental and nongovernmental alike. Many believe that the media is essential for democracy to thrive [47, 48]. As Blumler and Gurevitch [49] described, "*the media are thus responsible for providing the political information necessary to allow citizens to make political decisions and cast their ballot on the basis of informed choice*". Nonetheless, scholars have long argued that the media's coverage of democratic institutions tends to lower the public's confidence in these institutions by cultivating negative perceptions of those institutions [50–52]. There is a body of research that has sought to clarify the process of how what is called the "mediatization" of public organizations effects political institutions [53–56]. This research revealed that the incompatibility between the media and bureaucratic logic is linked to media-stress and fear among public servants [57, 58].

The messaging of the mass media impacts the opinions that citizens hold of public organizations and their support of their practices. Citizens are the ultimate beneficiaries of government action, even though national polls suggest that American citizens maintain a high level of skepticism and distrust of the federal government. According to the Pew Research Center [59], only 20% of the Americans believe that government can be trusted to "*do the right thing*" always or most of the time. However, environmental stresses may not impact all public organizations and employees equally. Organizations and employees who are more experienced with negative media attention and citizen criticism have developed effective coping and other organizational strategies that lessen the impact of this stress [60]. Like job and organizational stressors, environmental stressors are associated with work-related stress [41, 61]. The goal of this study is to explore whether public service motivation helps employees effectively cope with these stressors.

2.2 Public service motivation and work-related stress

Public service motivation is a need or internal call to service that attracts individuals to opportunities to contribute to the well-being of their communities [62, 63]. Scholars have found that PSM is related to a range of attitudes and behaviors in organizations, which includes job satisfaction [9, 14, 64, 65] and turnover [8, 11, 14, 65–70]. Consistent with the theory, some have hypothesized that PSM is a resource that helps public employees cope with stress and strain [14–16, 71]. For example, according to Bakker [13], "*Those who are prepared to make sacrifice for the good of society will be better able to deal with organizational stressors because they know that dealing with those stressors serves the higher goal of helping others. They will not be upset by daily hassles because they find their work important and meaningful.*" Hence, if this is the case, high levels of PSM should reduce the effects of stress on employees in public sector workplaces.

Regrettably, empirical research has not confirmed the Bakker [13] hypothesis. Three studies found that PSM was associated with higher job stress among government employees in Egyptian and the French-speaking region of Switzerland [14–16]. A study by Gould-Williams et al. [14] suggested that the beneficial effects of PSM on stress were seen indirectly through the person-organizational fit. The direct relationship that PSM had to stress was argued to indicate the dark side of PSM, which undermines employee well-being by raising performance expectations. However, Liu et al. [16] study presented a more nuanced explanation of the relationship between PSM, stress, and well-being. Using a sample of Chinese police officers, these scholars found that officers with high levels of PSM reported greater mental well-being in high-stress situations but reported lower physical well-being in low-stress situations. The authors reasoned that these findings were driven by the fact that PSM attracts individuals to stressful public service work that may satisfy their internal needs while contributing to elevated levels of physical fatigue. Findings by Liu et al. [16] highlight the fact that the association that PSM has to stress will depend on the type of stress under investigation and will not automatically lead to detrimental work outcomes. Hence, PSM's association with the job, organizational, and environmental-level stressors and their impact on work outcomes are likely to vary.

2.3 Work-related stress, job satisfaction, and turnover

Public service can be a stressful work environment given the complexity of the problems it addresses, the bureaucratic nature of its organizations, and the scrutiny it receives from its external environment. One question that deserves consideration is the extent to which the stress associated with the demands of public service work produces detrimental work outcomes. The general field has provided some answers. Job stress is associated with lower job satisfaction and higher turnover intentions [72–75]. However, Cavanaugh et al. [76] demonstrated that not all work-related stress produces detrimental consequences. According to the authors, challenge-related stress is associated with work-related demands that provide positive feeling and achievement, which may be stressful but offer potential gains for individuals. However, hindrance-related stress is associated with work-related demands that tend to constrain or interfere with an individual's work achievement and are not associated with potential gains. Unlike hindrance-stress, challenge-stress would produce positive work outcomes, because it does not hinder or interfere with employee work efforts or achievement needs, but instead promotes personal growth and triggers positive emotions [77]. So again, the relationship that work stress has to the attitudes and behavior of employees will depend on the type of stress in question. If this is the case, the job, organizational, and environmental stressors investigated in this study produced hindrance-related stresses and thus will be associated with high levels of PSM, lower job satisfaction, and higher turnover intentions.

For the sake of analysis, how are job, organizational, and environmental stresses related? While job, organizational, and environmental stressors produce distinct impacts on the work outcomes, these stressors are interrelated. One of the most important relationships represents the association between the organizational and environmental stressors. The stresses that employees experience in their work are inherently linked to the formal roles and demands of their jobs. Using this logic, the stresses that stem from the organizational and environment levels of analysis will magnify the stresses already present at the job level of analysis. Below are the hypotheses that were tested in this study.

Hypothesis 1: PSM will be positively related to job, organizational, and environmental stressors.

Hypothesis 2: Job-, organizational-, and environmental-level stressors will be interrelated. Namely, organizational and environmental stress will be positively related to job-level stress.

Hypothesis 3: Job, organizational, and environmental stressors will be associated with lower job satisfaction and higher turnover intentions.

3. Methodology

The data for this study was drawn in 2017 from a convenience sample of all frontline federal employees working as airport baggage and security screeners for the Transportation Security Administration (TSA) in the state of Oregon. The survey population were employed at the same occupational classification level and served on the front line of the agency. As frontline employees, their work required direct contact with citizens during their daily work. To stay abreast of the latest rules and regulations that governed their work, all employees were required to undergo monthly recertification training sessions. Agency officials integrated the survey instrument into one of these required training sessions. The employees were provided with a workspace and instructions on how to complete the survey. The survey instructed the employees that their participation in the study was completely voluntary; their individual answers would be kept confidential; they could refuse to answer any question that made them uncomfortable; and they could end the survey at any time with no penalty or loss. Five hundred and fifty-seven (N = 557) useable surveys were collected with a response rate of 97%. The study sample was representative of the study population in terms of age, gender, and full-time status.

Several major variables were collected in this study. See **Table 1** for a description of the variables and coding strategies. PSM was collected using the Kim [78] 12-item revision of the Perry [79] 24-item PSM scale, which had good internal validity (Cronbach's α = 0.843). Job, organizational, environmental stressors were all collected using multi-survey questions and summed. Work-related stress is assumed to increase as the experience that the respondents have in the job, organizational, and environmental stressors increases. These scales were found to have good internal/composite validity (Cronbach's α = 0.740, 0.874, 0.822, respectively). For the sake of parsimony, turnover intentions and job satisfaction were collected using single-item survey questions. While multi-item scales are preferred in some cases, empirical evidence suggest that single-item survey questions can produce reliable and robust data [80].

Label	Description/Survey question	Variable coding	Min	Max	Mean	SD
Age	What year were you born?	Year of birth – Year of study	19	74	41.94	13.1
Education	What is the highest level of education you have completed?	1) No College to 5) Masters/ Higher	1	5	2.69	0.983
Gender	What is your gender?	0) Male; 1) Female	0	1	0.447	0.498
Job Satisfaction (Sat)	How satisfied are you with your current job?	1) Extremely Dissatisfied to 6) Extremely Satisfied	1	6	4.03	1.43
Minority status	How would you describe your racial or ethnic group?	0) Minority; 1) Non-minority	0	1	0.754	0.431
Satisfaction	How satisfied are you with your current job?	1) Extremely Dissatisfied to 6) Extremely Satisfied	1	6	4.03	1.43
Public service motivation (PSM) [78]	Attraction to Public Policy (APM)	Sum PSM items 1,2,3	3	18	11.82	2.68
	Commitment to Public Interest (CPI)	Sum PSM items 4,5,6	3	18	13.03	2.55
	Compassion (COM)	Sum PSM items 7,8,9	3	18	12.09	2.54
	Self-sacrifice (SS)	Sum PSM items 12,13, 14	3	18	12.55	2.73

Label	Description/Survey question	Variable coding	Min	Max	Mean	SD
Turnover intentions	Within the next 2 years, how likely are you to leave your current organizational for a job in another organizational?	1) Extremely unlikely to 6) Extremely likely	1	6	3.69	1.8
Work experience	How many years have you worked for the TSA?		0	16	6.74	5.14
Job stress (JS)	I can count on my coworkers when I need help.	1) Strongly Agree to 6) Strongly Disagree	1	6	2.39	1.1
	Coworkers treat each other with respect.	1) Strongly Agree to 6) Strongly Disagree	1	6	2.86	1.2
	Employees in this organizational are treated fairly by their managers and supervisors.	1) Strongly Agree to 6) Strongly Disagree	1	6	3.78	1.4
Organizational stress (OS)	This organizational cares about my opinions	1) Strongly Agree to 6) Strongly Disagree	1	6	4.00	1.41
	The organizational really cares about my well-being.	1) Strongly Agree to 6) Strongly Disagree	1	6	3.80	1.46
	I am fairly rewarded for the amount of effort put forth.	1) Strongly Agree to 6) Strongly Disagree	1	6	3.90	1.45
Environmental stress (ES)	How concerned are you with the viewpoints that citizens hold about TSA?	1) Not Concerned at all to 4) Very Concerned	1	4	2.72	0.981
	How concerned are you with negative media coverage of TSA?	1) Not Concerned at all to 4) Very Concerned	1	4	2.83	1.06
	I am very interested in what others think about the TSA.	1) Strongly Disagree to 6) Strongly Agree	1	6	3.71	1.37

Table 1.
Description of study variables (N = 557).

As shown in **Figure 1**, this study investigated the relationships between PSM, three work-related stressors, job satisfaction, and turnover intentions. The analysis of this study was conducted in three stages. First, a bivariate correlation analysis was conducted to confirm the relationships among the study variables. Second, a structural equation modeling (SEM) in AMOS was used to explore the relationships among the study variables. Third, bootstrap analysis (2000 samples) was used to test the significances of potential mediation effects. Statistical significance was set at 0.05, two-tailed. All regression weights are standardized maximum likelihood estimates, unless otherwise noted.

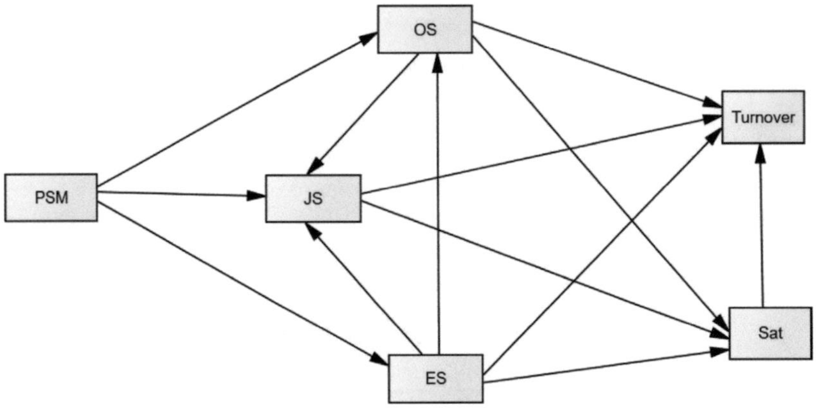

Figure 1.
Study model.

4. Findings

Table 2 displays the demographic characteristics of the sample. Most of the respondents were between 18 and 40 years old (52%), had some to no college experience (53%), were male (55%), identified as White (75%), and gained an average of seven years of work experience in the TSA. **Table 3** presents the respondents' experiences with the job, organizational, and environmental stressors. This data demonstrates that the respondents' experiences with work stress vary. The majority of the respondents indicate that they have relatively low levels of job stress. A vast majority of the respondents "*strongly to somewhat*" agree that their co-workers treat each other with respect (88%), can be counted on when help is needed (79%), and their organizational treats them fairly (62%).

There is also a high agreement among the respondents that environmental stress is high in their work. The vast majority of the respondents indicate that they are "*somewhat to very*" concerned about the citizens views (61%) and negative media coverage (61%). However, the respondents appear to disagree about the level of organizational stresses they experience. While the majority of the respondents "*strongly to somewhat*" disagree that their organization cares about their opinions and well-being and provides fair rewards, a lessor but considerable number of employees differ with these assessments.

Table 4 presents data regarding the correlations between the study variables. The correlations between demographic characteristics of the respondents and the work stressors are particularly interesting. Age and years of experience were both positively correlated with the job stressors. The respondents who were older and had more years of work experience reported experiencing less job stress than their counterparts who were younger and had fewer years of work experience. However, the opposite was true for the relationship between the environmental stressors and age. Concerns about the environmental stressors appeared to increase with age. Older respondents reported being more concerned about the environmental stressors than those who were younger. Also notable is the fact that the organizational stressors were unrelated to all the control/demographic variables in this study except for years of experience. The salience of the organizational stressors increased as the respondents' years of experience increased. The correlations among the work-related stressors were also

	N	%
Age		
18 to 30 years old	131	25%
31 to 40 years old	143	27%
41 to 50 years old	90	17%
51+ years old	167	31%
Education Level		
No College	35	6%
Some College	260	47%
AA/Technical	122	22%
BA	123	22%
Masters/Higher	17	3%
Gender		
Male	293	55%
Female	237	45%
Race and Ethnicity		
Black/African American	18	3%
Hispanic/ Latino	22	4%
White/Caucasian	399	75%
Asian/Pacific Islander	40	8%
Native American/ Alaska Native	5	1%
MultiRacial	47	9%
Work Experience		
1 year and less	130	23%
1 to 5 years	143	26%
5 to 10 years	130	23%
10 years and more	154	28%

Table 2.
Respondents characteristics and control variables.

noteworthy. The job and organizational stressors appear to work in similar directions. The respondents who indicated that they experienced elevated levels of job stress also reported elevated levels of organizational stress. However, the job and organizational stressors worked in opposing directions when compared to the environmental stressors. The respondents who reported experiencing high levels of the job or organizational stressors also reported experiencing lower levels of the environmental stressors.

Two SEM models were utilized to test the relationship between PSM, the work stressors, job satisfaction, and turnover intentions. The first model explored these relationships with control variables, while the second model excluded them. The first model had lower fit to the data and did not result in any meaningful differences regarding the relationships among the study variables. As a result, the second model

		Response categories					
Job stressors	I can count on my coworkers when I need help.	Strongly Agree	Agree	Somewhat Agree	Somewhat Disagree	Disagree	Strongly Disagree
		20%	40%	28%	6%	4%	2%
	Coworkers treat each other with respect.	Strongly Agree	Agree	Somewhat Agree	Somewhat Disagree	Disagree	Strongly Disagree
		10%	33%	36%	11%	6%	5%
	Employees in this organizational are treated fairly by their managers and supervisors.	Strongly Agree	Agree	Somewhat Agree	Somewhat Disagree	Disagree	Strongly Disagree
		4%	15%	33%	16%	14%	19%
Organizational stressors	This organizational cares about my opinions	Strongly Agree	Agree	Somewhat Agree	Somewhat Disagree	Disagree	Strongly Disagree
		3%	11%	27%	20%	18%	21%
	The organizational really cares about my well-being.	Strongly Agree	Agree	Somewhat Agree	Somewhat Disagree	Disagree	Strongly Disagree
		3%	17%	28%	18%	16%	18%
	I am fairly rewarded for the amount of effort put forth.	Strongly Agree	Agree	Somewhat Agree	Somewhat Disagree	Disagree	Strongly Disagree
		3%	16%	25%	19%	18%	19%
Environmental stressors	How concerned are you with the viewpoints that citizens hold about TSA?	Not Concerned at all	Slightly Concerned	Somewhat Concerned	Very Concerned		
		13%	26%	36%	25%		
	How concerned are you with negative media coverage of TSA?	Not Concerned at all	Slightly Concerned	Somewhat Concerned	Very Concerned		
		13%	26%	36%	25%		
	I am very interested in what others think about the TSA.	Strongly Disagree	Disagree	Somewhat Disagree	Somewhat Agree	Agree	Strongly Agree
		7%	14%	17%	33%	20%	9%

Table 3.
Work-related stressors percentage results by response category.

DOI: http://dx.doi.org/10.5772/intechopen.112707

	1	2	3	4	5	6	7	8	9	10	11
1. Age	1										
2. Education	0.022	1									
3. Experience	0.501**	−0.129**	1								
4. Gender	−0.089*	−0.065	−0.092*	1							
5. Minority Status	0.233**	−0.023	0.098*	−0.017	1						
6. Job Stress	−0.113**	−0.033	0.110**	0.019	−0.031	1					
7. Organizational Stress	−0.042	−0.045	0.198**	−0.020	−0.035	0.648**	1				
8. Environmental Stress	0.177**	0.016	0.082	0.056	0.070	−0.155**	−0.112**	1			
9. Satisfaction	0.126**	−0.057	−0.070	0.010	0.085	−0.525**	−0.560**	0.110**	1		
10. Turnover	−0.314**	0.080	−0.134**	−0.003	−0.145**	0.339**	0.371**	−0.095**	−0.405**	1	
11. PSM	−0.013	0.055	−0.121**	−0.049	−0.009	−0.229**	−0.255**	0.307**	0.181**	−0.059	1

** = $p \leq 0.05$; ** = $p \leq 0.01$.*

Table 4.
Bivariate correlations among study variables.

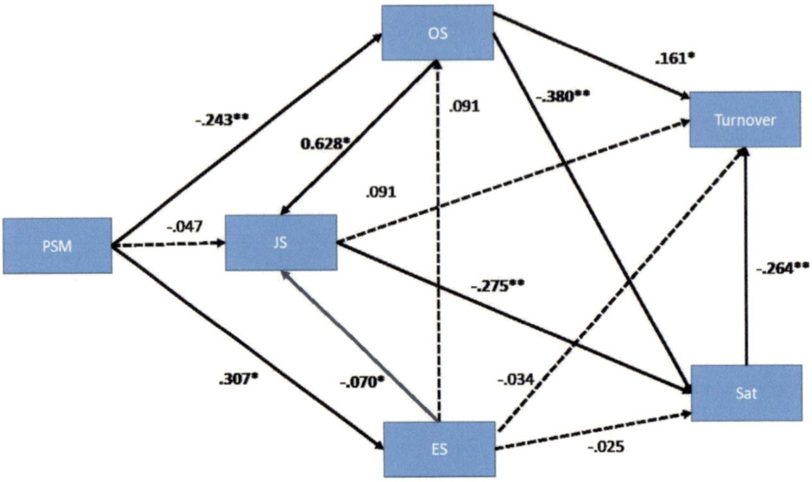

Figure 2.
*Standardized regression estimates (GFI = 0.998, NFI = 0.996, CFI = 0.998, RMSEA = 0.033) (** = * = p ≤ 0.05; ** = p ≤ 0.01).*

was adopted for parsimony and improved model fit. The fit indices indicate that the statistical model has a good fit to the data (GFI = 0.998, NFI = 0.996, CFI = 0.998, RMSEA = 0.033). The SEM findings are displayed in **Figure 2** as standardized regression estimate, and the significance of the estimates is presented in **Table 5**.

Three hypotheses were advanced in this study. Hypothesis 1 suggested that PSM would be positively associated with the job, organizational, and environmental stressors. The findings regarding this hypothesis were mixed. PSM only had a positive relationship with the environmental stressors, maintained negative relationships with

Model paths	β	P
ES ← PSM	0.307	***
OS←PSM	−0.243	***
OS←ES	−0.038	0.383
JS ← PSM	−0.047	0.171
JS ← ES	−0.070	0.039
JS ← OS	0.628	***
Sat ← JS	−0.275	***
Sat ← OS	−0.380	***
Sat ← ES	0.025	0.463
Turnover←JS	0.091	0.080
Turnover←OS	0.161	0.002
Turnover←ES	−0.034	0.375
Turnover←Sat	−0.264	***

*** = $p \leq 0.001$; ** = $p \leq 0.01$; * = $p \leq 0.05$.

Table 5.
Study variables standardized estimates by model paths.

the organizational-level stressors, and was not significantly related to the job-level stressors. While the respondents with high levels of PSM reported experiencing significantly higher levels of environmental stressors, they also reported significantly lower levels of the organizational level stressors than their counterpoints with lower levels of PSM. Even more, PSM's association with environmental stressors appears to be the strongest relationship, when compared to its association with the organizational stressors.

Hypothesis 2 posited that the job stressors would be positively associated with the organizational and environmental stressors. Once more, the findings of this were mixed. While both the organizational and environmental stressors were related to the job-level stressors, the directions of one of these relationships were different. Job-level stressors were positively related to the organizational stressors but negatively related to the environmental stressors. This suggests that the respondents who reported experiencing high levels of the job stressors were significantly more likely to report experiencing high levels of the organizational stressors but significantly more likely to report experiencing lower levels of the environmental stressors. Similarly unexpected was that no meaningful relationships were found between the organizational and environmental stressors.

Hypothesis 3 suggested that the job, organizational, and environmental stressors would be associated with lower job satisfaction and higher turnover intentions. The findings regarding this hypothesis were also mixed. As expected, the organizational stressors were related to both job satisfaction and turnover intentions. The respondents who experienced high levels of the organizational stressors were significantly more likely to report having lower job satisfaction and higher turnover intentions. However, while the job stressors were also negatively related to job satisfaction, they had no significant direct relationship with turnover intentions. Even more surprising was the finding that the environmental stressors were not directly related to either job satisfaction or turnover intentions.

The finding of this study also provided pertinent information regarding the significance of the mediations among the study variables and the work outcomes. Given the fact that the organizational stressors maintained significant direct relationships with both turnover intentions and job satisfaction, it is important to determine the extent to which these relationships were fully or partially mediated by the job stressors and/or the work outcomes. Bootstrapping was used to clarify this issue. A full mediation is present when the significance of the indirect pathway reduces the significance of the direct pathway, whereas a partial mediation is present when both the direct and indirect pathways are significant, even though one pathway may be dominant. As shown in **Table 6**, the findings revealed that the association that the organizational stressors had to job satisfaction and turnover intentions were partially

Analysis	Direct effect (x → y)	Indirect effect	Result
OS→ Sat → Turnover	0.075*	0.047**	Partial
OS→ JS → Sat → Turnover	0.075*	0.021**	Partial
OS → JS → Sat	−0.141**	−0.173**	Partial

*** = $p \leq 0.001$; * = $p \leq 0.05$; nm = not mediated.*

Table 6.
Bootstrap mediation analysis unstandardized results.

mediated by the job stressors and job satisfaction, respectfully. However, the direct relationship between organizational stressors and turnover was the most dominant path when considering the pathway through job satisfaction, whereas the indirect path though the job stressors was the dominate pathway in terms of its association with job satisfaction.

5. Conclusion

This book chapter presented a study that investigated how PSM is related to employee attitudes through its association with work-related stressors. This is one of the only known studies to explore the relationships that PSM has to a range of different types of stressors found in public service work organizations and environments. Unsurprisingly, the findings show that the job, organizational, and environmental stressors were detrimental to the work attitudes of employees, directly and indirectly. Employees who experienced high levels of job, organizational and job stressors were significantly more likely to report lower job satisfaction and higher turnover intentions. However, in contradiction to existing research [14, 15] and in support of Liu et al. [16], the influence that PSM appeared to have on job satisfaction and turnover intentions depended on the type of stress in question. PSM was associated with lower levels of organizational stressors, which increased job satisfaction and lowered turnover intentions. PSM had no direct relationship with the job stressors when organizational and environmental stressors were considered. Instead, PSM maintained indirect associations with the job stressors through its associations with the organizational and environmental stressors. The only potentially damaging impact PSM had on the work-related stressors was its association with the environmental stressors. The respondents with high levels of PSM were significantly more likely to report more concerns about the environmental stressors, which was associated with lower job stress concerns. However, outside of the respondents' job stress concerns, environmental stressors were not directly associated with their job satisfaction nor turnover intentions. There are several noteworthy implications of these findings.

Foremost, the findings of this study suggest that the connection that PSM has to work stress depends on the type of stress in question. Consistent with the findings of Liu et al. [16], this study demonstrated that PSM did not impact all work-related stressors in the same way. PSM appeared to increase the concerns that employees had regarding the environmental stressors, lowered concerns regarding the organizational, and had no direct relationship with their job stress concerns. These findings suggest that the association that PSM had to the stressors is neither monolithic nor uniform but is complex and often surprising. The findings also challenge the use of global measures of stress in PSM studies. While previous studies have found that PSM was associated with higher global measures of work-related stress, their results should be interpreted carefully. Considering the complex relationships that PSM has to the individualized categories of stress found in this study, the results of global measures of stress may be easily overgeneralized. Global measures of work stress may not be sensitive to the fine-tuned relationship that PSM has to the individualized dimensions of work stress.

Second, the findings of this study suggest that individuals with high levels of PSM have elevated concerns regarding the environmental stressors. The respondents who indicated that they possessed high levels of PSM were also significantly more likely to report experiencing high levels of environmental stress. While there are several potential explanations offered in the literature, Boardman and Sundquist [81] perceived that the public service efficacy theory (PPSE) is one of the most compelling. This theory suggests that employees with high levels of PSM are likely to believe that public organizations offer valuable contributions to the community because of their own attractions to public service missions and are inclined to believe that the members of the public who receive these benefits share their positive viewpoints. When the viewpoints of public employees and citizens conflict regarding the contributions of their work, increased stress will result. This suggests that public managers must ensure that they not only remind their employees of the value of their work, but also work to communicate this value to the communities that are being served.

Third, despite the elevated concerns that employees appear to have regarding the environmental stressors, the findings of this study may suggest that the environmental stressors were the least important predictors of the work attitudes and behaviors of employees included in this study. No meaningful differences were found between the environmental stressors, job satisfaction, and turnover intentions. Yet this finding should not be interpreted as an indication that environmental stressors were unimportant to the attitudes and behaviors of employees. On the contrary, the environmental stressors, such as negative media coverage and citizen criticism, are likely to influence employees' perceptions of prestige [82]. The perception of prestige theory argues that individuals are compelled to seek relationships that maintain and/or enhance positive self-images. Relationships that are detrimental to a positive self-image lead to lower job satisfaction [83, 84] and higher turnover intentions [85, 86]. As a result, it is critical that managers and supervisors foster strategies that help public employees cope with environmental stressors before they destructively affect their self-image.

Fourth, this study suggests that public employees prioritize work-related stresses differently. For example, the findings demonstrated that the environmental stressors were negatively related to the job stressors. That is, the respondents who reported feeling high levels of environmental stress also reported having significantly lower job stress. The reason for this finding is not entirely clear. From one perspective it could be that environmental stress is not as concerning to employees when their job stresses are high. Hence, when compared to the environmental stressors, the job stressors may be the most important to public employees. If this is the case, this would mean that the relationship that job stress has to environmental stress was misspecified in the study model. Job stress may work to impact environmental stress, rather than vice versa. However, on the other hand, the findings also support the opposite viewpoint that job stressors become less salient concerns when environmental stressors are high. It is clear that more research is needed to improve the field's understanding of the effects of environmental stressors on job stress, as well as other work outcomes unexplored in this study.

Relatedly, the work-related stressors were not equal in their influence on the work attitudes. While the organizational and job stressors were both related to job satisfaction and turnover intentions, the relationships that the organizational stressors had to these outcomes were stronger. This suggests the most effective way that managers can improve job satisfaction and turnover among public employees in high-stress situations is to address their organizational stress concerns. The organizational stressors investigated in this study centered on how much employees believed their organization cared about their opinions and well-being and offered fair rewards. The stress associated with the lack of these opportunities not only affected the respondents' job stress concerns but also significantly lowered their job satisfaction and raised their turnover intentions.

Furthermore, while this study's findings will add to the field of research on the benefits of PSM in public organizations, they should be interpreted cautiously. Two weaknesses should be acknowledged. For one, this study relied on a cross-sectional design that limited the confirmation of causality among the study variables. It was assumed that PSM modifies the experiences employees have regarding work-related stress when the opposite relationship may be the case. Work stress may vary the levels of PSM possessed by employees over time. While longitudinal or experimental research designs are better equipped to isolate and test causal relationships, this study does confirm that meaningful relationships between PSM and work stressors are present. A second weakness of this study is that it drew its data from a convenience sample of Transportation Security Agency branch in Portland, Oregon. Even though the results are comparable to similar organizations in similar circumstances, there may be limits to the generalizability of this study. This presents an opportunity for future research to confirm the findings of this study with data extracted from a broader sample of organizations.

In conclusion, the public sector is unique in terms of the kinds of stress that public employees are expected to work under. However, the results of this study suggest that these concerns can be effectively managed. This study supports the view that effective stress management is not a one-size-fits-all approach. Even though individuals with high levels of PSM may be better suited to handle some kinds of stressors of public service, they can be more sensitive to other types of stressors, namely those that originate from the social context of public organizations. As result, effective stress management must include not only the recruitment of individuals with high levels of PSM to public service, but also the development of strategies that help public servants who are working in environments of low citizen trust and hostile media coverage. Effectively managing these various sources of stress will go a long way toward reducing turnover, increasing satisfaction, and improving the well-being of public servants.

Author details

Leonard Bright
Bush School of Government and Public Service, Texas A and M University, College Station, United States

*Address all correspondence to: lbright@tamu.edu

References

[1] Ferry K. Workplace Stress Continues to Mount; 2019. Available from: https://www.kornferry.com/insights/this-week-in-leadership/workplace-stress-motivation

[2] Yaribeygi H et al. The impact of stress on body function: A review. EXCLI Journal. 2017;**16**:1057-1072

[3] Colligan TW, Higgins EM. Workplace stress. Journal of Workplace Behavioral Health. 2006;**21**(2):89-97

[4] Lambert EG, Lynne Hogan N, Barton SM. The impact of job satisfaction on turnover intent: A test of a structural measurement model using a national sample of workers. The Social Science Journal. 2001;**38**(2):233-250

[5] Lum L et al. Explaining nursing turnover intent: Job satisfaction, pay satisfaction, or organizational commitment? Journal of Organizational Behavior. 1998;**19**(3):305-320

[6] Mobley WH. Intermediate linkages in the relationship between job satisfaction and employee turnover. Journal of Applied Psychology. 1977;**62**(2):237-240

[7] Government OA, Public Sector Workers More Stressed than the Private Sector; 2018. Available from: https://www.openaccessgovernment.org/public-sector-workers-more-stressed-than-the-private-sector/54143/

[8] Bright L. Does public service motivation really make a difference on the job satisfaction and turnover intentions of public employees? American Review of Public Administration. 2008;**38**(2):149-166

[9] Homberg F, McCarthy D, Tabvuma V. A meta-analysis of the relationship between public service motivation and job satisfaction. Public Administration Review. 2015;**75**(5):711-722

[10] Lynggaard M, Pedersen MJ, Andersen LB. Exploring the context dependency of the PSM–performance relationship. Review of Public Personnel Administration. 2018;**38**(3):332-354

[11] Bright L. Does person-organization fit mediate the relationship between public service motivation and the job performance of public employees? Review of Public Personnel Administration. 2007;**27**(4):361-379

[12] Boyd N et al. Sense of community, sense of community responsibility, and public service motivation as predictors of employee well-being and engagement in public service organizations. The American Review of Public Administration. 2017;**48**(5):428-443

[13] Bakker AB. A job demands–resources approach to public service motivation. Public Administration Review. 2015;**75**(5):723-732

[14] Gould-Williams JS, Mostafa AMS, Bottomley P. Public service motivation and employee outcomes in the egyptian public sector: Testing the mediating effect of person-organization fit. Journal of Public Administration Research and Theory. 2015;**25**(2):597-622

[15] Giauque D, Anderfuhren-Biget S, Varone F. Stress perception in public organisations: Expanding the job demands–job resources model by including public service motivation. Review of Public Personnel Administration. 2013;**33**(1):58-83

[16] Liu B, Yang K, Yu W. Work-related stressors and health-related outcomes

in public service: Examining the role of public service motivation. The American Review of Public Administration. 2015;**45**(6):653-673

[17] Jiang Q, Lee H, Xu D. Challenge stressors, work engagement, and affective commitment among Chinese public servants. Public Personnel Management. 2020;**49**(4):547-570

[18] Deniz N, Noyan A, Ertosun ÖG. Linking person-job fit to job stress: The mediating effect of perceived person-organization fit. Procedia - Social and Behavioral Sciences. 2015;**207**:369-376

[19] Koolhaas JM et al. Stress revisited: A critical evaluation of the stress concept. Neuroscience & Biobehavioral Reviews. 2011;**35**(5):1291-1301

[20] Folkman S, Lazarus RS. Stress, Appraisal, and Coping. New York: Springer Publishing Company; 1984

[21] Karasek RA. Job demands, job decision latitude, and mental strain: Implications for job redesign. Administrative Science Quarterly. 1979;**24**(2):285-308

[22] Johnson JV, Hall EM. Job strain, work place social support, and cardiovascular disease: A cross-sectional study of a random sample of the Swedish working population. American Journal of Public Health. 1988;**78**(10):1336-1342

[23] French J, Rogers W, Cobb S. A Model Of Person-Environment Fit. Coping and Adaptation. New York: Basic Books Inc.; 1974

[24] Beehr TA, Newman JE. Job stress, employee health, and organizational effectiveness: A facet analysis, model, and literature review. Personnel Psychology. 1978;**31**(4):665-699

[25] Greenberg N, Carr JA, Summers CH. Causes and consequences of Stress1. Integrative and Comparative Biology. 2002;**42**(3):508-516

[26] Quick JD, Horn RS, Quick JC. Health consequences of stress. In: Job Stress. New York: Routledge; 2014. pp. 19-36

[27] Triplett R, Mullings JL, Scarborough KE. Work-related stress and coping among correctional officers: Implications from organizational literature. Journal of Criminal Justice. 1996;**24**(4):291-308

[28] West JP, West CM. Job stress and public sector occupations: Implications for personnel managers. Review of Public Personnel Administration. 1989;**9**(3):46-65

[29] Pendleton M et al. Stress and strain among police, firefighters, and government workers: A comparative analysis. Criminal Justice and Behavior. 1989;**16**(2):196-210

[30] Huckabee RG. Stress in corrections: An overview of the issues. Journal of Criminal Justice. 1992;**20**(5):479-486

[31] Burke RJ. Stress in Policing: Sources, Consequences and Interventions. London: Routledge; 2016

[32] Brown JM, Campbell EA. Stress and Policing: Sources and Strategies. Chichester: John Wiley & Sons; 1994

[33] Carpenter GSJ et al. Social support, stress, and suicidal ideation in professional firefighters. American Journal of Health Behavior. 2015;**39**(2):191-196

[34] Hamann DJ, Foster NT. An exploration of job demands, job control, stress, and attitudes in public, nonprofit, and for-profit employees. Review of Public Personnel Administration. 2014;**34**(4):332-355

[35] Tankha G. A comparative study of role stress in government and private hospital nurses. Journal of Health Management. 2006;**8**(1):11-22

[36] Cooper CL, Marshall J. Occupational sources of stress: A review of the literature relating to coronary heart disease and mental ill health. Journal of Occupational Psychology. 1976;**49**(1):11-28

[37] Motowidlo SJ, Packard JS, Manning MR. Occupational stress: Its causes and consequences for job performance. Journal of Applied Psychology. 1986;**71**(4):618

[38] Hurrell JJ Jr, Nelson DL, Simmons BL. Measuring job stressors and strains: Where we have been, where we are, and where we need to go. Journal of Occupational Health Psychology. 1998;**3**(4):368

[39] Bogg J, Cooper C. Job satisfaction, mental health, and occupational stress among senior civil servants. Human Relations. 1995;**48**(3):327-341

[40] Ivancevich JM, Matteson MT. Stress and Work: A Managerial Perspective. Glenview, Ill: Scott Foresman; 1980

[41] Schaufeli WB, Peeters MC. Job stress and burnout among correctional officers: A literature review. International Journal of Stress Management. 2000;**7**(1):19-48

[42] Warwick DP, Meade M. A Theory of Public Bureaucracy: Politics, Personality, and Organization in the State Department. Cambridge, Mass: Harvard University Press; 1980

[43] Lipsky M. Street-Level Bureaucracy: Dilemmas of the Individual in Public Service. New York: Russell Sage Foundation; 2010

[44] Jung CS. Why are goals important in the public sector? Exploring the benefits of goal clarity for reducing turnover intention. Journal of Public Administration Research and Theory. 2014;**24**(1):209-234

[45] Elovainio M, Kivimäki M. Occupational stresses, goal clarity, control, and strain among nurses in the Finnish health care system. Research in Nursing & Health. 1996;**19**(6):517-524

[46] Smock CD. The influence of psychological stress on the 'intolerance of ambiguity'. The Journal of Abnormal and Social Psychology. 1955;**50**(2):177-182

[47] Dumitrescu D, Mughan A. Mass media and democratic politics. In: Handbook of Politics. New York: Springer; 2010. pp. 477-491

[48] Eva, Opperhuizen A, Hans Klijn E, Schouten K. How do media, political and regulatory agendas influence one another in high risk policy issues? Policy & Politics. 2020;**48**(3):461-483

[49] Blumler J, Gurevitch M. Political communication systems and democratic values. In: The Crisis of Public Communication. London: Routledge; 2002. pp. 105-116

[50] Pfau M et al. The influence of individual communication media on public confidence in democratic institutions. Southern Communication Journal. 1998;**63**(2):91-112

[51] Gerbner G et al. The "mainstreaming" of America: Violence profile number 11. Journal of Communication. 1980;**30**(3):10-29

[52] Liu BF, Horsley JS, Yang K. Overcoming negative media coverage: Does government communication matter? Journal of Public Administration Research and Theory. 2012;**22**(3):597-621

[53] Mazzoleni G, Schulz W. "mediatization" of politics: A challenge

for democracy? Political Communication. 1999;**16**(3):247-261

[54] Thorbjornsrud K, Figenschou TU, Ihlen Ø. Mediatization in public bureaucracies: A typology. Communications: The European Journal of Communication Research. 2014;**39**(1):3-22

[55] Fredriksson M, Schillemans T, Pallas J. Determinants of organizational mediatization: An analysis of the adaptation of swedish government agencies to news media. Public Administration. 2015;**93**(4):1049-1067

[56] Schillemans T. Mediatization of Public Services. Germany: Peter Lang Frankfurt; 2012

[57] Bekkers V, Moody R, Edwards A. Micro-mobilization, social media and coping strategies: Some Dutch experiences. Policy & Internet. 2011;**3**(4):1-29

[58] Klijn EH et al. Public managers, media influence, and governance: Three research traditions empirically explored. Administration & Society. 2016;**48**(9):1036-1058

[59] Pew Research Center. Americans' Views of Government: Low Trust, but some Positive Performance Ratings; 2020. Available from: https://www.pewresearch.org/politics/2020/09/14/americans-views-of-government-low-trust-but-some-positive-performance-ratings/

[60] Schillemans T, Karlsen R, Kolltveit K. Why do civil servants experience media-stress differently and what can be done about it? Policy & Politics. 2019;**47**(4):599-620

[61] Stevens DJ. Origins of police officer stress before and after 9/11. The Police Journal. 2004;**77**(2):145-173

[62] Perry J, Wise L. The motivational bases of public service. Public Administration Review. 1990;**50**(3):367-373

[63] Vandenabeele W, Brewer GA, Ritz A. Past, present, and future of public service motivation researcH. Public Administration. 2014;**92**(4):779-789

[64] Naff KC, Crum J. Working for america does public service motivation make a difference? Review of Public Personnel Administration. 1999;**19**(4):5-16

[65] Kim S. Does person-organization fit matter in the public-sector? Testing the mediating effect of person-organization fit in the relationship between public service motivation and work attitudes. Public Administration Review. 2012;**72**(6):830-840

[66] Quratulain S, Khan AK. How does employees' public service motivation get affected? A conditional process analysis of the effects of person–job fit and work pressure. Public Personnel Management. 2015;**44**(2):266-289

[67] Liu B, Tang TL-P, Yang K. When does public service motivation fuel the job satisfaction fire? The joint moderation of person–organization fit and needs–supplies fit. Public Management Review. 2015;**17**(6):876-900

[68] Christensen RK, Wright BE. The effects of public service motivation on job choice decisions: Disentangling the contributions of person-organization fit and person-job fit. Journal of Public Administration Research and Theory. 2011;**21**(4):723-743

[69] Bright L. Where does public service motivation count the Most in government work environments? A preliminary empirical investigation and hypotheses. Public Personnel Management. 2013;**42**(1):5-26

[70] Caillier JG. Towards a better understanding of public service motivation and mission valence in public agencies. Public Management Review. 2015;**17**(9):1217-1236

[71] Knoop R. Relieving stress through value-rich work. The Journal of Social Psychology. 1994;**134**(6):829-836

[72] Arshadi N, Damiri H. The relationship of job stress with turnover intention and job performance: Moderating role of OBSE. Procedia-Social and Behavioral Sciences. 2013;**84**:706-710

[73] Jou R-C, Kuo C-W, Tang M-L. A study of job stress and turnover tendency among air traffic controllers: The mediating effects of job satisfaction. Transportation Research Part E: Logistics and Transportation Review. 2013;**57**:95-104

[74] Dodanwala TC, San Santoso D. The mediating role of job stress on the relationship between job satisfaction facets and turnover intention of the construction professionals. Engineering, Construction and Architectural Management. 2021;**29**(4):1777-1796

[75] Sesen H, Ertan SS. The effect of the employee perceived training on job satisfaction: The mediating role of workplace stress. European Journal of Training and Development. 2021;**46**(9):953-973

[76] Cavanaugh MA et al. An empirical examination of self-reported work stress among US managers. Journal of Applied Psychology. 2000;**85**(1):65

[77] Crawford ER, LePine JA, Rich BL. Linking job demands and resources to employee engagement and burnout: A theoretical extension and meta-analytic test. Journal of Applied Psychology. 2010;**95**(5):834

[78] Kim S. Revising Perry's measurement scale of public service motivation. American Review of Public Administration. 2009;**39**(2):149-163

[79] Perry J. Measuring public service motivation: An assessment of construct reliability and validity. Journal of Public Administration Research and Theory. 1996;**6**(1):5-22

[80] Wanous JP, Reichers AE, Hudy MJ. Overall job satisfaction: How good are single-item measures? Journal of Applied Psychology. 1997;**82**(2):247

[81] Boardman C, Sundquist E. Toward understanding work motivation: Worker attitudes and the perception of effective public service. The American Review of Public Administration. 2009:**39**(5):519-535

[82] Bright L. Does perceptions of organizational prestige mediate the relationship between public service motivation, job satisfaction, and the turnover intentions of Federal Employees? Public Personnel Management. 2020;**50**:009102602095281

[83] Tuna M et al. The effects of the perceived external prestige of the organization on employee deviant workplace behavior: The mediating role of job satisfaction. International Journal of Contemporary Hospitality Management. 2016;**28**(2):366-396

[84] Yim Y, Schafer BD. Police and their perceived image: How community influence officers' job satisfaction. Police Practice and Research: An International Journal. 2009;**10**(1):17-29

[85] Akgunduz Y, Bardakoglu O. The impacts of perceived organizational prestige and organization identification on turnover intention: The mediating effect of psychological empowerment.

Current Issues in Tourism. 2017:**20**(14): 1510-1526

[86] Shim DC, Park HH, Eom TH. Street-level bureaucrats' turnover intention: Does public service motivation matter? International Review of Administrative Sciences. 2017;**83**(3):563-582

Chapter 5

Organizational Culture as an Analytical Perspective on 'Organizational Failure'

Kazuyuki Maeda

Abstract

Under the knowledge-based economy, the new public management demands that the university as a source of wealth and well-being functions as an 'organization'. However, university reform has not functioned smoothly, and a situation of hybridisation has emerged, where heterogeneous ideologies of managerialism and collegiality coexist. Oliver Williamson states that 'the organizational failures' result when bounded rationality and opportunism, which are human nature, combine with environmental factors. And the current situation of hybridisation suggests the importance of focusing on the organizational culture that defines the mindset of organizational members. This paper proposes the 'organizational paradigm' as an analytical framework that integrates the thinking and behavioural styles of university members into the typology of organizational culture based on the Competing Values Framework by Cameron et al. and refers to the importance of organizational culture in university organizational reform through verification with the author's findings of quantitative analysis in Japanese universities.

Keywords: organizational culture, competing values framework, transaction cost, organizational paradigm, leadership

1. Introduction

The development of the knowledge-based economy is forcing a major shift in the organizational model of universities. As a unique, 'loosely coupled' organization, the interest that was directed towards the internal structure of the organization now shifts to a 'holistic model' as the relationship between universities and industry and the business community deepens [1]. In the state–university relationship, as well, the focus has been shifted from regulation of procedures to outcomes and results, a context of deregulation with an emphasis on the measurement of results. Underlying this change is the ideology of *managerialism*, which sees the public sector as something to be 'managed' and seeks to fulfil its responsibilities to its customers—consumers and taxpayers—through streamlined and standardised procedures [2]. The New Public Management (NPM) as the instrument of neoliberal policy is embodied by managerialism (see above); on the other hand, NPM has diverse objectives, such as strengthening the devolution of authority to local institutions by reducing the powers of central government [3], reducing state expenditure by promoting public sector organizational reform [4] and promoting the transition from bureaucratic to entrepreneurial organizations [5], so the concept is not clear [6]. However, the essence of NPM includes a desire to strengthen hierarchies based on direct control relationships or indirect governance based on strong contractual relationships between principal–agents [7], and university governance is becoming increasingly centralised in the trend of university reform [8].

Thus, as the organizational model of the university undergoes transformation, there is an emerging *hybridisatio*n within higher education institutions between the demands of modern management and traditional academic norms [9]. Milgrom and Roberts [10] point out that while the value maximisation criterion is presented as a condition for an organization to act as if it were an individual, universities are especially difficult to apply this criterion. In other words, the lack of value to be maximised is behind the emergence of hybridisation. Kezar and Lester [11] and Bess and Dee [12] point to the importance of focusing on the values when examining the organizational behaviour of universities.

The problems caused by hybridisation are not limited to the inner workings of university organizations. Global warming, biodiversity loss, pandemics and economic migration are compounding the human–environment system, and their solution requires not only interdisciplinary research but also transdisciplinary research involving multiple actors, such as policymakers and industry. University and research institutes play a central role in transdisciplinary research [13], but the promotion of collaborative research between different stakeholders is confronted with the same problems of the value maximisation as within the organization itself. The change to a holistic model due to the development of a knowledge-based economy has produced an environment of the organizational failures [14], which is different from the world of frictionless ideal [14], both inside and outside universities. The problem of hybridisation in university can be seen as a prototype of such a problem. However, no analytical framework has been established to systematically understand this problem, and an analytical perspective is required to address the organizational failures caused by differences in values.

This paper aims to study an analytical framework for examining the organizational failures, focusing on organizational culture, which is a representation of members' perceptions, and on universities, where maximising value is considered particularly difficult.

In conducting the above objectives, this paper is structured into six sections, including this section. Section 2 reviews previous research focusing on organizational culture in university along two trends in organizational culture research: interest in the cultural forms of organizational culture and interest in its impact on outcomes. On the one hand, in a knowledge-based economy, universities are required to be responsible for adapting to the external environment based on the transformation of values and ideologies, and in order to construct the analytical framework on 'organizational failure' that this paper aims at, it is necessary to assume a series of mechanisms: friction with neoliberal ideologies and dysfunctional environmental adaptation caused by this friction. This requires an integrative perspective on the two trends in organizational culture studies, but we will confirm that there is no previous research based on such an integrative perspective.

After reviewing the achievements of previous studies, this paper develops an argument for the integration of the two trends mentioned above. Section 3 deals with the issue of value as the basis of cultural forms, discusses the transformation of the research system under a knowledge-based economy, then refers to the subjective right 'academic freedom' and confirms that university reform is closely related to the issue of value. The frictions within university brought about by university reform are then identified as *intergroup conflict within organization* [15], and a premise is laid down for Section 5, which discusses 'organizational failures'. In the following Section 4, the concept of 'organizational paradigm' is introduced in joining the values discussed in Section 3 and their superstructure, organizational culture. It then focuses on the heterogeneity of the organizational paradigm as a source of hybridisation and presents the 'organizational paradigm analysis framework', which is typified into four categories based on previous research.

After organising the cultural forms, the first trend in organizational culture studies, the following Section 5 presents a second 'organizational failure framework' specific to university, which integrates the organizational paradigms discussed in the previous section, as a framework for analysing why organizational failures occur in university and the mechanisms by which they occur. This framework focuses on the mechanisms between organizational outcomes and organizational culture which is the second trend in organizational culture research, and the two trends are integrated in this section.

In this framework, the discussion is developed in three stages, based on problematic concerns in transaction cost theory. In the first stage, based on previous research, the basic concept of a framework for organizational failure based on transaction cost theory is presented. In the next stage, followed by the leader–follower relationship which can be regarded as a 'principal–agent' relationship, is regarded as a 'transaction' in light of the hybridisation problems currently occurring in university. Furthermore, reflecting the characteristics of university characterised by subcultural diversity, the stakeholder theory, which aims to establish relationships between stakeholders with different values, and the 'organizational paradigm analysis framework' developed in the previous section are used as support in the final stage. This section presents an 'organizational failure framework' specific to university, which sees leader–follower relationships with different organizational paradigms as 'transactions'.

The final section, Section 6, summarises the study and makes reference to its significance and limitations, as well as to its prospects and implications for future research.

2. Survey of previous research

Kitai [16] states that there are two trends in organizational culture research: interest in cultural forms, which are 'expressive aspects that transmit ideologies and values', and interest in the impact on outcomes, which focuses on 'the technical and tool aspects of the organization', but a similar trend can be observed in studies of organizational culture of university. Representative studies of the former type include Clark [17], who focused on the function of 'myths' in integrating the boundaries between departments within a university organization and between inside and outside the organization, and Becher [18], who raised doubts about the uniformity found in market-based institutions and revealed the diversity of academic culture as a disciplinary community. Subcultural diversity is an organizational characteristic of universities, and De Zilwa [19] found that subcultures and values differ between groups according to their proactivity to adapt to the external environment, while Sporn [20], who examined subcultures in the Vienna University of Economics, found the similar facts. In addition to these subcultures between disciplines, another problematic issue with regard to the integration of organizational goals is the difference in subcultures between faculty and staff, which is also related to the hybridisation on which this paper focuses. Swenk [21] identified a lack of recognition of contradictions between faculty and staff as a cause of conflict between them; Kuo [22] points out that conflicts between faculty and staff are more complex than in other organizations due to the existence of an organizational culture based on their academic nature.

As for the latter regarding the 'technical and tool aspects of the organization' that organizational culture provides, Cameron and Freeman [23], who examined the relationship between nine organizational outcomes and the congruence, strength and type of organizational culture, and Smart and John [24], who conducted a follow-up study of the same, are representative quantitative studies.

Representative qualitative studies of universities that refer to the instrumental functions of organizational culture include Tierney [25], who defined them by several sub-concepts such as leadership, trust, strategy and mission, and Kezar [26], who also noted that in universities, leadership, relationships and trust are more important than rules and procedures. Barkin and Collins [27] also point out that Audit Culture, based on neoliberal ideology, has led to a diversification of indicators for measuring educational outcomes in the field of international education. This has led to a situation referred to as 'rubric shopping', whereby convenient indicators are selected according to different educational objectives.

The above-mentioned previous studies were conducted in Europe and the USA, but hybridisation is also taking place in East Asia. Chan, Yang and Wai Lo [28] reveal the fact that there is a cultural clash with Chinese state control in university in Taiwan, where neoliberal ideals in the West are prevalent. In Japan, where the author has been studying organizational culture, university reforms have progressed, starting with the incorporation of national and public universities in 2004, but the incorporation of national universities, which was the main focus of reform, was a 'peculiar system' [29] in which authority was significantly more concentrated in the hands of university presidents than in other countries. Furthermore, since the 2010s, 'selection and concentration' in the strengthening of management systems and allocation of funds has progressed throughout the entire higher education sector, including private universities, but it is difficult to say that the university reform has been successful. In this context, an increasing number of studies have focused on organizational culture, but only a limited number of studies have focused on the types of organizational culture that are critically important for examining the situation of hybridisation. First, a previous study focusing on organizational values and ideologies [30] examined the characteristics of the organizational culture of national, private and public universities established by local governments, using the CVF scale. While in Japan, national universities have a particularly high prestige as research-oriented universities, private universities have university management in line with their founding principles, and public universities are strongly controlled by local governments; the results in this study showed that above characteristics in each founder.

Similarly, Maeda [31] focused on the instrumental aspects of organizational culture using the CVF scale. This study conducted a quantitative study using a multilevel model on faculty members at a private universities and revealed the mechanisms that generate and suppress conflict as a factor of opportunistic behaviour and revealed the fact that an organizational culture that emphasises research reduces conflict, while an organizational culture that emphasises competition between universities and centralisation of power in the university executive reinforces conflict.

In addition, in order to clarify the degree to which organizations are able to prevent opportunity-based behaviour, it is necessary to focus on efficiency rather than on organizational effectiveness, which focuses on attainment. A review article focusing on efficiency in educational institutions is De Witte and López-Torres [32], but there are no previous studies internationally that have used CVF to identify the relationship between organizational culture and efficiency, such as Cameron and Freeman [23], mentioned above, and Smart and John [24] who have focused on organizational outcomes rather than on efficiency. Thus, the relationship between organizational culture and efficiency has not been clarified, but Maeda [33] examines two types of efficiency, short-term resource allocation and long-term management improvement performance, for private universities using the data envelopment analysis to identify private universities with high management capacity and suggests that a highly competition-oriented organizational culture has a strong influence on organizational efficiency.

In a knowledge-based economy, where responses to the external environment are required, a framework that integrates the relationship between cultural forms and performance is currently sought, but as noted above, previous studies focusing on organizational culture have found two separate trends. There is a lack of previous research focusing on a framework that integrates the two interests.

3. Knowledge-based economy and academic freedom

Unlike classical economics, which rejects state intervention in individual freedom, neoliberalism actively evaluates the role of the state as far as it concerns appropriate market development, and the main feature of its ideology is that it regards knowledge as capital [34]. The higher education sector is undergoing a transformation at all levels—political, economic and philosophical—and the transformation of the organizational model towards a 'holistic model' [1] of the university must be understood in this context. It is also a transformation from a 'public good knowledge/learning regime' to an 'academic capitalist knowledge/learning regime' [35]. Marginson [36] points out that as long as NPM, the policy instrument of neoliberalism, exercises power based on 'freedom as control', the 'freedom as power' described by Amartya Sen is necessary as a corresponding force to that power. In other words, the heterogeneity of values surrounding 'freedom'—'freedom as control' on the part of administrators, who pursue organizational values and rely on legitimacy based on laws and regulations, and 'academic freedom', which is also a self-subjective right on the part of faculty—exists, while power-based enforcement against heterogeneous values is intensifying, The essential challenge of hybridisation in universities in a knowledge-based economy can be said to lie in such a situation. Currently, in university, the management of objectives, such as setting organizational goals, strategic planning and effective resource allocation, has become increasingly important [4], and a situation has arisen where the management of objectives has itself become an end in itself. Kogan [37] points to this ideology, in which ends and means are inverted, as 'managerialism' and distinguishes it from management. Birnbaum [38] also points out that 'governance' is a concept that describes organizational structures and procedures to achieve an 'effective balance' under different systems based on different validities, but a distinction between governance and managerialism should also be made.

March and Simon [15] identified three types of origins of 'intergroup conflict within organization': a difference in goals, a difference in perceptions of realty and a positive felt need for joint decision-making. Also, there are stages in the methods of resolving these conflicts. The methods of conflict resolution at the individual level include persuasion and problem-solving, but when the conflict cannot be resolved between members, the level of the problem shifts to the organizational dimension. This solution then becomes 'bargaining' and 'politics' [12, 15], but these problem-solving methods are difficult to apply between members who have different perceptions on the value dimensions of goals and perceptions of realty. Bess and Dee [12] state that it is important that administrators and faculty members in universities do not aim to follow the same conceptual framework, but rather work together to transcend the conceptual frameworks attributed to their respective positions and to find a shared commitment. They point to the importance of *Appreciative Inquiry* as a solution method, which is a 'communication technique', allowing for conflict between groups and attempting to overcome the factors causing that conflict through dialogue. Lu [39] refers to the importance of members with different values exploring shared values through examples of practice in US universities and states that 'institutional restraint' is more important than 'institutional neutrality' in this practice.

The increasing hybridisation that value differences bring about is not only limited to within universities but also between university and business organizations. Geiger [40] states that while the knowledge-based economy is advancing, the culture between academic and industrial research is fundamentally different, with industrial research tending towards application and disclosure, whereas universities have a different interest: the advancement and diffusion of systematic knowledge. Difficulties exist in industry–academia collaboration in the form of differing values, with companies expecting university researchers to contribute to the task and universities expecting companies to contribute to research funding and student support. In overcoming inter-sectoral conflicts based on cultural differences, efforts are required to search for a compromise between the two sides through negotiations.

The shift to a 'holistic model' based on the development of a knowledge-based economy has led to hybridisation, where heterogeneous values coexist inside and outside university, resulting in inter-group conflicts within organization and inter-organizational conflicts caused by value differences.

4. Organizational paradigm analysis framework

4.1 Organizational paradigm

The previous section referred to a situation in which a hybridisation of 'freedom as control' by government and university administrators and 'academic freedom' in university faculty members has emerged. The above situation is closely related to the issue of bounded rationality brought about by their values. In this section, the concept of *organizational paradigm* will be introduced to systematically combine values and organizational culture as sources of bounded rationality and to position organizational culture as an analytical perspective of *organizational failure*.

Transaction cost theory, which is the theoretical basis for the mechanism of 'the organizational failures', incorporates concepts related to organizational culture, such as 'atmosphere', which enables 'supplying *a satisfying exchange relation*' [14]. Milgrom and Roberts [10] also stated that 'implicit contracts', which are closely related to corporate culture, correspond to a shared set of values, ways of thinking and beliefs and serve 'An important adjunct to incomplete written contract'. Focusing on organizational culture as a factor in the forming of bounded rationality at the organizational level, not only among individual members, is useful in examining *the organizational failures* in universities, which encompasses intergroup conflict within organizations due to differences in values.

On the other hand, the concept of organizational culture is multivalent, Schein [41] identified the elements of organizational culture as 'articfacts', 'espoused beliefs and values' and 'underlying assumptions'. Tierney [25] who noted 'organizational culture is as slippery a term as the word culture' pointed out the elements of organizational culture generally agreed upon by organizational culture researchers as 'environment', 'mission', 'socialisation', 'information', 'strategy' and 'leadership'. However, in all of these, the concepts of values and mission are included in the elements of organizational culture. Another term that has the same meaning as values and worldviews is *paradigm*. Bess and Dee [12] point out that 'underlying assumptions', which Schein [41] defines as part of organizational culture, are most closely related to the concept of *paradigm*. Thomas Kuhn used the term *paradigm* to examine the history of the development of science, which Kuhn defined as meaning 'universally recognized scientific achievements that for a time provide model problems and solutions to a community of practitioners' [42]. The concept of paradigms has also been the focus of attention in organizational theory, but Kagono [43] criticised that 'what has been called a paradigm in previous discussions can be adequately substituted by the concept of a common worldview or organizational ideology' and that 'the inherent implication of the concept is developmental' and proposed the concept of *organizational paradigm*, which defines the thinking and behavioural patterns of organizational members.

Kagono [43] explains that the organizational paradigm consists of three elements and defines a *metaphor* as an assumption of thinking that is unquestionably accepted by the members as legitimate within organization members. And the metaphor itself is composed of the following subcomponents.

> *'The members of a company themselves share a variety of metaphors about the company, about the relationship between the company and the market, and about the relationship between the company and its members' [43].*

The second and third components of the metaphor's upper structure are then explained as follows.

> *'The second is the paradigm as values and norms that more concretely indicate how members of an organization should behave in different situations. It is the level corresponding to what we have called the daily theory and is a similar expression to which we have called organizational culture in organizational theory. Finally, it is an exemplar or example that concretely represents the daily theory' [43].*

Organizational paradigm have robustness and can lead to a decline in the organization's adaptability to its environment. Hence, for an organization to survive in the long term, it must undergo a *paradigm shift* [43]. Milgrom and Roberts [10] describe the difficulties of making changes in corporate culture, which are closely related to implicit contracts, as being equivalent to '*breaking old contracts and implementing new ones, all without the benefit of being able to discuss the terms of either contract very explicitly*'. In the light of this point, it will be understood that *organizational paradigm* and *implicit contract* are synonymous concepts. The current situation in university can be described as the coexistence of two types of contract between administrators and faculty members based on different values that have not been discussed on both sides.

The above-mentioned *appreciative inquiry* [12], which creates a *new contract*, may be one solution to this situation.

4.2 Typology of organizational paradigm

In this section, the concept of *organizational paradigm* is used to attempt a typology of the values of university members and the organizational culture that arises from them. The 'organizational paradigm analysis framework' based on the above typologies will be presented as a frame of reference for understanding why organizational failure occurs in universities. In examining this analytical framework, reference is made to the university typologies of Olsen [44] and McNay [45], who formulated a typology of universities in terms of adaptability to the society surrounding the university. Furthermore, the 'Competing Values Framework' (CVF) [46] is additionally taken into account in making the connection with the organizational culture arising from the values of the members. Considering the consistency between the concepts in these previous studies, an attempt is made to integrate them into the 'organizational paradigm analysis framework'.

First, Olsen [44] in Table 1 (p. 30: hereafter 'Olsen Table 1') describes four types of university and governance based on the two dimensions of *autonomy* and *conflict*: a rule-governed community of scholars, a representative democracy, an instrument for national political agendas and a service enterprise embedded in competitive markets. In terms of the low autonomy typology, low conflict is a 'rule-governed community of scholars' based on traditional value norms, while high conflict is a 'representative democracy' based on the participation of diverse members. The low conflict in the high autonomy typology is an 'instrument for national political agendas' that acts as an administrative organization, while the last high autonomy–high conflict is a 'service enterprise embedded in competitive markets'. The 'community of scholars', which is based on academic values, is classified as an 'institution', while the other types of 'representative democracy' are an 'instrument' for individuals and groups within the university to realise democracy, while the 'national political agendas' promote the government's national policy, and the 'service enterprise' type is organised as an 'instrument' to meet the needs of external stakeholders and 'customers' in a competitive environment (p. 29). The top row of the organizational paradigm analysis framework (**Table 1**) is defined on the basis of the above. As noted above, Kagono [43] states that the organizational paradigm is composed of three concepts: the '*metaphor*', the 'daily theories' meaning the *organizational culture* and the '*exemplar or example*' meaning representations of actual reality, of which only *metaphor* and *organizational culture* related to the perceptions of the members were placed in the leftmost column. Furthermore, the sub-concepts of metaphor are also discussed above Kagono [43] and are divided into the following categories: 'the ideal state of the university', 'the relationship between the university and its members' and 'the relationship between the university and society'. In the upper row, the 'daily theory', organizational culture, was placed. Next, in the second column, the 'constitutive logic' in Olsen (Table 1) was used for 'the ideal state of the university'. For 'the relationship between the university and its members', as it was difficult to find an evaluation perspective equivalent to Olsen's (Table 1). The author used the 'dominant unit', the 'internal references' and the 'administrator roles of servant of...' from McNay [45] in Table 9.1 (p. 109: hereafter 'McNay (Table 9.1)'). For 'the relationship between the university and society', we used the 'reasons for autonomy' from Olsen (Table 1) and the 'models of universities as organizations' from McNay (Table 9.1) , together with Figure 9.1 (p. 106) from [45],

Dimension of organizational paradigm		Institution	Instrument		
		A rule-governed community of scholars	**A representative democracy**	**An instrument for national political agendas**	**A service enterprise embedded in competitive markets**
Organizational culture					
Competing values framework		Flexibility and discretion		Stability and control	
		External focus and differentiation	Internal focus and integration	Internal focus and integration	External focus and differentiation
		Adhocracy	Clan	Hierarchy	Market
Metaphor					
The relationship between the university and society	Reasons for autonomy	Constitutive principle of the university as an institution: authority to the best qualified	Mixed (workplace democracy, functional competence, *realpolitik*)	Delegated and based on relative efficiency	Responsiveness to 'stakeholders' and external exigencies, survival
	Models of universities as organizations	Bureaucracy	Collegium	Corporation	Enterprise
	Nature of change	Reactive adaptation	Organic innovation	Proactive transformation	Tactical flexibility
The relationship between the university and its members	Dominant unit	Faculty/committees	Department/individual	Institution/senior management team	Sub unit/project teams
	Internal references	The rules	The discipline	The plans	Market strength/students
	Administrator roles: servant of ...	The committee	The community	The chief executive	The client, internal and external
The ideal state of the university	constitutive logic	Identity based on free inquiry, truth finding, rationality and expertise	Interest representation, elections, bargaining and majority decisions	Administrative: implementing predetermined political objectives	Community service. Part of a system of market exchange and price systems

Source: [44–46]. Refer to Section 4.2.

Table 1.
The organizational paradigm analysis framework.

which shows the four types of university models. In integrating McNay (Table 9.1) and Olsen (Table 1) for the above items, based on the suitability of each type, the 'bureaucracy' corresponds to the 'community of scholars', the 'collegium' to the 'representative democracy', the 'corporation' to the 'instrument for national political agendas' and the 'enterprise' to the 'service enterprise'. Based on the above, the 'organizational paradigm analysis framework' was constructed.

Next, we refer to organizational culture. Cameron and Quinn [46] defined the competing value framework (CVF) based on two dimensions of organizational culture, external/internal and stability/flexibility, and proposed four organizational culture typologies: adhocracy, market, hierarchy and clan. Adhocracy is concerned with *innovative and pioneering initiatives* (p. 43), which it states represents the characteristics of an organization's emphasis on *mainly in the business of developing new products and services and preparing for the future* (p. 43). The same external focus dimension, market emphasis on stability and control than adhocracy. Market's special character lies in its *transactions with (mainly) external constituencies* (p. 39), which differs from the hierarchy's emphasis on internal constituencies. The most important aspect of market culture is the emphasis on *transaction costs* which Williamson [14] proposes (p. 39). Hierarchy assumes Weber's bureaucracy, an organizational characteristic that emphasises *stable, efficient, highly consistent products and services* (p. 37). This assumption provides validity when the external environment is stable, sectional functions are integrated and members are under control (p. 37). The clan is an organizational cultural characteristic exemplified in Japan during its period of rapid economic growth (1960s to early 1970s) and derived from the Japanese-style management of *shared values and goals, cohesion, participativeness, individuality and a sense of 'we-ness'* (p. 41).

Based on the above typologies, the organizational culture in CVF corresponds to adhocracy as 'community of scholars', clan as the 'representative democracy', hierarchy as the 'instrument for national political agendas' and market as the 'service enterprise'.

5. Organizational failures framework in university

5.1 Organizational failures framework in profit organization

The purpose of this section is to present an analytical framework for clarifying the inherent mechanisms related to 'the organizational failures' in universities. In order to proceed with this discussion, we first identify the analytical framework of 'the organizational failures' presented by Williamson [14], on which the above-mentioned author's analytical framework relies.

Five factors were identified by Williamson [14] as contributing to the failure to construct the world of *frictionless ideal* [14] in organizations. Among them, the combination of the thick arrows shown in **Figure 1**—Bounded rationality and uncertainty/complexity, as well as opportunism and the exchange relationship between small numbers—are the main factors in the organizational failures. On the other hand, information impactedness is a derivative factor, primarily arising from uncertainty and opportunism, which themselves produce small numbers. And these transactions take place inside the *atmosphere*. Similar to the above, bounded rationality based on value and opportunism based on value differences can arise in university, but these mechanisms cannot be explained in the diagram below and require a specific framework.

5.2 Transaction cost theory as a constructive 'stakeholder theory'

In creating an analytical framework for the organizational failures in universities, we next draw on Casson [47], who examined leader–follower relationships in the

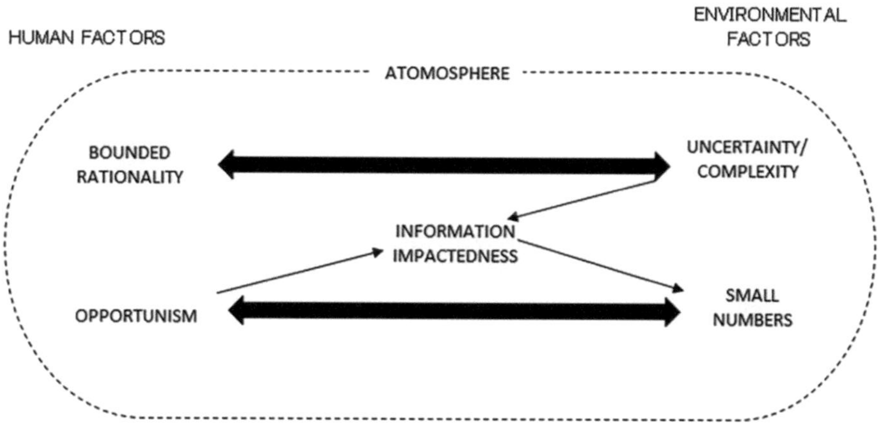

Figure 1.
The organizational failures framework. Source: [14] p. 40, Figure 3.

intellectual professions from the perspective of transaction cost theory. Casson [47] states that leader–follower relationships can be seen as *transactions* in which *the follower agrees (informally) to work hard in return for some benefit – emotional or material – conferred by the leader* (p. 48).

This perspective is even more valid in universities where hybridisation around value is occurring, and it is possible to view the relationship between university administrators and faculty as such a *transaction*. The introduction of a perspective simultaneously brings attention to the invisible costs of transaction in resolving intergroup conflict within organizations. Casson [47] defined the costs required for leaders to exert influence over their followers as the manipulation costs. Furthermore, Casson [47] divided the manipulation costs into the fixed costs that depend on the number of followers and the variable costs that depend on leader's intensity and not on the number of followers. The above costs were defined as the direct costs, in addition to which lost profits due to follower negligence were defined as the indirect costs. And through comparing the transaction costs of *manipulating these followers* with the costs of monitoring, he argues that in intellectual work such as research and professional services (except in cases where intellectual negligence can cause serious harm, such as clinical medical safety), it is more important to make leadership work than to increase monitoring costs.

It should be noted that *transaction costs have the limitation that the cost of transacting are real; they are not always easily separated from other kind of cost*s (p. 34) [10], but the interest of this paper is not the quantitative measurement of transaction costs for the purpose of comparing costs and benefits. As Montgomery and Snyder [48], who measured library administrative costs, pointed out that the most important factor for minimising costs is not detailed cost measurement, but increasing the number of users using existing resources. A detailed cost–benefit analysis focusing on transaction costs for a university would not only be of little research significance from a practical perspective but also, as Milgrom and Roberts [10] point out, itself be almost impossible to attempt.

However, this does not diminish the value of applying transaction cost theory to a university. Although the phenomenon that transaction cost theory initially intended to address was the problem of vertical integration, sometimes referred to as 'the canonical TCE case' [49]. Ketokivi and Mahoney [49] notes that transaction cost theory is beneficial in providing 'a useful contrast and counterpoint' perspective to other organizational theories that focus on 'competence- and power-based theories of the firm'. Casson [47] could be said to have offered a new perspective on leader–follower relationships, not of power or competence, but of *transaction*.

While the leader–follower mentioned above can be positioned as a 'stakeholder' within the university, a theoretical system that focuses on the relationships between different stakeholders, such as customers, suppliers, communities, employees and financial institutions, and tries to understand capitalism through these overall relationships is called as *stakeholder theory*; this theory focuses on issues of value creation and transactions, the ethics of capitalism and management mindset [50]. This theory is considered a useful theory in a university where moving towards a 'holistic model' and simultaneously generating 'hyblidisation' based on the differences of values among members. But a few studies in university governance research have focused on stakeholder theory [51]. Ketokivi and Mahoney [52], on the other hand, point out that the principles of stakeholder theory—cooperation, involvement and responsibility—are underpinned by problematic concerns such as opportunism, trust and pre-regulation of potential conflicts and that these problematic concerns in the basic principles of stakeholder theory are consistent with transaction costs theory. And Ketokivi and Mahoney [52] conclude that *transaction cost theory can indeed be applied as a constructive stakeholder theory*. The significance of applying transaction cost theory to a university with intergroup conflict within organization under heterogeneous values is not in the vertical integration or the comparison of costs and benefits, but in clarifying the mechanisms of construction and failure of 'cooperation, involvement and responsibility' among stakeholders as a *constructive stakeholder theory*.

Figure 2 shows the organizational failures framework in university. The outermost dotted line represents the organizational culture as a whole in a university. However, there are university administrators (leaders) and faculty members (followers) with heterogeneous organizational paradigms underneath. These stakeholders have an organizational culture that is a subculture, and underlying this culture is a metaphor that they believe in about the nature of the university, the relationship between the university and its members and society. This metaphor then forms a bounded rationality.

On the other hand, the executive and administrative staff of the university (leaders) try to exert influence through governance (organizational structures and procedures) or leadership and elicit 'cooperation, involvement and responsibility' from the faculty (followers). However, opportunism can easily occur in intellectual work where 'monitoring' does not function effectively. This mechanism shows 'the organizational failures' in university that this paper assumes.

At the lowest part, in 'organizational outcomes', efficiency will be a stronger indicator of the consequences of 'the organizational failures' than effectiveness. On the other hand, what is even more important for organizational research, and what researchers truly want to know, is *why organizations fail*. In determining this cause, the organizational culture and the value perceptions of its members will provide useful information. The metaphor of the constituency is different when the dominant organizational culture of the faculty is adhocracy, which emphasises creativity and innovation, and when it is market, which emphasises gaining competitive advantage. Therefore, when similar governance and leadership is applied to these universities in eliciting faculty collaboration and engagement, the responses may be quite different. Similar results may be observed across different establishers (national, local and private). Furthermore, different academic disciplines will have different metaphors, and the occurrence of

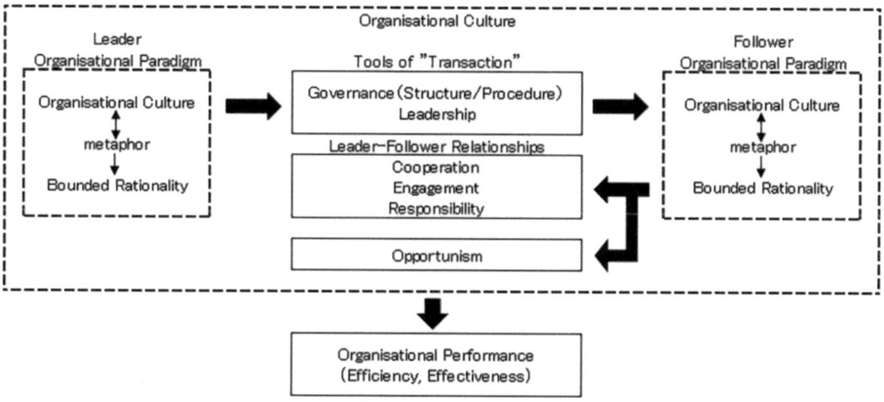

Figure 2.
The organizational failures framework in university. Source: Author.

opportunism will differ depending on whether tenure is granted or not. By using 'the organizational paradigm analytical framework' presented in this paper together with 'the organizational failures framework in university', organizational culture can be an analytical perspective for fact-finding on the organizational failures in universities.

6. Conclusion and discussion

This paper has focused on the heterogeneity of values surrounding 'freedom'—'freedom as control' on the part of management and 'academic freedom' on the part of faculty—as an essential issue of hybridisation that has emerged in universities in a knowledge-based economy and has proposed two analytical frameworks to treat organizational culture arising from this as an analytical perspective of organizational failure. In the first framework, the concept of organizational paradigm was introduced in an attempt to connect metaphors, which are the perceptions of values held by university members, with the concept of organizational culture arising from them, and a categorisation of these paradigms was attempted, and an 'organizational paradigm analysis framework' was presented. The second analytical framework presented in this paper is the 'organizational failure framework' specific to university in order to examine why organising in universities has not progressed easily and to avoid organizational failure. This framework proposed the necessity to focus not only on governance and leadership, such as procedures and structures, but also on the type of organizational paradigm that leaders and followers have.

We would like to mention the significance of this research in light of the above. Universities are required to be responsive to their external environment, and in order to achieve this, we must focus on conflicts of values. Organizational culture studies have two trends: interest in the cultural form of organizational culture and interest in its impact on outcomes, but in order to examine the above issues, it is necessary to integrate the two trends, but until now, no such efforts have been made. The significance of this study was the integration of these two trends into a single framework, with regard to cultural forms in the 'organizational paradigm analysis framework' and the impact on outcomes in the 'organizational paradigm analysis framework'. Effective policy recommendations will be possible through the hypotheses formulated by the NPM and the execution of analyses based on the two frameworks.

On the other hand, a limitation of this study is that it does not incorporate the perspective of comparing transaction costs based on a quantitative perspective within the 'organizational failure framework'. However, this is an unavoidable consequence. As mentioned in Section 5, universities are composed of stakeholders with diverse values and cannot maximise value by measuring quantitative costs and benefits, so there is little significance in incorporating such a perspective into this framework. Rather, the purpose of this framework is to present a framework for pre-regulation [52] against opportunism and potential conflicts that obstruct 'cooperation, involvement and responsibility', which is also a principle of stakeholder theory, as described in Section 5, and the above problematic concerns overlap with those of transaction cost theory. It will be necessary to clarify the limitations of the above based on the characteristics of university. Another limitation in this study is that the framework focuses on the relationship between leaders and followers but does not reflect the perspective of organizational learning, especially among followers.

Three directions for future research should be mentioned. First, with regard to the 'organizational paradigm analysis framework', the validity as a constitutive concept of organizational paradigm and the differences between types of organizational paradigm should be clarified through empirical research on the linkage between metaphor and organizational culture. Second, with regard to the 'organizational failure framework', it is important to examine the homogeneity or heterogeneity of organizational paradigms between the university executive (leaders) and the university faculty and staff (followers), as well as the types of these paradigms. Based on the above findings, it is important to identify how the effective 'transactions' of governance and leadership between leaders and followers, aimed at establishing cooperation and engagement, vary according to the organizational paradigm. As a research direction, the last point I would like to make is the importance of research based on property rights: Jones [53] provides valuable insights into the relationship between organizational culture, transaction costs and property rights, but from an empirical perspective, it is important to clarify the relationship between the organizational paradigm that leaders have and property rights. Because property rights provide a legitimate basis for the exclusion of followers who do not 'go along with a leader's will', and leaders may rely on that legitimacy to guide followers towards the achievement of arbitrary organizational objectives. This perspective is crucial in deterring organizational opportunism and realising organizational responsiveness to the external environment through leader–follower alignment.

As the organizational model of universities shifts towards a 'holistic model' [1] in a knowledge-based economy, a focus on organizational culture will provide a useful analytical perspective in clarifying intergroup conflict within organizations regarding their 'values'. Although this paper has focused on the internal university, the two analytical frameworks presented in this paper can also be extended to the analytical framework of failures in collaboration between industry and universities and in 'transdisciplinary research' [13]. Kandawinna, Mallawaarachchi and Vijerathne [54], who examined the requirements for the formation of 'public–private partnerships', which are partnerships between universities and industry, found that organizations with different interests can be successful in achieving common objectives through discussion and communication. This finding shows the importance of formulating the metaphor between stakeholders. On the other hand, the effectiveness of the means of establishing 'transactions' between these stakeholders will vary depending on the objectives and commerciality of the collaborative projects they work on. Organizational culture may provide an analytical perspective when building these relationships runs into difficulties.

Author details

Kazuyuki Maeda
Research Institute for Humanity and Nature, Kyoto, Japan

*Address all correspondence to: kmaeda458@gmail.com

References

[1] Peterson MW. The study of colleges and universities as organizations. In: Gumport PJ, editor. Sociology of Higher Education. Baltimore: Johns Hopkins University Press; 2007

[2] Ekman M, Lindgren M, Packendorff J. Universities need leadership, academics need management: Discursive tensions and voids in the deregulation of Swedish higher education legislation. Higher Education. 2018;**75**(2):299-321. DOI: 10.1007/s10734-017-0140-2

[3] Enders J, Boer, De H, Liudvika L. On striking the right notes: Shifts in governance and the organisational transformation of universities. In: Amaral A, Bleiklie I, Musselin C, editors. From Governance to Identity a Festschrift for Mary Henkel. Dordrecht: Springer; 2008. pp. 113-130

[4] Sporn B. Governance and administration: Organizational and structural trends. International Handbook of Higher Education. 2007;**1**:141-157. DOI: 10.1007/978-1-4020-4012-2_9

[5] Bleiklie I, Svein M. The university as Enterprise and academic Co-determination. In: Amaral A, Bleiklie I, Musselin C, editors. From Governance to Identity a Festschrift for Mary Henkel. Dordrecht: Springer; 2008. pp. 57-80

[6] Maassen P. The modernisation of European higher education: National Policy Dynamics. In: Amaral A, Bleiklie I, Musselin C, editors. From Governance to Identity a Festschrift for Mary Henkel. Dordrecht: Springer; 2008. pp. 95-112

[7] Ferlie E, Musselin C, Adnresani G. The steering of higher education systems: A public management perspective. Higher Education. 2008;**56**:325-348

[8] Allen DK. Organisational climate and strategic change in higher education: Organisational insecurity. Higher Education. 2003;**46**(1):61-92. DOI: 10.1023/A:1024445024385

[9] Amaral A. Transforming higher education. In: Amaral A, Bleiklie I, Musselin C, editors. From Governance to Identity a Festschrift for Mary Henkel. Dordrecht: Springer; 2008. pp. 81-94

[10] Milgrom PR, Roberts J. Economics, Organization, and Management. New Jersey: Prentice Hall; 1992

[11] Kezar A, Lester J. Organizing Higher Education for Collaboration: A Guide for Campus Leaders. 1st ed. San Francisco: JOSSEY-BASS A Wiley Imprint; 2009

[12] Bess JL, Dee JR. Bridging the Divide between Faculty and Administration: A Guide to Understanding Conflict in the Academy. 1st ed. New York and Abingdon: Routledge; 2014

[13] OECD. Addressing societal challenges using transdiciplinary research. Policy Papers. 2020;**88**:39-51

[14] Williamson OE. Markets and Hierarchies Analysis and Antitrust Implications. New York: The Free Press; 1975

[15] March JG, Simon HA. Organizations. 2nd ed. John Wiley & Sons; 1993

[16] Kitai A. Organizational culture enhancing: Multi-level approach (*Gakushu wo unagasu soshikibunka maruchi reberu apurochi ni yoru jisshou bunseki*). Tokyo: Yuhikaku; 2014

[17] Clark BR. The organizational saga in higher education. Administrative Science Quarterly. 1972;**17**(2):178-184

[18] Becher T. Academic Tribes and Territories Intellectual Enquity and the Cultures of Disciplines. First ed. The Society for Research into Higher Education & Open University Press; 1989

[19] De Zilwa D. Organisational culture and values and the adaptation of academic units in Australian universities. Higher Education. 2007;**54**(4):557-574. DOI: 10.1007/s10734-006-9008-6

[20] Sporn B. Managing university culture: An analysis of the relationship between institutional culture and management approaches. Dordrecht: Higher Education. 1996;**32**(1):41-61. DOI: 10.1007/BF00139217

[21] Swenk J. Planning failures: Decision cultural clashes. The Review of Higher Education. 1999;**23**(1):1-21. DOI: 10.1353/rhe.1999.0025

[22] Kuo H. Understanding relationships between academic staff and administrators: An organisational culture perspective. London: Journal of Higher Education Policy and Management. 2009;**31**(1):43-54. DOI: 10.1080/13600800802559278

[23] Cameron KS, Freeman SJ. Cultural congruence, strength, and type: Relationships to effectiveness. Leeds, England: Research in Organizational Change and Development. 1991

[24] Smart JC, John EP, St. Organizational culture and effectiveness in higher education: A test of the "culture type" and "strong culture" hypotheses. USA: Educational Evaluation and Policy Analysis. 1996;**18**(3):219-241. DOI: 10.3102/01623737018003219

[25] Tierney WG. The Impact of Culture on Organizational Decision Making: Theory and Practice in Higher Education. Virginia: Stylus Publishing, LLC; 2008

[26] Kezar A. What is more important to effective governance: Relationships, trust, and leadership, or structures and formal processes? USA: New Directions for Higher Education. 2004;**2004**(127):35-46. DOI: 10.1002/he.154

[27] Barkin G, Collins L. Assessing study abroad: Rubric shopping, managerialism, and audit culture at the neoliberal university. USA: Frontiers: The Interdisciplinary Journal of Study Abroad. 2023;**35**(1):52-81. DOI: 10.36366/frontiers.v35i1.766

[28] Chan SJ, Yang CC, Wai Lo WY. Adopting neoliberal values in Taiwan's higher education governance: A hybridisation process. Discourse: Studies in the Cultural Politics of Education. 2023;**44**(3):425-440. DOI: 10.1080/01596306.2023.2200078

[29] Oba J. Revision of the school education law and the National University Corporation law and governance of national universities (*Gakkou Kyouikuhou Kokuritsu Daigaku Houjinhou no Kaisei to Kokuritsu Daigaku no Gabanansu*). Tokyo: University Evaluation Research (*Daigaku Hyouka Kenkyu*). 2015;**11**(253-272)

[30] Maeda K. Empirical research on the relationship between organizational culture and presidential leadership (*Soshikibunka to Gakutyou Ridashippu ni kansuru Jisshouteki Kenkyu*). Hiroshima: Research in Higher Education (*Daigaku Ronshu*). 2017;**49**:85-100

[31] Maeda K. Can managerialism promote organisational transformation in private universities? International Journal

of Chinese Education. 2022;**10**(3):1-18. DOI: 10.1177/22125868211067288

[32] De Witte K, López-Torres L. Efficiency in education. A review of literature and a way forward. Document de Treball. 2015;**15**(1):1-40

[33] Maeda K. Empirical research on environmental adaptations of Japanese private universities: Focusing on the relationship between economies of scale and transaction costs (*Shiritsu Daigaku no Kankyou Tekiou ni Kansuru Jisshouteki Kenkyu*). Bulletin of the graduate School of Humanities and Social Sciences (*Kyouikugaku Kenkyu*). Hiroshima: Hiroshima University. Studies in Education. 2020;**1**(731-740)

[34] Olssen M, Peters MA. Neoliberalism, higher education and the knowledge economy: From the free market to knowledge capitalism. Journal of Education Policy. 2005;**20**(3):313-345. DOI: 10.1080/02680930500108718

[35] Slaughter S, Rhoades G. Academic Capitalism and the New Economy: Markets, State, and Higher Education. Johns Hopkins University Press; 2009

[36] Marginson S. Academic creativity under new public management: Foundations for an investigation. Educational Theory. 2008;**58**(3):269-287. DOI: 10.1111/j.1741-5446.2008.00288.x

[37] Kogan M. Frame-work paper: The issues. In: Managerialism and Evaluation in Higher Education. UNESCO Forum Occasional Paper Series. Vol. 2004. Paris; 2004. Available from: http://specialcollections.nust.na:8080/greenstone3/library/sites/localsite/collect/unesco/index/assoc/HASH8f80.dir/Managerialism_and_evaluation_in_higher_education.pdf;jsessionid=DD0B63DCE5AF8EA42BF1BDBFAEC0A1E2

[38] Birnbaum R. The End of Shared Governance: Looking Ahead or Looking Back. Conference Paper, (July); 2003. pp. 1-31. Available from: https://senate.oregonstate.edu/sites/senate.oregonstate.edu/files/birnbaumsgtf.pdf

[39] Lu A. Should College Administrators Take Political Positions? The Chronicle of Higher Education. 2022. Available from: https://www.chronicle.com/article/the-apolitical-university?sra=true&cid=gen

[40] Geiger RL. Knowledge and Money: Research Universities and the Paradox of the Marketplace. Stanford University Press; 2004

[41] Schein E. Organizational Culture and Leadership. 3rd ed. Jossey-Bass A Wiley Imprint; 2004. DOI: 10.1080/09595230802089917

[42] Kuhn TS. The Structure of Scientific Revolutions: With An Introductory Essay by Ian Hacking. 4th ed. Chicago: The University of Chicago Press; 2012

[43] Kagono T. Organizational epistemology. 5th ed. Chikura Shobou; 2004

[44] Olsen JP. The institutional dynamics of the European university. In: Maassen P, Olsen JP, editors. University Dynamics and European Integration. Dordrecht: Springer; 2007. pp. 25-54. DOI: 10.1007/978-1-4020-5971-1_2

[45] McNay I. From the collegial academy to corporate Enterprise: The changing cultures of universities. In: Schuller T, editor. The Changing University? Society for Research into Higher Education; 1995. pp. 105-115

[46] Cameron KS, Quinn RE. Diagnosing and Changing Organizational Culture Based on the Competing Values Framework. Revised ed. JOSSEY-BASS A Wiley Imprint; 2006

[47] Casson M. The Economics of Business Culture: Game Theory, Transaction Costs, and Economic Performance. New York: Oxford University Press; 1991

[48] Montgomery JR, Snyder JK. Costing a library. Research in Higher Education. 1989;**30**(1):47-87

[49] Ketokivi M, Mahoney JT. Transaction cost economics as a theory of the firm, management, and governance. Oxford Research Encyclopedia of Business and Management. 2017;**February**:1-24. DOI: 10.1093/acrefore/9780190224851.013.6

[50] Freeman RE, Harrison JS, Wicks AC, Parmar BL, de Colle S. Stakeholder Theory: The State of the Art. Cambridge University Press; 2010

[51] Avci Ö, Ring E, Lynette M. Stakeholders in U.S. higher education: An analysis through two theories of stakeholders. Bilgi Ekonomisi ve Yönetimi Dergisi. 2015;**10**(2). Available from: https://dergipark.org.tr/en/download/article-file/323147

[52] Ketokivi M, Mahoney JT. Transaction cost economics as a constructive stakeholder theory. Academy of Management Learning & Education. 2016;**15**(1):123-138. DOI: 10.5465/amle.2015.0133

[53] Jones GR. Transaction costs, property rights, and organizational culture: An exchange perspective. Administrative Science Quarterly. 1983;**28**(3):454-467. DOI: 10.2307/2392252

[54] Kandawinna N, Mallawaarachchi H, Vijerathne D. Successful delivery of public-private partnership (PPP) in the construction projects of Sri Lankan higher education sector. In: Proceedings of the 10th World Construction Symposium. 2022:782-793. DOI: 10.31705/WCS.2022.63

Section 2

Digital Transformation Outcomes

Chapter 6

The Role of Organizational Climate in Cultural Transformation

Jacek Grodzicki

Abstract

Each enterprise operates in a different way and has a different work system and culture. So, each enterprise has different requirements, action plans, and organizational systems. In order for an organization to have better functionality and to be innovative and effective, it is important to analyze the system of operation, the duties assigned to employees, and the organizational climate. This will help to examine what affects the functionality of the enterprise and the efficiency of the employees. Hence, it is important to know what the organizational climate is and how to study it. In this context, the chapter will explore the most common dimensions of organizational climate and understand their correlations with organizational culture in the broadest sense.

Keywords: organizational climate, engagement, employee well-being, employee commitment, job satisfaction, organizational culture

1. Introduction

In recent years, business organizations have been experiencing a significant acceleration of organizational change, both in terms of structure and employment needs. In addition, a different approach of young employees to work itself from the previous one is becoming a problem. Balance is becoming an overriding value. For generation X or Z, the amount of pay is less important than for earlier generations of workers. It is increasingly common that the choice of a workplace is determined by information about the climate in a given organization. The level of employee commitment and efficiency also depends on it [1]. This is causing more and more organizations to see the need to build the work environment in such a way that employees feel comfortable in it. So that they can use all their potential and creativity for the good of the organization. This is their key to success in a competitive market today [2]. However, it is worth remembering that the organizational climate is something impermanent, which changes quickly, depending on the needs and expectations of employees. On their ability and willingness to work together. In contrast, organizational culture is the basis for how individuals act within an organization. It is something that employees find and to which they must adapt. According to Schneider, the difference between the two concepts is that organizational climate describes events and experiences and reveals patterns of employee behavior, while culture is a set of shared values, assumptions, and beliefs that exist within an organization. It seems, therefore, that culture should be viewed as something deeper within the organization. Something based on the values, beliefs, and assumptions of its employees. Organizational climate, on the other hand, as measured by a number of dimensions, is merely a piecemeal examination of these areas over a period of time [3]. Organizational culture is built over years, and the changes it undergoes are inherently slow. Interestingly, however, it is the organizational climate that is one of the more powerful factors in these changes.

2. The concept of organizational climate

The work environment is created primarily by people. Humans are the most important element for an enterprise to function, and relationships largely determine the work climate and productivity. The work climate has a major impact on an employee's daily performance and career. A person acquires knowledge throughout life, and importantly this takes place primarily in the work environment. A pleasant environment in which employees work has a positive impact on performance and well-being. Employers who create a pleasant work environment and good employee relations find it easier to attract new employees. This is because their positive image reinforces the company's good reputation in the social environment.

The work environment includes many factors that affect well-being, work comfort, and productivity. These are divided into two groups: physical factors and psychosocial factors. Physical factors — otherwise known as the material work environment. They are designed to provide comfortable conditions and safety for the employee. Employees have little influence on this, but the environment in which they perform their work translates into their productivity and well-being. Therefore, it is an extremely important element to provide adequate working conditions for the employees and create a relaxed and pleasant zone, where everyone feels comfortable. Psychosocial factors—these are interpersonal relationships. They are formed at the stage of each employee's daily life. They are extremely important as they largely determine how people employed by the organization will feel in the work environment, and how this will translate into their work. This aspect of human functioning in an organization, along with satisfaction and satisfaction analysis, that is, the area of organizational climate research.

While there are various proposals in the academic literature on this area of research, the dominant approach defines organizational climate as the majority of employees' shared assessment of practices, procedures, and events that shape perceptions of an organization. Organizational climate is a tool for understanding human behavior in organizations [4]. Research on organizational climate dates back to Kurt Lewin's work in the 1950s [5]. The concept became particularly popular in the 1960s and 1970s [6]. The organizational climate is shaped by a variety of factors, including the leadership style, organizational culture, communication patterns, and the physical environment. It is important for organizations to create a positive and supportive climate that promotes employee well-being, engagement, and productivity [7]. According to Guion, this climate relates to both the attributes of the organization and the perception of the individual, and that it is simply an alternative to affective responses to the organization, such as job satisfaction [8]. Thus, one can agree with Taguiri that organizational climate is a set of measurable characteristics of the work environment in which the people studied function. These dimensions are something that employees perceive directly or indirectly that affect their motivation and behavior ([9], p. 362-381).

It is worth noting at this point that, in general, several groups of proposals for organizational climate can be singled out [10]. One of them is the subjective concept, which focuses on the individual feelings of employees. According to this concept, it is the sum of all the feelings, relationships, and perspectives of individual employees that creates a differentiated organizational climate. This is a dynamic and impermanent process. The climate evolves with the changes that naturally occur in employee groups. Another is the interactionist concept, which views climate as a phenomenon that can be created by a group of employees. The important thing is that, according to this concept, it is not just the sum of individual employee perspectives, but the sum of the relationship between individual employee perspectives, group perspectives, and the organizational environment. Other proposals can be categorized as a concept that is referred to as managerial because it focuses on the responsibility of managers for building the organizational climate. It is primarily concerned with creating positive vertical relationships (manager-subordinate). This is the basis for a good atmosphere in the organization and translates into work efficiency. It is also worth noting that the concept is focused on satisfaction and performance. It focuses primarily on the needs of the employee. The main idea here is to recognize the climate itself, which allows you to more reliably assess the needs and expectations of employees, and then respond accordingly. The last one worth mentioning is the cultural concept, which depicts the organizational climate as a "manifestation" of the organizational culture. This means that with the help of the visible organizational climate certain theses can be formulated about a given organizational culture.

It is worth noting that at different times different currents and directions of interest in the organizational climate emerged, which translated into differences in the selection and study of climate components. The debate on organizational climate research that has been going on since the 1970s in the pages of scientific journals has been not so much about how to measure it, but what to measure [1]. Cilliers and Kossuth summarized the research of many authors and concluded that organizational dimensions at the formal level are structure, policies, goals, management practices, task specialization, decision-making, standards, and rewards. At the informal level, organizational climate refers to identity, employees' needs, accountability, the process of social communication, information exchange, support, or ways of resolving conflicts [11]. Analyzing the emerging subsequent research results in this area confirmed these observations. Although, of course, there are some differences between the various areas that are studied. Thus, for example, C.M. Tustin based his research on such dimensions as [12]:

- Interpersonal communication, both horizontally and vertically;
- reciprocal relations between colleagues;
- level of identification with the organization;
- level of fairness in the context of access to benefits and the process of awarding them itself;
- assessment of the employee's level of responsibility for tasks performed;
- assessment of employee participation in decision-making;
- opportunities for development and career building;
- assessment of existing risks and the need for change.

While Martins and Martins, for example, analyzed such dimensions as [13]:

- level of satisfaction with the physical equipment of workplaces;
- the evaluation of the perception of the organization's goals and the level of satisfaction with their achievement;
- evaluation of the management system;
- assessment of the sense of fair treatment;
- general job satisfaction and factors that keep an employee in an organization.

However, it can be noted that there are common areas in all studies on organizational climate. These are [14]:

Autonomy — understood as the ability to make independent decisions about goals, methods, or priorities.

Relationships — a sense of belonging to a community and a desire to help each other;

Trust — primarily in relation to superiors;

Responsibility — in relation to task completion;

Support—primarily from superiors to support risk-taking by subordinates;

Recognition— the level of recognition of individual employees' contribution to the bottom line;

Fairness— a sense of justice on 3 levels-procedural, distributive and relational;

Change—the ability to use new solutions or employees' own creativity without risk of punishment.

Based on these eight areas, individual researchers try to tailor their question proposals to achieve the broadest and most coherent picture of relations within an organization. At this point, it is worth taking a closer look at the various elements of the organizational climate.

A positive organizational climate is characterized by open communication, collaboration, trust, and a shared commitment to achieving common goals. On the other hand, a negative climate can be characterized by fear, mistrust, conflict, and a lack of cooperation. Organizations can analyze and assess their climate through surveys, focus groups, and other methods of gathering employee feedback. The feedback can then be used to identify areas for improvement and develop strategies for creating a more positive and supportive climate. For example, surveys conducted among users of a recruitment service showed that 65 percent of Poles believe that the atmosphere in a company can become a reason for resigning from a job, even if there is no other offer of employment. It turns out that the majority of Polish employees are not satisfied with relations in companies. A bad atmosphere at work causes frustration and a decrease in their commitment. The most common reason such a state is the behavior of co-workers and the boss [15].

The organizational climate can become conducive to develop the potential and competencies of the employees and provide opportunities for fulfillment. There is a need for an enhanced role of managers who should feel responsible for building a positive motivating work culture, which would ensure optimum utilization of the capabilities of the team members, leading to self and organizational effectiveness ([16], p. 33-43).

At a time, when the employee is an organization's greatest asset, employers' concern for a good organizational climate is becoming a necessity. Organizational climate is a measure of verifying working conditions and the level of motivation of an employee team. A positively perceived work environment is often tantamount to an increase in employee performance, while an organizational climate that negatively affects employees promotes job burnout. Among the costs to the company of employee burnout are employee inactivity and the need to redirect tasks assigned to them to other team members who are not necessarily prepared and have the necessary aptitude to perform them. Interpersonal relationships can become uncomfortable for an employee, for example, when he or she becomes a victim of bullying or sexual abuse. The result can be resignation and psychological problems [17].

Another important issue worth investigating is the level of utilization of an employee's potential. According to T. Amabile, creativity is influenced primarily by the employee's knowledge of the field in which he or she moves on a daily basis and the motivation associated with the performance of a given task [18]. The employer does not have much influence on the first aspect, and he can only try to hire people who are specialists in a particular field and have creative aptitude. He does, however, have the opportunity to influence the motivation and commitment of the employee. It is worth remembering that an employee who is skilled in a particular field is not always ready to fully engage. This is influenced by several factors such as motivating the employee to be innovative, the system of mobilizing the team for new challenges and projects, the way the work is done, the tools the employee is given to perform the tasks, enabling the employee to act independently, and believing in the team. The employee motivation system is extremely important in the work environment. It improves the employee's psychological comfort, as well as facilitates problem-solving and improves interpersonal relations and atmosphere and well-being. It affects effective performance and commitment. Every employee values comfort at work, wants to be appreciated, supported, but also to be able to work independently, to have his opinion respected. This gives a sense of satisfaction and a desire to work. Reverse actions, such as disrespecting an employee's opinion, constant criticism, or excessive control, can be a threat to the well-being of the team and can reduce the sense of comfort, efficiency, and motivation. For a company to grow, it should be open to new ideas and projects. Employees should be given the opportunity to think independently so that they can create innovative solutions. This involves the extra time they must be given to perform activities unrelated to their current tasks. Team members should not feel stress or pressure when creating something new. Feedback on the work done is needed so that the employee knows if their actions are leading in the right direction. The evaluation should be positive so that the employee is motivated to continue.

"The best places to work are distinguished by the fact that you like the people you work with, trust them, and take pride in what you do." It turns out that companies that interact well with their employees, trust them, and give them opportunities for development are considered the best places to work. Employees feel safe there and want to give as much as they can form themselves to make the company grow and be as profitable as possible. Good relations between employees and also with the supervisor integrate the team for innovative action [19]. The relationship between employees and supervisor plays an extremely important role against the background of the entire enterprise. It should be based on cooperation, openness, and trust. The atmosphere in the group reflects their individual feelings, which affect the productivity and functionality of employees.

3. Organizational climate and management functions

It is worth noting that the organizational climate is linked in a certain way to all management functions. It is particularly important for employees to have their opinions and feelings taken into account right from the planning stage. They feel they are full members of the organization when they are reliably informed about the goals the company is aiming to achieve when they have a real influence on the actions taken. Employee participation in the decision-making process regarding the organization's development directions and ways to implement the adopted strategies triggers an above-average level of commitment in employees. By participating in the planning of activities, they feel they are equal participants in events and members of the community that the organization should create.

In the process of organizing, many elements have to do with shaping the organizational climate. These include clear and lucid organizational arrangements, an appropriate division of authority, a defined space of autonomy and responsibility, and a well-known promotion system. Inadequate distribution of competencies in the organization, or uneven distribution of responsibilities and tasks among employees has a destructive effect on the organizational climate, making horizontal cooperation in the organization difficult. A predetermined scope of competence at the time of hiring helps avoid unnecessary tensions within the work team. Entrusting new tasks should be consulted with them in advance, which provides an opportunity to jointly develop a method to achieve the set goal and resolve any dilemmas.

The formation of the organizational climate is also influenced by elements related to controlling as a function of management. Particularly, noteworthy are employees' feelings about the rigorousness of verifying the level of performance of tasks assigned to them. Here the question arises about the level of autonomy of employees in the choice of methods and tools used to perform tasks, and the power of superiors to maintain deadlines for their performance. On the one hand, one can see the desire to increase the area of autonomy, but on the other hand (especially in countries with a high level of dimension —Power distance), there is still pressure to control the actions of subordinate employees. This is strongly correlated with the management style adopted. Such actions negatively affect employees and reduce their efficiency and block creativity. This negatively affects the organizational climate and detracts from employee motivation.

Of all the management functions, motivation contains the most elements that influence organizational climate building. There is a feedback loop between organizational climate and motivation. Organizational climate affects the level of employee motivation, and the methods of motivation used in an organization have a significant impact on the creation of organizational climate. The more positive employees feel about their work environment, the more they tend to identify with the organization. In an era of chronic labor shortages, efforts to retain existing staff become extremely important. It is worth remembering that the costs incurred by staff turnover are increasing and ultimately affect the overall assessment of the organization. It is also important from the point of view of building a positive image that serves to attract more job applicants. In a favorable atmosphere, there are no difficulties with team integration and greater openness to new challenges is noticeable. In a well-integrated group of employees, raising the requirements arising from the development of the company's activities is not a problem, even raising the level of job satisfaction [20].

Given the low capital intensity of intangible motivation tools, such as concern for improving the organizational climate, it is difficult to replace them with something else that brings similar results in the form of increasing employee efficiency. Job satisfaction can be defined as an emotional reaction that an employee has toward a job that is the result of his or her comparison of actual outcomes with expected outcomes. Job satisfaction has also been defined in terms of attitudes that individuals have toward their jobs [21]. Sempane, Rieger, and Roodt stating that job satisfaction refers to the individual's perception and evaluation of the job. According to these authors, the individual's perception is influenced by his or her unique circumstances such as needs, values, and expectations. Therefore, jobs are evaluated by people on the basis of factors that are important to them. Although the definitions of job satisfaction are varied, it is generally considered to be an attitude or feeling that one has about one's job that is either positive or negative [22]. There are numerous studies investigating the relationship between organizational climate and job satisfaction, with many researchers finding evidence to support this relationship [23]. It is worth citing at this point the work of Brief who found that an organizational climate that is characterized by features such as a high degree of autonomy, building good relationships among employees, showing interest and concern for employees, recognizing employees' achievements, and showing them respect results in higher employee satisfaction. So do salary, benefits, and promotion opportunities, which are elements of the organizational climate [7].

4. Organizational culture and organizational climate

Analyzing the concept of organization culture, one can see that it concerns both the quality of life of the people associated with the organization and the methods of its further development. It assumes the existence of interdependencies between such areas as nature, society, and the economy [24]. Harmonizing the relationship between these planes requires both the development of new, more efficient, and environmentally friendly technologies, the introduction of restrictions on the exploitation of environmental resources, as well as a widespread change in the way of life and a revision of the prevailing hierarchy of values. These aspirations, among others, can be seen in changes in the culture of organizations. Where the issue of employee satisfaction is playing an increasingly important role [25]. Incidentally, this interest in social relations in the workplace contributed to the discovery of the aforementioned correlation occurring between job satisfaction and performance and organizational climate. Organizational climate is often combined with organizational culture by researchers. It is part of organizational culture, actually what employees create among themselves [26]. Organizational climate defines more the relationships and rules among employees, which are not necessarily predetermined by the organization. Organizational climate is a concept that focuses mainly on employees. It is also an issue that separates the concepts of organizational culture and organizational climate. Culture is a much deeper aspect that focuses on subconscious and abstract behaviors within a team. Climate, on the other hand, is more observable as it involves realized actions that are evident in behaviors and habits within a team of employees. Organizational climate refers to how employees perceive particular features of an organization's culture. Unlike culture, which sets behavioral boundaries, climate has a direct impact on behavior within the organization and when dealing with external contractors. The quality of the organizational climate can have a real impact on the proper functioning of a company. Mainly due to the fact that employees are less likely to be stressed, which means future job burnout. These employees are more willing to learn new things, that is, take part in training courses or otherwise develop their skills. The organizational climate has a significant impact on the development of companies through the formation of a positive organizational culture. It is the surface of culture and reflects employees' subjective feelings about the atmosphere in the workplace [27]. Creating a positive climate promotes employee motivation and success. Managers should pay attention to the organizational climate and take measures to build a positive atmosphere in the workplace. Finally, it is worth noting that if employees perceive their organization as morally excellent, based on optimism, trust, compassion, honesty, and forgiveness, they are more likely to engage in pro-organizational behaviors, such as mutual aid and support. In addition, the perception of the organization as a place with an "ethical climate" directly influences the overall willingness to work together, deeper than just performing work tasks together [28]. That's why it is so important to know about ethics, that is, the personal beliefs of individual employees as to what behavior is right and what behavior is not within generally accepted norms. This is especially true when an organization seeks to embed new patterns of behavior in the organization's culture. It should be remembered that culture is transmitted to employees in various forms, the most important of which are: material symbols and language, rituals, and anecdotes.

The original culture of an organization emerges due to the philosophy of the founder of a particular organization. It exerts a strong influence on the selection of the workforce. The activities that the organization's top managers carry out create a common climate and outline what is allowed and what is not. This culture is reflected in the formulated mission, the sense of social responsibility, and the operation of a strong organizational system. The organization's culture is reinforced by human resource management practices. It is also reinforced by the selection process, the actions of the top management, and socialization methods. The culture of an organization consists of permanent elements. Therefore, it is difficult to change. It develops over several or even a dozen years. It is deeply rooted in the values to which employees are attached [29].

Today, with changes in the socioeconomic environment occurring so rapidly and unpredictably, organizations cannot wait for these changes to remodel organizational culture on their own. With the increasing impact of globalization and the new challenges posed by the different expectations of the next generation than before, organizations must try to implement new ideas into their culture themselves. But for this, they need clear and researchable criteria and dimensions, and this is what is contained in the field of organizational climate research. This is where the need for change can be seen most quickly. Hence, the apparent emphasis in well-managed organizations on conducting organizational climate monitoring. It is through it that changes can be responded to in a timely manner. It is worth remembering that one of the biggest challenges of today's organizations is to get and keep talented employees. This is not possible without ensuring that they work in a friendly and rewarding atmosphere.

5. Conclusion

Work has become an area, where people seek satisfaction, personal fulfillment, and opportunities for growth. The organizational climate provides the foundation for these expectations. A friendly open and supportive work environment fosters creative thinking, and effective communication and increases employee engagement.

Understanding these needs has led companies to focus on employees and engage in building a positive social environment, that is, a good organizational climate. However, the speed and multidirectionality of changes in the socioeconomic environment and the emerging different expectations of new generations of employees are forcing changes in the functioning of the organization. The first stage is to try to implement new ideas in the area of organizational climate. The next is to introduce more permanent changes that are related to organizational culture. This is because the latter is the basis of the organization's operation at all levels. It is something that arises in the course of the organization's development and defines the norms and value systems that stimulate employees. As an established system of patterns of thought and action in the organization, it is not subject to such rapid changes as the organizational climate. Therefore, in order to know the intensity and direction of new proposals for the perception of the shape of organizational culture, it is worth analyzing emerging changes in the area of organizational climate.

Acknowledgements

University of Gdansk, Faculty of Economy, ArmiiKrajowej 119/121, Sopot, Poland.

Conflict of interest

The author declares no conflict of interest.

Author details

Jacek Grodzicki
University of Gdansk, Sopot, Poland

*Address all correspondence to: jacek.grodzicki@ug.edu.pl

References

[1] James L, Jones A. Organizational climate: A review of theory and research. Psychological Bulletin. 1974;**12**:1096-1112

[2] Brown SP, Leigh TW. A new look at psychological climate and its relationship to job involvement, effort and performance. Journal of Applied Psychology. 1996;**81**(4):358-368

[3] Schneider B. The psychological life of organizations. In: Ashkanasy NM, Wilderom CPM, Peterson MF, editors. Handbook of Organizational Culture and Climate. California: Sage; 2000. pp. xvii-xxi

[4] Ashforth BE. Climate formation: Issues and extensions. Academy of Management Journal. 1985;**10**(4):837-847

[5] Schneider B. Organisational Climate and Culture. San Francisco: Josey Bass; 1990

[6] Litwin GH, Stringer RA. Motivation and Organisational Climate. Cambridge: Harvard University; 1968

[7] Brief AP. Attitudes in and around Organizations. California: Sage; 1998

[8] Guion R. A note on organisational climate. Organisational Behaviour and Human Performance. 1973;**9**:120-125

[9] Forehand G, Von Gilmer B. Environmental variations in studies of organisational behaviour. Psychological Bulletin. 1964;**62**:361-382

[10] Kundu K. Development of the conceptual framework of organizational climate. Vidyasagar University Journal of Commerce. 2007;**12**:99-108

[11] Cilliers F, Kossuth S. The relationship between organisational climate and salutogenic functioning. SA Journal of Industrial Psychology. 2002;**28**(1):8-13

[12] Tustin CM. A consensus approach to the measurement of organizational climate. The Journal of Individual Psychology. 1993;**19**:1-4

[13] Martins EC, Martins N. Organisational surveys as a tool for change. Parttwo: A case study. Zuid Afrika: HR Future. 2001;**1**(4):46-49

[14] Martins N, von der Ohe H. Organizational climate measurement – new and emerging dimensions during a period of transformation. In: South African Journal of Labour Relations. Spring/Summer; 2005. p. 48

[15] Available from: www.szybkopraca.pl [Accessed: February 21, 2021]

[16] Bhaskar RK, Choudhry N. Work culture: A study of selected organizations in India. Abhigyaan; 1997;**15**(4)

[17] Oleksa-Marewska K. Shaping an organizational climate that nullifies job burnout vs. employee retention in the organization. Prace Naukowe Uniwersytetu Ekonomicznego we Wrocławiu. Wrocław, Poland; 2018:164

[18] Amabile TM. A model of creativity and innovation in organizations. In: Staw B, Sutton R, editors. Research in Organizational Behavior. Vol. 22. Elsevier Science; 2000

[19] Burchell M, Robin J. The Great Workplace: How to Build it, How to Keep it, and Why it Matters. San Francisco: Josey Bass; 2011

[20] Schneider B, Snyder RA. Some relationships between job satisfaction and organizational climate. Journal of Applied Psychology. 1975;**60**(3):318-328

[21] Weiss HM. Deconstructing job satisfaction: Separating evaluations, beliefs and affective experiences. Human Resource Management Review. 2002;**12**(2):173-194

[22] Sempane ME, Rieger HS, Roodt G. Job satisfaction in relation to organisational culture. The Journal of Individual Psychology. 2002;**28**(2):23-30

[23] Friedlander F, Margulies N. Multiple impacts of organizational climate and individual value systems upon job satisfaction. Personnel Psychology. 1969;**22**(2):171-183

[24] Giovannini E, Linster M. Measuring sustainable development. In: Achievements and challenges. OECD; 2005

[25] Wiley JW, Brooks SM. The high performance organisational climate. Howworkers describe top-performing units. In: Ashkanasy NM, Wilderam CPM, Peterson MF, editors. Handbook of Organisational Culture & Climate. London: Sage; 2000

[26] Govender KK. The relationship between the type of organisational socialization role and the organisational climate: A path analytical study. The Journal of Individual Psychology. 1998;**24**(3):1-6

[27] Smolarek M, Sipa M. Organizational climate as a manifestation of organizational culture in small businesses Zeszyty Naukowe Wyższej Szkoły Humanitas. Poland: Zarządzanie; 2015;**4**:301-315

[28] Shin Y. CEO ethical leadership, ethical climate, climate strength, and collective organizational citizenship behavior. Journal of Business Ethics. 2012;**1**:299-312

[29] Robbins S, Judge T. Organizational Behavior. 18th ed. Financial Times Prentice Hall; 2018

Chapter 7

The Role of Employee Behavior and Organizational Culture in Strategy Implementation and Performance in a VUCA World

Dinko Herman Boikanyo

Abstract

This paper examines the crucial role of employee behavior and organizational culture in successfully implementing strategies and achieving high performance in a VUCA world. It emphasizes the importance of effective strategy execution in dynamic environments. Drawing on social cognitive theory, goal-setting theory, and self-determination theory, the paper explores how employee behavior influences strategy implementation, highlighting the significance of goal clarity, feedback mechanisms, and employee participation. Factors such as intrinsic motivation, autonomy, competence, and relatedness are discussed for fostering employee engagement and commitment. The impact of organizational culture on strategy implementation is investigated using the Competing Values Framework, organizational socialization theory, and Schein's model of organizational culture. The paper delves into the interplay between employee behavior, organizational culture, and strategy implementation, discussing theories such as person-organization fit and cultural congruence. Strategies for overcoming VUCA challenges are provided, including sense-making theory, change management frameworks, and resilience theory. Measurement and evaluation of strategy implementation and performance are addressed through the balanced scorecard approach, organizational network analysis, and employee engagement theories. Real-life case studies and examples offer practical insights into the interrelationships among employee behavior, organizational culture, strategy implementation, and performance in diverse contexts.

Keywords: employee behavior, organizational culture, performance, strategy implementation, VUCA

1. Introduction

In today's rapidly evolving business landscape, organizations confront unprecedented challenges driven by the volatile, uncertain, complex, and ambiguous (VUCA) nature of the world [1]. These challenges necessitate a fundamental reevaluation of conventional approaches to strategy implementation and performance management [2]. Within this context, the roles played by employee behavior and organizational culture have emerged as pivotal factors that can significantly influence an organization's success in navigating the complexities of a VUCA world [3].

The primary objective of this chapter is to delve into the intricate relationship between employee behavior, organizational culture, strategy implementation, and performance within the VUCA framework. It seeks to provide a comprehensive understanding of how these interconnected elements influence one another and, in turn, shape an organization's ability to thrive in an environment characterized by volatility, uncertainty, complexity, and ambiguity.

The contemporary business landscape is characterized by unprecedented levels of volatility, uncertainty, complexity, and ambiguity (VUCA) [4, 5]. Rapid technological advancements, shifting consumer preferences, global economic fluctuations, and political uncertainties create a challenging environment for organizations across industries [2]. In this dynamic context, effective strategy implementation becomes paramount for organizations to navigate uncertainties, capitalize on opportunities, and achieve sustainable performance [6, 7].

The success of strategy implementation is contingent upon the behavior of employees and the prevailing organizational culture [8, 9]. Employee behavior plays a pivotal role in translating strategic objectives into actions and outcomes [10, 11]. It encompasses the attitudes, actions, and decisions made by individuals at all levels of the organization [12, 13]. Similarly, organizational culture, defined as the shared values, beliefs, and norms that guide behavior within an organization [14, 15], influences the collective mindset, behaviors, and actions of employees during strategy execution [16, 17].

Understanding the interplay between employee behavior, organizational culture, and strategy implementation is essential for organizations to effectively navigate the VUCA world. By aligning employee behavior with strategic objectives and fostering a culture that supports strategy execution, organizations can enhance their ability to adapt, innovate, and achieve superior performance outcomes [18].

While prior research has examined the individual effects of employee behavior and organizational culture on strategy implementation, there is a need for a comprehensive conceptual framework that integrates these two critical factors [19]. This conceptual paper aims to fill this gap by synthesizing recent literature and theoretical frameworks to develop a holistic understanding of the role of employee behavior and organizational culture in strategy implementation and performance in the VUCA world.

The paper is structured as follows: Firstly, the theories surrounding employee behavior and its impact on strategy implementation will be explored. Social cognitive theory, which emphasizes the role of cognitive processes, self-efficacy, and observational learning in shaping employee behavior [20] will be discussed. Additionally, goal-setting theory will be delved into, which highlights the importance of setting clear and challenging goals, providing feedback, and fostering employee motivation [21]. Furthermore, we will examine self-determination theory, which emphasizes the role of intrinsic motivation, autonomy, competence, and relatedness in driving employee engagement and commitment to strategic initiatives [22].

Secondly, the literature on organizational culture and its influence on strategy execution will be delved into. The Competing Values Framework is explored, which categorizes organizational culture into four types: clan, adhocracy, hierarchy, and market, each with distinct characteristics and implications for strategy implementation [3]. Additionally, organizational socialization theory is discussed, which highlights the role of socialization processes and organizational rituals in shaping employees' beliefs, values, and behaviors [23]. Moreover, Schein's model of organizational culture is explored, which emphasizes the existence of three levels of culture (artifacts, espoused values, and basic underlying assumptions) and their impact on strategy implementation [15].

Next, there will be an integration of these factors to examine their mutual influence and their joint impact on strategy implementation outcomes. Person-organization fit theory will be discussed, which emphasizes the importance of aligning individual values and behaviors with the organizational culture to enhance strategy execution [24]. Furthermore, cultural congruence theory is explored, highlighting how a strong alignment between employee behavior, organizational culture, and strategic goals leads to improved performance [25]. Additionally, social exchange theory is examined, which explores the reciprocal relationship between employees and the organization, emphasizing the role of trust, reciprocity, and commitment in fostering desired behaviors during strategy implementation [26].

Recognizing the challenges organizations face in a VUCA world, strategies to overcome them will be discussed. Sensemaking theory is explored, emphasizing the role of employee behavior and organizational culture in making sense of ambiguity and complexity during strategy implementation [27]. Additionally, discussing change management theories, including Lewin's change model and Kotter's 8-step model, offering frameworks for addressing resistance, fostering employee buy-in, and adapting to dynamic VUCA conditions [28, 29]. Moreover, discussing resilience theory, underscoring the importance of individual and organizational resilience in navigating the uncertainties and disruptions associated with a VUCA world [30].

Lastly, highlighting the importance of measuring and evaluating strategy implementation and performance. The balanced scorecard approach will be discussed, which offers a comprehensive set of metrics and indicators across financial, customer, internal processes, and learning and growth perspectives to assess strategy outcomes [31]. Furthermore, exploring organizational network analysis, a valuable tool for understanding communication patterns, social networks, and the influence of employee behavior and organizational culture on strategy execution [32]. Additionally, considering employee engagement theories and measurement tools, recognizing the impact of engaged employees on strategy implementation success [33].

This paper's relevance and importance are underscored by several key considerations:

- *Adapting to a VUCA world*: As the world becomes increasingly VUCA, organizations must adapt swiftly and effectively to remain competitive [34]. This paper will illuminate the strategies required not only to survive but to thrive in this challenging environment.

- *Maximizing human capital*: Employees represent an organization's most valuable asset. Understanding how their behavior impacts strategy execution and performance is critical in leveraging this resource optimally [35].

- *Culture as a competitive advantage*: Organizational culture has emerged as a critical competitive advantage [36]. In a VUCA world, a strong culture that fosters innovation, agility, and resilience is essential. This paper will explore how organizations can cultivate such cultures.

- *Enhancing leadership and management practices*: Leaders and managers play a pivotal role in shaping employee behavior and culture [37]. This paper will provide insights into effective leadership and management strategies for a VUCA world.
- *Practical implications*: The findings of this research will have practical implications for leaders, managers, and policymakers [38]. It will offer actionable insights and recommendations to enhance strategy implementation and organizational performance.
- *Academic contribution*: This paper contributes to the academic discourse by providing a comprehensive analysis of the relationship between employee behavior, organizational culture, strategy implementation, and performance, particularly in the context of a VUCA world [39].

2. Methodology

This chapter aims to explore and synthesize existing literature related to the topic. The methodology employed in this study is rooted in a comprehensive review of peer-reviewed articles, books, reports, and other scholarly sources pertinent to the chosen topic. The process followed a systematic approach to identify, select, and analyze relevant literature to develop a holistic understanding of the conceptual underpinnings and theoretical frameworks that surround the topic.

2.1 Ethical considerations

Given that this study relied solely on existing literature, ethical approval was not required. However, proper citation practices were observed to acknowledge the contributions of the authors of the selected works.

In conclusion, this conceptual paper aims to provide a comprehensive and detailed examination of the vital role played by employee behavior and organizational culture in effectively implementing strategies and achieving high performance in a VUCA world. By synthesizing theories, frameworks, and practical insights, the paper offers valuable guidance to organizations seeking to navigate the complexities and uncertainties of the modern business landscape. The insights derived from this paper will contribute to the existing body of knowledge and provide a foundation for future empirical research in this domain.

3. Understanding the VUCA world

3.1 Definition and characteristics of a VUCA world

The term VUCA, coined by the U.S. Army War College, refers to a world characterized by volatility, uncertainty, complexity, and ambiguity [4, 5]. Volatility refers to the rapid and unpredictable changes that organizations encounter in the business environment, such as sudden shifts in market trends, technological advancements, and geopolitical events. Uncertainty reflects the lack of predictability and the difficulty in making accurate forecasts due to factors like rapid market fluctuations and disruptive innovations. Complexity highlights the intricate interdependencies and interconnectedness of various elements within the business environment, making it challenging to fully understand and navigate. Ambiguity arises from the existence of multiple interpretations, perspectives, and information gaps, creating a lack of clarity and consensus.

3.2 Impact of VUCA on organizations and their strategic management processes

The VUCA world has profound implications for organizations and their strategic management processes. Organizations operating in such an environment face increased levels of risk and uncertainty, making it difficult to rely on traditional long-term planning and linear decision-making processes [2]. The dynamic nature of the VUCA world necessitates a shift toward more agile and adaptive strategic approaches.

VUCA conditions introduce significant challenges, including rapidly changing customer preferences, disruptive technologies, and competitive landscapes [5]. Organizations must continuously scan their external environment, gather relevant data, and monitor market trends to stay abreast of the evolving dynamics. In addition, political and regulatory uncertainties can introduce unexpected shifts in the business landscape, requiring organizations to be vigilant and responsive.

3.3 The need for agility, adaptability, and resilience in strategy implementation

In the face of volatility, organizations need to be agile to effectively respond to and capitalize on changing conditions [40]. Agility enables organizations to sense market shifts, make rapid decisions, and swiftly execute strategies. It involves developing capabilities such as rapid experimentation, flexibility, and the ability to pivot quickly based on emerging opportunities or threats [41]. By embracing agility, organizations can stay ahead of the competition and seize new opportunities.

Uncertainty in the VUCA world demands adaptability from organizations. The ability to adapt involves continuously scanning the environment, monitoring trends, and remaining flexible in strategy formulation and execution [42]. Organizations must be willing to challenge their assumptions, adjust their strategies based on new information, and reconfigure their resources and capabilities to align with evolving market conditions [43]. Adaptability enables organizations to effectively navigate uncertain environments and stay resilient in the face of unforeseen challenges.

Complexity in the VUCA world necessitates organizational resilience. Resilience enables organizations to withstand disruptions, recover quickly from setbacks, and adapt their strategies and operations to changing circumstances [44]. Building resilience involves fostering a culture of learning, promoting collaboration and knowledge sharing, and developing robust systems and processes that can absorb shocks and adapt to unexpected events [45]. Resilience allows organizations to bounce back stronger and take advantage of emerging opportunities, even in the face of adversity.

4. Employee behavior and strategy implementation

4.1 Importance of employee behavior in strategy execution

The success of strategy implementation heavily relies on the behavior and actions of employees within an organization. Employees are the ones responsible for executing the strategic initiatives, translating strategic plans into action, and driving the desired organizational outcomes [46]. Their behavior influences the efficiency, effectiveness, and overall success of strategy implementation efforts. Therefore, understanding and managing employee behavior is crucial for achieving strategic objectives.

4.2 Social cognitive theory

Social cognitive theory provides insights into how individual attitudes, self-efficacy, and motivation influence employee behavior during strategy implementation. Attitudes play a key role in shaping employee behavior. Positive attitudes toward the strategy, its goals, and its potential outcomes are more likely to motivate employees to align their actions with the strategic objectives [47]. By fostering a positive attitude among employees, organizations can enhance their commitment and engagement in strategy implementation.

Self-efficacy, a central construct in social cognitive theory, refers to an individual's belief in their capabilities to perform specific tasks or behaviors. Employees with high self-efficacy are more likely to take on challenging tasks, persist in the face of obstacles, and actively contribute to the implementation of strategic initiatives [48]. Building employee self-efficacy through training, support, and skill development programs can enhance their confidence and willingness to engage in behaviors that drive strategy execution.

Motivation is another critical factor in social cognitive theory. Employees' motivation to participate actively in strategy implementation is influenced by their beliefs about the value and importance of the strategy, as well as the perceived rewards and consequences associated with successful implementation [22]. Intrinsic motivation, driven by internal factors such as personal satisfaction and fulfillment, is particularly important for long-term engagement and commitment to strategy implementation. Organizations can foster intrinsic motivation by creating a supportive work environment, offering opportunities for growth and development, and recognizing and rewarding employees' contributions to strategy execution.

4.3 Goal-setting theory

Goal-setting theory highlights the role of clear goals, feedback, and employee participation in driving behavior alignment with strategic objectives. Clear and specific goals provide employees with a sense of direction and purpose, guiding their efforts toward achieving desired outcomes [21]. Well-defined goals help employees understand the relevance of their tasks to the broader strategic agenda and encourage them to align their behavior accordingly.

Regular feedback and performance evaluations are essential in goal-setting theory. Feedback enables employees to monitor their progress, identify areas for improvement, and make necessary adjustments in their behavior [31]. It provides employees with information about the effectiveness of their actions in contributing to the strategic goals, enhancing their understanding of what is expected and helping them stay on track.

Employee participation in the goal-setting process can significantly impact their commitment and motivation to achieve strategic objectives. When employees are involved in setting their own goals and have a say in determining how to accomplish them, they develop a sense of ownership and responsibility for their performance [49]. This participatory approach increases employees' engagement and commitment to strategy implementation efforts.

4.4 Self-determination theory

Self-determination theory emphasizes the importance of providing employees with autonomy, competence, and relatedness to enhance their intrinsic motivation and engagement in strategy implementation. Autonomy refers to employees' sense of control and independence in their work. Allowing employees to have autonomy in decision-making, task execution, and problem-solving empowers them to take ownership of their responsibilities and fosters a sense of accountability for strategy execution [50].

Competence represents employees' belief in their abilities to perform effectively in their roles. Providing employees with the necessary resources, training, and support to develop their skills and competencies enhances their confidence and motivation to contribute to the successful implementation of the strategy [51]. Organizations should invest in employee development programs and provide ongoing learning opportunities to enhance their competence and enable them to effectively execute the strategic initiatives.

Relatedness refers to the sense of connection and belongingness employees experience within the organization. When employees feel valued, supported, and connected to their colleagues and leaders, they are more likely to be engaged and motivated in strategy implementation [50]. Organizations can foster a sense of relatedness by promoting teamwork, open communication, and collaboration, which enhance employees' motivation to contribute to the collective goals of the organization.

5. Organizational culture and strategy implementation

5.1 Definition and elements of organizational culture

Organizational culture refers to the shared values, beliefs, assumptions, and norms that guide the behaviors and actions of individuals within an organization [15]. It represents the unique personality and character of an organization and influences how employees think, behave, and interact with each other and with external stakeholders. Organizational culture is composed of various elements, including symbols, rituals, stories, language, norms, and the overall organizational climate [3]. These elements shape the collective identity and provide a framework for decision-making and behavior within the organization.

5.2 Competing values framework

The Competing Values Framework (CVF) provides a model for understanding different types of organizational culture and their implications for strategy implementation [3]. The CVF identifies four types of culture: clan, adhocracy, hierarchy, and market. Clan culture emphasizes collaboration, teamwork, and a focus on employee development. Adhocracy culture values innovation, flexibility, and risk-taking. Hierarchy culture emphasizes stability, control, and a clear chain of command. Market culture focuses on competitiveness, results-orientedness, and external market forces. Each type of culture has distinct strengths and weaknesses in relation to strategy implementation. For example, a clan culture may foster employee engagement and commitment, while a market culture may drive a focus on performance and results.

5.3 Organizational socialization theory

Organizational socialization theory explains how culture shapes employee values, beliefs, and norms, which in turn influence their behavior during strategy implementation [9]. As employees enter and adapt to an organization, they learn the cultural values and expectations through socialization processes. This socialization influences their perception of what behaviors are desirable and acceptable in the organization, shaping their actions during strategy execution. For instance, if the organizational culture emphasizes innovation and risk-taking, employees are more likely to engage in proactive and creative behaviors to support strategy implementation.

5.4 Schein's model of organizational culture

Schein's model of organizational culture highlights three levels of culture: artifacts, espoused values, and basic underlying assumptions [15]. Artifacts are the visible and tangible aspects of culture, such as physical symbols, rituals, and behaviors. Espoused values represent the stated beliefs and norms that are promoted by the organization. Basic underlying assumptions are the deeply embedded, unconscious beliefs and values that guide behavior but may not be explicitly acknowledged. These levels interact and influence each other, shaping the organization's culture and its impact on strategy implementation. For example, if the artifacts and behaviors reflect a culture of collaboration and adaptability, employees are more likely to exhibit cooperative and flexible behaviors during strategy implementation.

In conclusion, organizational culture plays a crucial role in strategy implementation. The Competing Values Framework helps identify different types of culture and their implications for strategy execution. Organizational socialization theory explains how culture shapes employee values and behavior. Schein's model of organizational culture highlights the levels of culture and their impact on strategy implementation. Understanding the elements of culture and their influence on behavior can help organizations align their culture with strategic objectives and create an environment conducive to effective strategy implementation.

6. The interplay between employee behavior, organizational culture, and strategy implementation

6.1 Examining how employee behavior and organizational culture interact to shape strategy implementation outcomes

The interplay between employee behavior and organizational culture is a critical factor in determining the success of strategy implementation. Employee behavior is influenced by the prevailing organizational culture, while at the same time, employee behavior contributes to shaping and reinforcing the culture [52]. This dynamic interaction highlights the importance of understanding how these two factors interconnect to drive strategy execution outcomes.

6.2 Person-organization fit theory

Person-organization fit theory emphasizes the importance of aligning individual values and behaviors with the organizational culture to enhance strategy execution

[24]. When employees' values, beliefs, and behaviors align with the organizational culture, they experience a sense of fit and compatibility, which leads to positive outcomes such as higher job satisfaction, commitment, and performance [53]. Employees who share similar values and beliefs with the organization are more likely to exhibit behaviors that are consistent with the desired cultural norms, thereby facilitating successful strategy implementation.

6.3 Cultural congruence theory

Cultural congruence theory suggests that a strong alignment between employee behavior, organizational culture, and strategic goals leads to improved performance [54]. When employee behavior is congruent with the values, norms, and expectations of the organizational culture, it creates a work environment where employees feel a sense of belonging and identification. This alignment fosters employee engagement, commitment, and a shared focus on achieving strategic goals. In turn, this enhances communication, coordination, and collaboration among employees, facilitating the smooth execution of strategy.

6.4 Social exchange theory

Social exchange theory examines the reciprocal relationship between employees and the organization and how it influences behavior, trust, and commitment during strategy implementation [55]. According to this theory, employees evaluate the exchange relationship with the organization based on the perceived fairness and support they receive. When employees perceive that the organization values and supports their contributions, they are more likely to reciprocate by exhibiting positive behavior and higher levels of commitment. In the context of strategy implementation, a supportive organizational culture that recognizes and rewards employees' efforts fosters a positive social exchange relationship. This, in turn, leads to increased motivation, cooperation, and dedication to achieving strategic objectives.

The interplay between employee behavior, organizational culture, and strategy implementation is a complex and dynamic process. The alignment between individual values, behaviors, and the organizational culture is crucial for successful strategy execution. Organizations need to ensure that their employees' values and behaviors are consistent with the desired cultural norms and strategic goals. This can be achieved through effective recruitment, selection, and onboarding processes that focus on assessing and aligning values and cultural fit. Furthermore, fostering a positive social exchange relationship by providing a supportive work environment and recognizing employees' contributions enhances their commitment and engagement in strategy implementation.

Recent research has increasingly recognized the interplay between employee behavior and organizational culture [44]. Lengnick-Hall et al. [44] argued that building a capacity for organizational resilience in a VUCA world involves aligning employee behaviors with a culture that encourages adaptability and knowledge sharing. Furthermore, Hitt et al. [39] explored how leaders can leverage both culture and behavior to drive strategic change and improve performance. These findings underscore the synergy between behavior and culture as a key driver of success in turbulent environments.

Despite the wealth of research in this area, several gaps persist in the literature. First, while existing studies provide valuable insights, they often lack a holistic view that integrates employee behavior, organizational culture, and strategy implementation in a VUCA context. Second, limited attention has been given to practical implications and actionable strategies for managers and leaders to navigate these challenges effectively. Finally, the dynamic nature of the VUCA world requires continuous adaptation, necessitating a focus on longitudinal research that examines the evolving relationship between behavior, culture, and performance.

7. Overcoming challenges in a VUCA world

7.1 Identifying specific challenges faced by organizations in strategy implementation within VUCA environments

Strategy implementation in a VUCA world poses unique challenges for organizations. VUCA environments are characterized by volatility, uncertainty, complexity, and ambiguity [34]. These challenges include rapidly changing market conditions, disruptive technologies, unpredictable customer demands, and geopolitical uncertainties. In such dynamic contexts, organizations need to navigate through these challenges to effectively implement their strategies.

7.2 Sensemaking theory

Sensemaking theory highlights the role of employee behavior and organizational culture in sensemaking processes to navigate ambiguity and complexity during strategy implementation [27]. Sensemaking involves interpreting and understanding the VUCA environment and its implications for strategy. Employee behavior influenced by the organizational culture plays a crucial role in sensemaking activities. Employees who actively seek information, engage in dialog, and share diverse perspectives contribute to collective sensemaking, enabling organizations to make sense of the VUCA world and align their actions with strategic goals.

7.3 Change management theories

Change management theories provide frameworks and strategies to address resistance, foster employee buy-in, and adapt to dynamic VUCA conditions. Lewin's change model emphasizes the importance of unfreezing existing behaviors, implementing change, and refreezing new behaviors [29]. Kotter's 8-step model offers a structured approach that includes creating a sense of urgency, building a guiding coalition, and empowering employees to embrace change [28]. These change management theories help organizations overcome resistance to change, enhance employee engagement, and facilitate the successful implementation of strategies in VUCA environments.

7.4 Resilience theory

Resilience theory explores how individual and organizational resilience can mitigate the negative impact of VUCA on strategy implementation and performance [56]. Individual resilience refers to the ability of employees to adapt, bounce back from setbacks, and thrive in challenging circumstances. Organizational resilience involves building agile structures, fostering a learning culture, and developing robust systems to respond to VUCA challenges. Resilience enables organizations to anticipate, absorb, and adapt to VUCA conditions, minimizing disruptions and enhancing strategy implementation outcomes.

In a VUCA world, organizations face numerous challenges during strategy implementation. Sensemaking theory highlights the role of employee behavior and organizational culture in making sense of complex and ambiguous environments. Change management theories provide frameworks to address resistance and foster adaptability in VUCA conditions. Resilience theory emphasizes the importance of individual and organizational resilience in mitigating the negative impact of VUCA and maintaining strategy implementation effectiveness.

8. Measuring and evaluating strategy implementation and performance

8.1 Key metrics and indicators for assessing strategy implementation success in a VUCA world

Measuring and evaluating strategy implementation success in a VUCA world requires organizations to consider a range of metrics and indicators that go beyond traditional financial measures. Key metrics may include customer satisfaction, market share, innovation rate, employee productivity, and adaptability to changing market conditions [57]. These indicators provide a comprehensive view of strategy execution outcomes and help organizations assess their ability to navigate the challenges of a VUCA environment.

8.2 Balanced scorecard approach

The balanced scorecard approach offers a framework for evaluating the impact of employee behavior and culture on strategy outcomes by considering multiple perspectives. This approach includes financial, customer, internal process, and learning and growth perspectives [31]. By incorporating these perspectives, organizations can assess how employee behavior and organizational culture contribute to financial performance, customer satisfaction, operational efficiency, and employee development. The balanced scorecard approach provides a holistic view of strategy implementation outcomes and enables organizations to identify areas for improvement and alignment.

8.3 Organizational network analysis

Organizational network analysis (ONA) examines social networks and communication patterns within an organization to understand the influence of employee behavior and culture on strategy execution [58]. By mapping formal and informal networks, ONA helps identify key influencers, information flows, and collaboration patterns. It provides insights into how employee behavior and organizational culture impact the exchange of knowledge, decision-making processes, and coordination efforts during strategy implementation. ONA helps organizations identify both strong and weak ties in the network, facilitating effective communication and collaboration to support strategy execution.

8.4 Employee engagement theories

Employee engagement is a crucial factor in strategy implementation success. Various models and tools can be used to measure and assess employee engagement and its impact on strategy implementation outcomes. For example, the Gallup Q12 survey measures employee engagement by assessing factors such as clear expectations, supportive management, and growth opportunities [59]. The Job Demands-Resources model [60] examines the balance between job demands and resources to understand employee engagement. These models provide insights into the relationship between employee engagement, behavior, and strategy execution outcomes, helping organizations identify areas where engagement can be improved.

In measuring and evaluating strategy implementation and performance in a VUCA world, organizations should adopt a multidimensional approach that goes beyond financial metrics. The balanced scorecard approach provides a comprehensive framework for assessing the impact of employee behavior and culture across various dimensions. Organizational network analysis offers insights into the influence of behavior and culture on communication and collaboration networks. Employee engagement theories provide tools to measure and understand the relationship between engagement, behavior, and strategy execution outcomes.

9. Conceptual framework

In today's volatile, uncertain, complex, and ambiguous (VUCA) world, organizations must navigate multifaceted challenges to remain competitive and achieve their strategic objectives. Central to this endeavor is understanding the intricate relationship between employee behavior and organizational culture and how these elements collectively influence strategy implementation and organizational performance. This conceptual framework seeks to provide a structured perspective on this relationship, elucidating the key dimensions and their interconnections. The framework is shown in **Figure 1** and the dimensions are discussed in the **Figure 1**.

9.1 Key dimensions of the framework

9.1.1 Employee behavior

- *Alignment with strategy*: The extent to which employee behaviors are consistent with the organization's strategic objectives.

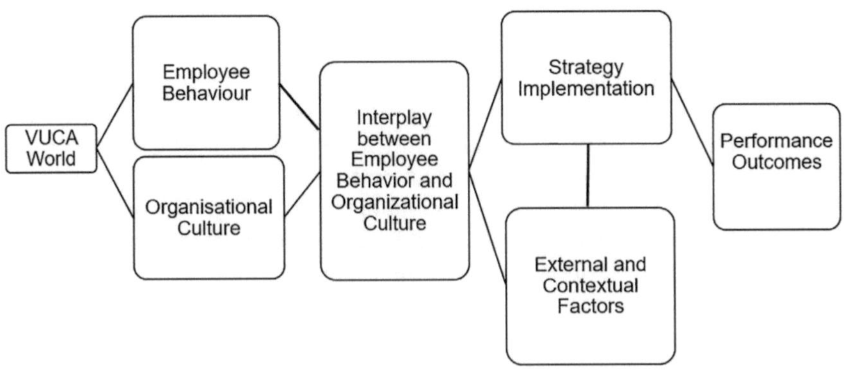

Figure 1.
Conceptual framework. Source: Author's compilation.

- *Proactiveness*: The degree to which employees exhibit initiative and take proactive steps to contribute to strategy execution.

- *Adaptability*: The organization's ability to encourage and accommodate adaptive behaviors among employees in response to changing conditions.

- *Ownership and accountability*: The sense of responsibility and ownership that employees feel toward the successful implementation of the organization's strategy.

9.1.2 Organizational culture

- *Cultural types*: The predominant cultural types within the organization, such as clan, adhocracy, market, or hierarchy [3].

- *Cultural values*: The core values, beliefs, and norms that shape employee attitudes and behaviors.

- *Innovation and learning*: The extent to which the culture encourages innovation, experimentation, and continuous learning [36].

- *Leadership influence*: Leaders play a crucial role in shaping and reinforcing the ezculture by serving as role models and setting cultural expectations [37].

9.1.3 Interplay between employee behavior and organizational culture

- *Alignment*: The degree to which employee behavior aligns with and reflects the cultural values and expectations of the organization.

- *Mutual reinforcement*: How employee behaviors, when consistent with the culture, reinforce and strengthen the cultural norms, and vice versa.

- *Cultural evolution*: The dynamic nature of culture and behavior reflects how changes in one can drive changes in the other over time [39].

9.1.4 Strategy implementation and performance outcomes

- *Efficiency and effectiveness*: The successful execution of strategic initiatives leads to efficient processes and effective results.

- *Adaptability and resilience*: The organization's capacity to adapt to changing circumstances and maintain performance levels in the face of disruption.

- *Competitive advantage*: How the alignment of employee behavior and culture contributes to a sustainable competitive advantage.

- *Employee satisfaction and engagement*: The impact on employee satisfaction, engagement, and retention as a result of alignment with organizational culture and strategic goals.

9.1.5 External and contextual factors

- *Industry and market dynamics*: How industry-specific factors influence the relationship between behavior, culture, and strategy.
- *Regulatory environment*: The impact of external regulations on an organization's culture, employee behavior, and strategic choices.
- *Globalization*: The influence of global factors, such as international markets and cultural diversity, on the interplay between behavior, culture, and strategy.

This conceptual framework provides a structured lens to analyze the role of employee behavior and organizational culture in strategy implementation and performance, considering important dimensions and their interrelationships. By examining these components and their interactions within the context of external and contextual factors, organizations can better understand and leverage the dynamics at play in a VUCA world, ultimately driving strategic success and resilience.

10. Case studies and examples

Illustrating real-life case studies or examples highlighting the relationship between employee behavior, organizational culture, strategy implementation, and performance in a VUCA world can provide valuable insights into the practical application of theories and concepts discussed earlier.

10.1 Case study 1: Google's innovation culture

Google is known for its innovative culture, which has played a significant role in its success. The company encourages employee behavior that fosters creativity, risk-taking, and continuous learning. This behavior is influenced by Google's organizational culture, which emphasizes collaboration, experimentation, and a supportive work environment [61]. The social cognitive theory helps explain how individual attitudes, self-efficacy, and motivation influence employee behavior during strategy implementation. In Google's case, employees' belief in their capabilities, combined with a culture that supports innovation, drives their behavior to experiment with new ideas and contribute to the company's continuous improvement [62].

10.2 Case study 2: Zappos' customer-centric culture

Zappos, an online shoe and clothing retailer, is renowned for its customer-centric culture. The company focuses on creating a positive customer experience and has built its organizational culture around this principle. Zappos emphasizes employee behavior that prioritizes customer satisfaction, going above and beyond expectations. This behavior is influenced by the organizational socialization theory, which states that culture shapes employee values, beliefs, and norms. Zappos' culture instills the importance of exceptional customer service and empowers employees to make decisions that align with the company's customer-centric values [63]. The goal-setting theory further supports Zappos' approach by highlighting the role of clear goals, feedback, and employee participation in driving behavior alignment with strategic objectives. Zappos sets clear goals related to customer satisfaction, provides regular feedback, and involves employees in decision-making processes to ensure that their behavior is aligned with the company's strategic focus [21].

10.3 Case study 3: Southwest Airlines' employee engagement

Southwest Airlines is recognized for its strong employee engagement, which has contributed to its success as a low-cost airline. The company's organizational culture, characterized by a fun and supportive work environment, fosters employee behavior that is aligned with the company's strategy. The self-determination theory emphasizes the importance of providing employees with autonomy, competence, and relatedness. Southwest Airlines allows its employees to have a degree of autonomy in decision-making, provides training and development opportunities to enhance competence, and promotes a sense of camaraderie and teamwork among employees [22]. This approach enhances employees' intrinsic motivation and engagement in strategy implementation, leading to improved performance.

These case studies demonstrate how employee behavior and organizational culture interact to shape strategy implementation outcomes. The theories and concepts discussed earlier, such as social cognitive theory, goal-setting theory, and self-determination theory, play a vital role in understanding and explaining the relationship between employee behavior, culture, and strategy execution. These examples highlight the practical application of these theories in real-life organizations, providing insights into how specific behaviors and cultural attributes influence strategy implementation and performance in a VUCA world.

11. Some empirical studies

Empirical studies provide valuable insights into the relationship between employee behavior, organizational culture, and strategy implementation in various contexts. Here are a few recent studies that shed light on this topic:

- *Study 1*: Dinh T. Q., & Nguyen H. T. [64] explored the impact of employee behavior and organizational culture on strategy implementation success in Vietnamese manufacturing firms. The study found that positive employee behaviors, such as commitment, initiative, and teamwork, were positively associated with successful strategy implementation. Additionally, a supportive and adaptive organizational culture that encourages collaboration and innovation enhanced the effectiveness of strategy implementation.

- *Study 2*: Marique G., et al. [65] examined the influence of organizational culture on strategy implementation in Belgian small and medium-sized enterprises (SMEs). The study found that organizations with a clan culture, characterized by a supportive and nurturing environment, had higher levels of employee commitment and engagement in strategy execution. This positive organizational culture facilitated better alignment between employee behavior and strategic objectives, leading to improved strategy implementation outcomes.

- *Study 3*: Vasilaki A., et al. [66] investigated the role of employee behavior in strategy implementation in the hospitality industry. The study found that employees' proactive behavior, such as seeking opportunities for improvement and taking initiative, positively influenced the effectiveness of strategy implementation. Moreover, the study highlighted the importance of a supportive organizational culture that encourages and rewards such proactive behaviors to enhance strategy execution success.

- *Study 4*: Mutonyi, Slatten Liean and Gonzalez-Pinero [67] examined the impact of organizational culture on strategy implementation outcomes in the healthcare sector. The study revealed that a culture characterized by shared values, open communication, and employee involvement positively influenced employee behavior during strategy implementation. This alignment between culture and behavior led to improved strategy execution and performance in healthcare organizations.

These empirical studies demonstrate the significance of employee behavior and organizational culture in strategy implementation and highlight the positive outcomes associated with their alignment. They provide evidence that supportive and adaptive cultures, along with positive employee behaviors, enhance strategy execution success across different industries and countries.

12. Recommendations

Thriving in VUCA environments requires organizations to cultivate a culture that promotes desired employee behaviors and adaptability. Here are some recommendations:

- *Clearly communicate strategic objectives*: Ensure that employees have a clear understanding of the organization's strategic objectives and their role in achieving them. This clarity helps align employee behavior with strategic goals and fosters a sense of purpose and direction.

- *Encourage employee involvement and participation*: Involve employees in the strategy development process and decision-making. This promotes a sense of ownership and empowers employees to contribute their ideas and perspectives. Employee involvement enhances commitment and motivation, leading to proactive behavior in strategy implementation.

- *Provide continuous learning and development opportunities*: Offer training programs and learning opportunities to enhance employees' skills and knowledge. This fosters a culture of continuous learning and adaptability, enabling employees to navigate VUCA challenges effectively.

- *Foster collaboration and teamwork*: Create an environment that encourages collaboration, information sharing, and teamwork. This helps break down silos and promotes collective problem-solving and innovation. Collaboration enhances employee engagement and facilitates the integration of diverse perspectives, leading to more effective strategy implementation.

- *Recognize and reward desired behaviors*: Recognize and reward employees who exhibit desired behaviors aligned with the organization's strategic objectives. This can be done through formal recognition programs, incentives, or career advancement opportunities. Recognitions and rewards reinforce the desired behaviors and motivate employees to continue their efforts in strategy implementation.

- *Lead by example*: Leaders play a crucial role in shaping organizational culture and employee behavior. Leaders should model the desired behaviors, demonstrate adaptability, and promote a positive and inclusive culture. By leading by example, leaders inspire employees to emulate these behaviors and create a culture of continuous improvement and resilience.

- *Encourage risk-taking and learning from failure*: VUCA environments require organizations to be open to experimentation and learning from failures. Encourage employees to take calculated risks, embrace innovation, and view failures as opportunities for growth and learning. Create a safe space where employees feel comfortable sharing their ideas and learning from their experiences.

- *Foster open and transparent communication*: Establish open channels of communication where employees feel comfortable sharing their thoughts, concerns, and ideas. Transparent communication helps build trust, promotes engagement, and facilitates timely information flow, enabling employees to adapt and respond effectively to VUCA challenges.

- *Promote flexibility and agility*: Encourage employees to embrace flexibility and adaptability in their work. Provide them with the necessary resources and support to respond quickly to changing circumstances and make informed decisions. This flexibility enables employees to navigate uncertainties and seize opportunities in a VUCA world.

- *Foster a learning culture*: Create a culture that values continuous learning and encourages employees to acquire new knowledge and skills. Support employees in pursuing professional development opportunities, such as training programs, workshops, conferences, and online courses. A learning culture enables employees to stay ahead of emerging trends and technologies and adapt to dynamic market conditions.

- *Emphasize cross-functional collaboration*: Break down departmental barriers and foster collaboration across different functions and teams. Encourage employees to collaborate with colleagues from diverse backgrounds and disciplines to solve complex problems and drive innovation. Cross-functional collaboration enhances organizational agility and enables a holistic approach to strategy implementation.

- *Encourage innovation and experimentation*: Foster an environment that encourages innovation and experimentation. Provide employees with the freedom to explore new ideas, take calculated risks, and learn from failures. Implement mechanisms such as innovation labs, idea incubators, or designated time for creative pursuits to stimulate innovation and entrepreneurial thinking.

- *Promote diversity and inclusion*: Embrace diversity and create an inclusive workplace where employees feel valued and respected. Encourage diverse perspectives, ideas, and experiences, as they contribute to a richer understanding of complex issues and better decision-making. A diverse and inclusive culture enhances adaptability and problem-solving capabilities in a VUCA world.

- *Establish feedback and performance management systems*: Implement regular feedback mechanisms to provide employees with constructive feedback on their performance. Set clear performance goals aligned with the organization's strategic objectives and provide ongoing feedback to support employee growth and development. This promotes accountability, continuous improvement, and alignment of individual behaviors with organizational goals.

- *Foster a supportive and well-being-oriented environment*: Prioritize employee well-being and create a supportive work environment. Offer programs and initiatives that promote work-life balance, stress management, and mental health support. Recognize the importance of employee well-being in enhancing engagement, productivity, and resilience in the face of VUCA challenges.

- *Continuously monitor and adapt*: Regularly assess the effectiveness of strategies, employee behaviors, and cultural initiatives in the context of VUCA environments. Monitor key performance indicators, solicit employee feedback, and conduct periodic organizational assessments to identify areas for improvement and adapt strategies accordingly.

By implementing these recommendations, organizations can foster the desired employee behaviors and cultivate an adaptive culture that thrives in VUCA environments. It is important to remember that every organization is unique, and strategies should be tailored to the specific context and needs of the organization.

13. Conclusion

In conclusion, this paper has explored the critical role of employee behavior and organizational culture in strategy implementation and performance within the context of a volatile, uncertain, complex, and ambiguous (VUCA) world. The findings highlight the significance of aligning employee behavior and organizational culture with the strategic objectives of an organization to achieve optimal performance and navigate the challenges posed by a VUCA environment.

Firstly, it is evident that employee behavior plays a crucial role in strategy implementation and performance. Organizations need to foster a culture of commitment, engagement, and proactive problem-solving among employees. This involves providing clear communication, empowering employees, and fostering a sense of ownership and accountability. By aligning individual behaviors with strategic goals, organizations can enhance the effectiveness and efficiency of strategy execution.

Secondly, organizational culture has a profound impact on strategy implementation and performance. A strong and adaptive culture that values innovation, agility, and continuous learning is essential in a VUCA world. Organizations must promote an environment that encourages risk-taking, knowledge sharing, and collaboration, allowing employees to adapt and respond swiftly to changing circumstances. A culture that supports flexibility and resilience enables organizations to effectively implement strategies and achieve sustainable performance in the face of uncertainty and complexity.

Furthermore, the interplay between employee behavior and organizational culture is critical. The alignment of individual behaviors with the prevailing culture fosters a shared sense of purpose and direction. When employees exhibit behaviors that are consistent with the desired culture, it enhances organizational cohesion, employee satisfaction, and overall performance. Leaders and managers play a vital role in shaping and reinforcing the culture, serving as role models and providing necessary support and resources to employees.

Some practical implications are as follows:

- To achieve optimal performance in a VUCA world, organizations must prioritize aligning employee behavior and organizational culture with strategic objectives.

- Promoting a culture that encourages adaptive behaviors and embraces change is crucial for effectively responding to VUCA challenges and opportunities.

- This alignment leads to improved strategy implementation, employee engagement, and overall organizational performance.

Future research should focus on further exploring the dynamic relationship between employee behavior, organizational culture, strategy implementation, and performance. Specific areas for investigation could include:

- Developing practical frameworks and strategies for organizations to thrive in VUCA environments.

- *Cross-cultural analysis*: Investigate how cultural differences influence the relationship between employee behavior, organizational culture, and strategy implementation in various regions and industries. Understand how cultural nuances impact adaptability and performance in a VUCA environment.

- *Leadership styles and organizational culture*: Explore the impact of different leadership styles (e.g., transformational, transactional, servant leadership) on shaping and sustaining organizational culture. Examine how leadership behavior aligns with or diverges from the desired culture and its effects on strategy execution and performance.

- *Technology and digital transformation*: Study how the integration of technology, such as AI, automation, and digital tools, influences employee behavior and organizational culture in the context of strategy implementation in a VUCA world. Investigate the role of digital culture and its implications.

- *Employee well-being and resilience*: Research the relationship between employee well-being, mental health, and their ability to adapt to VUCA environments. Explore how organizational culture can foster resilience and support employees in times of uncertainty.

- *Change management strategies*: Examine the effectiveness of various change management strategies in aligning employee behavior and culture with evolving strategic objectives. Identify best practices for leading and facilitating organizational change in VUCA settings.

- *Performance metrics and measurement*: Develop comprehensive performance metrics and measurement frameworks that consider the impact of employee behavior and culture on strategy implementation. Explore novel methods for assessing performance in dynamic environments.

- *Knowledge management and learning organizations*: Investigate how knowledge management practices and the creation of learning organizations impact strategy execution and performance in a VUCA world. Examine the role of continuous learning and knowledge sharing.

- *Sustainability and CSR*: Explore the link between organizational culture, employee behaviors related to sustainability, and corporate social responsibility (CSR) initiatives. Assess how a culture of sustainability influences strategy implementation and long-term performance.

- *Crisis management and resilience*: Analyze how employee behavior and organizational culture contribute to crisis management and resilience in VUCA scenarios. Identify strategies for building and maintaining resilience during crises.

- *Long-term vs. short-term focus*: Investigate the tension between short-term and long-term strategic objectives and how employee behavior and culture contribute to organizations' ability to balance these priorities in a VUCA world.

- *Case studies and industry-specific analysis*: Conduct in-depth case studies and industry-specific analyses to provide practical insights into how different organizations address the challenges of VUCA through their culture and employee behavior.

- *Global workforce and remote work*: Examine the impact of a global and remote workforce on organizational culture and employee behavior in VUCA environments. Explore strategies for fostering cohesion and alignment in distributed teams.

In conclusion, this paper underscores the importance of aligning employee behavior and organizational culture with strategic objectives to navigate the challenges of a VUCA world successfully. Theoretical and practical implications emphasize the need for organizations to embrace adaptability and change to achieve sustainable performance.

The successful implementation of strategies and achievement of high performance in a VUCA world require organizations to prioritize the alignment of employee behavior and organizational culture. By promoting a culture that encourages adaptive behaviors and embraces change, organizations can effectively respond to the challenges and opportunities presented by a volatile and uncertain environment. This, in turn, leads to improved strategy implementation, employee engagement, and overall organizational performance. Future research should continue to explore the dynamic relationship between employee behavior, organizational culture, strategy implementation, and performance to develop practical frameworks and strategies that organizations can adopt to thrive in a VUCA world.

Author details

Dinko Herman Boikanyo
Department of Business Management, University of Johannesburg, Johannesburg, South Africa

*Address all correspondence to: hermanb@uj.ac.za

References

[1] Kaplan RS, Norton DP. The Execution Premium: Linking Strategy to Operations for Competitive Advantage. Boston, Massachusetts: Harvard Business Press; 2008

[2] Eisenhardt KM, Sull DN. Strategy as simple rules. Harvard Business Review. 2001;**79**(1):106-116

[3] Cameron KS, Quinn RE. Diagnosing and Changing Organizational Culture: Based on the Competing Values Framework. 3rd ed. San Francisco: Jossey-Bass; 2011

[4] Mitra T, Kapoor R, Gupta N. Studying key antecedents of disruptive technology adoption in the digital supply chain: An Indian perspective. International Journal of Emerging Markets. 2022. DOI: 10.1108/IJOEM-07-2021-1052 [Ahead-of-print]

[5] O'Reilly CA, Tushman ML. Organizational ambidexterity: Past, present, and future. Academy of Management Perspectives. 2013;**27**(4):324-338

[6] Liedtka JM. Strategy implementation: An overview. In: The Palgrave Encyclopedia of Strategic Management. London Borough of Camden: Palgrave Macmillan; 2018. pp. 1-7

[7] Teece DJ. Business models and dynamic capabilities. Long Range Planning. 2018;**51**:40-49. DOI: 10.1016/j.lrp.2017.06.007

[8] Edmondson AC. The Fearless Organization: Creating Psychological Safety in the Workplace for Learning, Innovation, and Growth. Hoboken, NJ: John Wiley & Sons; 2018

[9] Bauer TN, Bodner T, Erdogan B, Truxillo DM, Tucker JS. Newcomer adjustment during organizational socialization: A meta-analytic review of antecedents, outcomes, and methods. Journal of Applied Psychology. 2007;**92**(3):707-721

[10] Chen G, Rong K, Wu Y. Reconceptualizing strategic management in the digital age: A fuzzy cognitive map approach. Journal of Business Research. 2019;**99**:238-246

[11] Chen S, Chang Y, Lai Y. Strategic ambiguity, employee behaviors, and organizational performance. Journal of Business Research. 2019;**96**:238-249

[12] Gong Y, Law KS, Chang S, Xin KR. Employee behavior in organizations: A multilevel perspective. Annual Review of Organizational Psychology and Organizational Behavior. 2021;**8**:209-232

[13] Gong Y, Wang H, Huang JC, Cheung SY. Proactive strategic behavior: A review and extension of the literature. Journal of Management. 2021;**47**(4):781-818

[14] Denison DR, Haaland S, Goelzer P. Corporate culture and organizational effectiveness: Is Asia different from the rest of the world? Organizational Dynamics. 2012;**41**(4):287-295

[15] Schein EH. Organizational Culture and Leadership. 4th ed. San Francisco, CA: Jossey-Bass; 2010

[16] Lund DB. Organizational culture and job satisfaction. Journal of Business & Industrial Marketing. 2003;**18**(3):219-236

[17] Smircich L. Concepts of culture and organizational analysis. Administrative

Science Quarterly. 1983;**28**(3):339-358. DOI: 10.2307/2392246

[18] Knippenberg DV, Knippenberg BV, Cremer DD. Leadership, affect, and emotions: A state of the science review. The Leadership Quarterly. 2017;**28**(1):21-34

[19] Lunenburg F. Self-efficacy in the workplace: Implications for motivation and performance. International Journal of Management, Business, and Administration. 2011;**14**(1)

[20] Bandura A. Social Foundations of Thought and Action: A Social Cognitive Theory. Upper Saddle River, NJ: Prentice Hall; 1986

[21] Locke EA, Latham GP. A Theory of Goal Setting and Task Performance. Englewood Cliffs, NJ: Prentice Hall; 1990

[22] Deci EL, Ryan RM. The "what" and "why" of goal pursuits: Human needs and the self-determination of behavior. Psychological Inquiry. 2000;**11**(4):227-268

[23] Van Maanen J, Schein EH. Toward of theory of organizational socialization. Research in Organizational Behavior. 1979;**1**:209-264

[24] Kristof AL. Person-organization fit: An integrative review of its conceptualizations, measurement, and implications. Personnel Psychology. 1996;**49**(1):1-49

[25] O'Reilly C, Chatman J, Caldwell D. People and organizational culture: A profile comparison approach to assessing person-organization fit. Academy of Management Journal. 1991;**34**:487-516. DOI: 10.2307/256404

[26] Blau PM. Exchange and Power in Social Life. New York: Wiley, Transaction Publishers; 1964

[27] Weick K. Sensemaking in Organizations. Thousand Oaks, CA: Sage Publications; 1995

[28] Kotter JP. Leading Change. Boston: Harvard Business School Press; 1996

[29] Lewin K. Field theory in social science: Selected theoretical papers. In: Cartwright D, editor. New York: Harper & Row; 1951

[30] Masten AS, Best KM, Garmezy N. Resilience and development: Contributions from the study of children who overcome adversity. Development and Psychopathology. 1990;**2**:425-444. DOI: 10.1017/S0954579400005812

[31] Kaplan RS, Norton DP. The balanced scorecard: Measures that drive performance. Harvard Business Review. 1992;**70**(1):71-79

[32] Cross R, Borgatti SP, Parker A. Making invisible work visible: Using social network analysis to support strategic collaboration. California Management Review. 2002;**44**(2):25-46

[33] Macey WH, Schneider B. The meaning of employee engagement. Industrial and Organizational Psychology. 2008;**1**(1):3-30

[34] Bennett N, Lemoine GJ. What VUCA really means for you. Harvard Business Review. 2014;**92**(1/2):27-29

[35] Gong Y, Kim TY, Lee DR, Zhu J. A multilevel model of team goal orientation, information exchange, and creativity. Academy of Management Journal. 2010;**53**(2):434-449

[36] Denison DR, Spreitzer GM. Organizational culture and organizational development: A competing values approach. Research

in Organizational Change and Development. 1991;**5**:1-21

[37] Schein E. Organizational Culture and Leadership. 3rd ed. San Francisco, CA: Jossey-Bass; 2004

[38] Gittell JH, Douglass A. Relational bureaucracy: Structuring reciprocal relationships into roles. Academy of Management Review. 2012;**37**(4):709-733

[39] Hitt MA, Ireland RD, Hoskisson RE. Strategic Management: Competitiveness and Globalization. 5th ed. Cincinnati: International Thomson Publishing; 2001

[40] Doz YL, Kosonen M. Embedding strategic agility: A leadership agenda for accelerating business model renewal. Long Range Planning. 2008;**41**(3):315-334

[41] Helfat C, Finkelstein S, Mitchell W, Peteraf M, Singh H, Teece D, et al. Dynamic Capabilities: Understanding Strategic Change in Organizations. Malden, MA: Blackwell; 2007

[42] Eisenhardt KM, Martin JA. Dynamic capabilities: What are they? Strategic Management Journal. 2000;**21**(10-11):1105-1121

[43] Tushman ML, O'Reilly CA. Ambidexterity as a dynamic capability: Resolving the innovator's dilemma. Research in Organizational Behavior. 2007;**27**:1-44

[44] Lengnick-Hall CA, Beck TE, Lengnick-Hall ML. Developing a capacity for organizational resilience through strategic human resource management. Human Resource Management Review. 2011;**21**(3):243-255

[45] Sutcliffe KM, Vogus TJ, Dane E. Organizational resilience: A capability-based conceptualization. Academy of Management Annals. 2016;**10**(1):535-615

[46] Brouthers KD, Nakos G, Dimitratos P. SME entrepreneurial orientation, international performance, and the moderating role of strategic alliances. Entrepreneurship Theory and Practice. 2018;**42**(5):737-760

[47] De Clercq D, Haq IU, Azeem MU, Raja U. Does employees' positive psychological capital strengthen their work engagement? A self-determination perspective. Journal of Business Research. 2018;**84**:416-425

[48] Bandura A. Self-Efficacy: The Exercise of Control. New York: W.H. Freeman and Company; 1997

[49] Kristof-Brown AL, Zimmerman RD, Johnson EC. Consequences of individuals' fit at work: A meta-analysis of person–job, person–organization, person–group, and person–supervisor fit. Personnel Psychology. 2005;**58**(2):281-342

[50] Gagné M, Deci EL. Self-determination theory and work motivation. Journal of Organizational Behavior. 2005;**26**(4):331-362

[51] Rigotti T, Schyns B, Mohr G. A short version of the occupational self-efficacy scale: Structural and construct validity across five countries. Journal of Career Assessment. 2019;**27**(1):130-147

[52] O'Reilly CA, Doerr B, Chatman JA. The promise and problems of organizational culture: CEO personality, culture, and firm performance. Group & Organization Management. 2014;**39**(6):595-625

[53] Edwards JR, Cable DM. The value of value congruence. Journal of Applied Psychology. 2009;**94**(3):654-677

[54] Chatman JA, Caldwell DF. Leading culture change in organizations. Journal of Applied Behavioral Science. 2014;**50**(4):481-511

[55] Cropanzano R, Mitchell MS. Social exchange theory: An interdisciplinary review. Journal of Management. 2005;**31**(6):874-900

[56] Luthans F, Youssef-Morgan CM, Avolio BJ. Psychological Capital and beyond. New York: Oxford University Press; 2015

[57] Sahin E, Robinson D. Building a resilient strategy for a VUCA world. MIT Sloan Management Review. 2021;**62**(1):14-16

[58] Obstfeld D, Borgatti SP, Davis J. Network ethnography: A mixed-methods approach for the study of social networks in organizations. Organizational Research Methods. 2019;**22**(2):491-515

[59] Gallup. Q12 Employee Engagement Survey. 2021. Available from: https://www.gallup.com/workplace/285674/q12-employee-engagement-survey.aspx

[60] Bakker AB, Demerouti E. The job demands-resources model: State of the art. Journal of Managerial Psychology. 2007;**22**(3):309-328

[61] Kim H. The analysis of innovation management in google. Journal of Economics and Management Sciences. 2020;**3**:10-19. DOI: 10.30560/jems.v3n4p10

[62] Bandura A. Social cognitive theory of self-regulation. Organizational Behavior and Human Decision Processes. 1991;**50**(2):248-287

[63] Chatman JA. Matching people and organizations: Selection and socialization in public accounting firms. Administrative Science Quarterly. 1991;**36**(3):459-484

[64] Dinh TQ, Nguyen HT. Employee behavior and organizational culture: Impacts on strategy implementation in Vietnamese manufacturing firms. Journal of Asian Business and Economic Studies. 2020;**27**(1):9-25

[65] Marique G et al. Strategy implementation and organizational culture in Belgian SMEs. Journal of Organizational Change Management. 2019;**32**(4):462-483

[66] Vasilaki A et al. The role of employee behavior in strategy implementation: The case of the hospitality industry. Journal of Hospitality Marketing & Management. 2021;**30**(4):500-520

[67] Mutonyi BR, Slåtten T, Lien G, González-Piñero M. The impact of organizational culture and leadership climate on organizational attractiveness and innovative behavior: A study of Norwegian hospital employees. BMC Health Services Research. 13 May 2022;**22**(1):637. DOI: 10.1186/s12913-022-08042-x. PMID: 35562748; PMCID: PMC9102259

Chapter 8

Interplay between Technology and Culture in Driving Change for Employee Satisfaction

Peter Paul Kithae

Abstract

Technology and society have been in constant interplay since the early man's invention of simple tools. Among modern interplays are e-press, digital technologies, and the internet of things (IoT). Based on a critical review of existing literature, the study investigated how organizational culture is driving employee's actions to embrace change through technological innovation, and how this interplay result to organizational competitiveness. The study used qualitative design to collect data, which was manually analyzed using the researcher's insight and research skills to bring out the main themes. After analysis, the study found that technology is a key driver of innovation, and innovation is an enabler for organizations' to consistently achieve superior performance. In organizations, technological innovation and culture interact to influence organizational behavior which drives economic change, productivity and long term growth. When embraced by organizational employees, technological innovation can lead to high employee performance. The study concludes that people through culture shift, have adopted technological innovation for their organizational superior performance. The study recommends that governments train their organizations and help them buy technologies in form of digital computers and Information Communication Technologies for connecting individuals, promotion of values, mutual respect, and innovation.

Keywords: change, customer satisfaction, interplay between technology and culture, organizational excellence, technological innovation, technology and society

1. Introduction

Culture has been seen to refer to the shared patterns of beliefs, values, customs, behaviors, and artifacts that characterize a group or society [1]. It has been found that employees tend to be attracted to those organizations with a culture that values their work and focuses on organizational wellbeing; and that there is a positive relationship between organizational culture, job satisfaction and the organizational commitment of employees [2]. According to Griswold [1], culture encompasses the concept of social roles, relations, cosmological ideas, and material possessions that a group of people acquire over generations through their individual and collective efforts. Likewise, Samovar et al. [3] sees culture encompassing the learned behaviors and shared experiences of individuals within a relatively large social group, which are passed down through social learning. As a result, culture represents the way of life of a particular group, including their behaviors, unquestioned beliefs, cherished values, and symbolic expressions that are transmitted through communication and imitation from one generation to the next [3]. While studying Americans best run companies in 2006; Peters and Waterman [4] observed that organizational culture influences a variety of organizational and individual outcomes including productivity, performance, commitment and self-confidence.

According to Samovar et al. [3], culture can be seen as a form of symbolic communication, comprising the collective skills, knowledge, attitudes, values, and motives of a group, as well as the patterns and tangible manifestations in artifacts, traditional concepts, and shared mental programming that distinguish members of one group from others. When positive culture is implemented in an organization, it has been seen to contribute immensely to shaping employees′ perceptions and behavior, as well as the principles that apply to members of an organization in south Asian firms [5]. This study investigated the role of organizational culture in driving employee's actions; how organizations drive cultural change through technological innovation and the symbiotic relationship between technological innovation and organizational competitiveness.

1.1 Statement of the problem

Despite the many initiatives started by the governments, the united nation organizations, and other world bodies aimed at improving customer satisfaction in their working relationship with their employers, gaps still exist regarding what drives employees' commitment towards their organizations [2], Specifically, bilateral agreements, laws and binding treaties are signed at international forums between governments on the safety, security and wellbeing of employees while at work, yet at national levels employees continue being unlawfully laid off, given low salaries and exposed to dehumanizing working conditions [6]. Technological innovations worldwide is improving enormously creating enhanced organizational production processes and majority of employees desire to adopt to new technologies as opposed to existing technology [7], yet working conditions within their employer premises remain deplorable [6]; and that the relationship between technological innovation and organizational cultural change [6], and that there exists a strong relationship between technology and culture in driving change for employee satisfaction whereas Bagozzi, Davis and Warshaw observes that actual usage of technology may not be a direct or immediate consequence of the desire, attitude or intention to use the technology [8]. This study therefore investigates the symbiotic relationship between technology and culture in driving change for employee satisfaction.

1.2 Study objectives

The study's general objective was to investigate the symbiotic relationship between technology and culture in driving change for employee satisfaction while its specific objectives were to analyze the role of organizational culture in driving employee's actions; evaluate how organizations drive cultural change through technological innovation and assess the symbiotic relationship between technological innovation and organizational competitiveness.

The study findings are expected to help organizations and their employees to adopt positive technological innovations for employee satisfaction, assist government of Kenya and other stakeholders to formulate good policies which can result in positive organizational culture change for employee satisfaction as a result of technological innovation; and finally enrich existing theories for use by other researchers and academicians in disseminating knowledge in the field of symbiotic relationship between technology and culture in driving change for employee satisfaction.

2. Theoretical background and informing literature review

The study is anchored on the technology acceptance model which postulates that people's behavior is a factor that is influenced by the *desire to use* technology. The model suggests that when users are presented with a new technology, there is a myriad of issues that influence their decision of how and when to use it, namely: *Perceived usefulness* which according to Davis F [9] is "*the degree to which a person sees that using a specific system would enhance his job performance* and, *Perceived ease-of-use*, which is "*the degree to which a person believes that using a particular system would be free from effort*" [9]. As a result, *external variables* such as social influence come to play when determining the attitude. When these external factors are in place, people will have the desire and positive propensity to use the technology. However, this intention may change depending on one's age and gender.

The technology acceptance model is one of the users' acceptances and usage of technology model according to Venkatesh V. [10]. Since its development in the early 1989, it has replaced many of the TRA's attitude measures. It has strong behavioral elements which assume that when someone forms a desire to act, that he will be free to act without limitation. The model is a widely adopted concept to demonstrate the acceptance of new technology fields. It attempts to demonstrate and predict people's behaviors with their beliefs, attitudes, and behavioral intention. In it, perceived ease of use, perceived usefulness and considered general beliefs play a significant role than salient beliefs in attitudes towards utilizing a particular technology [7]. However, the model has been criticized in that there are many constraints in the real world which curtails the freedom to act. Likewise, attitude towards usage and intentions to use may be ill-formed or lacking which implies that actual usage may not be a direct or immediate consequence of such attitudes and intentions [8].

3. Research methodology

The study used a descriptive research design to collect qualitative data. According to Mugenda and Mugenda, this in-depth design has been used successfully by other researchers to design and communicate their findings. Secondary data was primarily gathered through a literature review (desk research). To bring out the main themes, data was manually analyzed using the researcher's insight and research skills. The emerging themes were then operationalized for content analysis and to make sense and determine the significance of the study. Following the necessary explanations based on the findings, the conclusions and recommendations were summarized.

4. Study findings and discussions

According to Hofstede [11] there are five dimensions of culture, which are Individualism or collectivism, Power distance, avoidance of uncertainty, masculinity or femininity, and long-term or short-term orientation. Individualism and collectivism refer to the degree of importance individuals place on their relationships with others within a society. In highly individualistic cultures such as Kenya, Nigeria, and Britain, people tend to prioritize their individual identities and actions over group affiliations [12]. These cultures emphasize self-reliance rather than dependence on the collective. Conversely, in highly collectivist cultures like Tanzania and Pakistan, individuals primarily identify themselves as members of a group [13]. They are expected to dedicate themselves to the welfare of the community, and the community, in turn, is expected to provide support and protection in times of need.

Culture plays a significant role in how power disparities are perceived and accepted within a society. It influences the level of inequality considered normal or acceptable. In countries where power disparities are prevalent, the culture tends to view such inequalities as a regular part of social dynamics. One way to observe these differences in power distance is through the manner in which individuals address each other. In high-power-distance countries such as Japan and Mexico, individuals use formal titles when communicating [14]. On the other hand, in the United States, it is common for individuals to address each other by their first names in most situations, whereas such informality might be considered disrespectful in other cultures [15].

Cultural orientation refers to how cultures cope with uncertainty about the future. A strong cultural preference for structure situations is referred to as high uncertainty avoidance. Individuals in countries such as Portugal and Greece, for example, rely heavily on technology, religion, and law to provide them with a sense of security and rules on how to behave. Individuals in countries with low uncertainty avoidance, such as Jamaica and Singapore, appear to take each day as it comes [11]. Cultural orientation highlights the significance placed on traditionally masculine or feminine practices and qualities. In a "masculine" culture, there is a strong emphasis on achievement, financial success, assertiveness, and competition. On the other hand, a "feminine" culture places a greater value on relationships, service to others, care for the vulnerable, and environmental preservation. Japan and Germany are examples of masculine cultures, whereas Norway and Sweden are considered feminine cultures.

Cultural values can be oriented towards either the future (long-term) or the present and past (short-term). Cultures with a long-term orientation place importance on persistence and saving, as they believe it will yield benefits in the future. Several Asian countries, such as China and Japan, are examples of cultures that exhibit a long-term orientation. Short-term orientations, such as those found in West African, American, and Russian cultures, encourage respect for past tradition while also fulfilling social obligations in the present [16]. In today's world, a distinction between strong and weak cultures has become more prevalent. The argument posits that strong cultures have a greater impact on employee behavior and are directly associated with lower turnover rates. In a strong culture, the organization's core values are deeply ingrained and widely shared among its members. The strength of the culture is determined by the extent to which individuals wholeheartedly embrace and commit to these core values. According to this definition, a strong culture exerts significant influence on member behavior due to the high level of cohesiveness and intensity, creating an internal environment characterized by strong behavioral control. Nordstrom serves as an example of a company with a highly robust service culture in the retail industry. Employees at Nordstrom have a clear understanding of the expectations placed upon them, and these expectations play a substantial role in shaping their behavior [17].

4.1 Culture influence of organizational behavior

Employee turnover should be reduced as a result of a strong culture. A strong culture demonstrates that members agree on what the organization stands for. Such unity of purpose fosters loyalty, cohesiveness, and organizational commitment. These characteristics, in turn, reduce employees' proclivity to leave the organization. A strong organizational culture reduces the need for management to extensively rely on formal rules and regulations to govern employee behavior. A culture is considered weak when its members are unaware of its behavioral rules, traditions, rituals, and beliefs, or when there is inconsistency between behavior and stated values. This may be due to lack of knowledge of what the organization stands for. Weak cultures work against an organization's success [18]. In contrast, weak cultures frequently result in poor performance. Weak cultures also have a slew of unhealthy traits that can stymie an organization's ability to achieve its goals and succeed.

Scholars the world over have identified weak cultures to have some of the following traits: *Isolated/narrow thinking*: When an organization avoids looking outside itself for best approaches and practices, it exhibits this trait. These organizations' employees believe they have all the answers [19]. This type of inward thinking can keep a company from making necessary procedural and cultural changes; and, *Resistance to change:* When an organization is suddenly confronted with a rapidly changing environment, this trait becomes apparent. The organization is concerned with maintaining the status quo, avoiding mistakes, and avoiding risks. It is the culture's leadership that allows these factors to paralyze and pervade the organization, rather than focusing on success and innovation.

On how employees Learn Culture, the following have been suggested by many scholars;

Story telling: This practice involves the transmission of significant stories across generations within specific cultures. For example, during Henry Ford II's tenure as chairman of Ford Motor Company, it was challenging to find a manager who had not heard the story of Mr. Ford reminding his executives, in moments of excessive confidence, that "it is my name that is on the building." The underlying message was unmistakable: Henry Ford II held the ultimate authority and leadership within the organization [20]. Similarly, Nike employs several senior executives who actively serve as organization storytellers. These individuals dedicate a significant amount of their time to sharing stories that effectively convey the essence and values of Nike as a company [21]. For instance, they might recount the tale of Bill Bowerman, the co-founder and former Oregon track coach, who famously used his wife's waffle iron to pour rubber and create a better running shoe. These anecdotes, while entertaining and often eliciting laughter, are intended to exemplify Nike's spirit of innovation. New employees, on the other hand, might hear stories about the challenges faced by running star Steve Prefontaine in his pursuit to professionalize the sport and obtain improved performance equipment. These narratives highlight Nike's commitment to supporting athletes. Such stories are prevalent within many organizations and typically encompass a range of events, including those involving the organization's founders, rule-breaking, remarkable success stories, downsizing, employee relocations, responses to past mistakes, and the organization's ability to adapt and overcome challenges. By grounding the present in the past, these stories serve to explain, legitimize, and reinforce current practices;

Rituals: Rituals are repetitive sequences of actions that serve to express and reinforce the core values of an organization, prioritize goals, identify important individuals, and establish a sense of expendability. One well-known example of an organization ritual is Wal-Mart's company chant, which involves employees enthusiastically chanting the letters of the company's name. This ritual, initiated by the company's founder, Sam Walton, was designed to motivate and unify the workforce [22] while emphasizing the significance of employees in driving the company's success. Similar organization chants are also employed by other organizations such as IBM, Ericsson, Novell, Deutsche Bank, and PricewaterhouseCoopers. These rituals serve to unite employees and reinforce the founders' beliefs in the pivotal role of their workforce for achieving organizational objectives;

Material symbols: This involves construction of infrastructures in such a way to depict certain ranks or positions in the organization. For instance, Alcoa's headquarters do not appear to be typical organization headquarters for any "Tom and Dick" [23]. Even high-level executives have minimal individual offices within Alcoa, as the company predominantly utilizes cubicles, communal spaces, and meeting rooms. This informal organization layout serves as a symbolic representation of Alcoa's emphasis on transparency, equality, creativity, and adaptability. It communicates to employees that these values are highly valued within the organization. Some corporations provide limousines for top executives, as well as organization jet when traveling by air. While some individuals may not have the privilege of traveling in luxury limousines or private jets, they may still have access to company-provided transportation such as a car or air travel. However, the car provided may be a Chevrolet, and when flying, they may occupy seats in the economy section of commercial airliners. Material symbols encompass various aspects such as the physical arrangement of organization headquarters, the automobiles provided to top executives, and the presence or absence of organization aircraft. They also include factors like office size, the quality of furnishings, executive privileges, and attire. These material symbols serve as a means of communication to employees, indicating the individuals who hold significance within the organization, the level of egalitarianism preferred by top management, and the expected behaviors, ranging from conservative to risk-taking, participative to authoritarian, social to individualistic [20];

Language: Language plays a significant role in identifying and preserving the culture or subculture within organizational units and organizations. Learning and using specific terminology within a culture demonstrates acceptance and contributes to its preservation. For instance, employees at Knight-Ridder Information utilize terms like "accession number" (assigned to individual records in a database), "KWIC" (key-words-in-context), and "relational operator" (searching a database for names or key terms in a specific order). Similarly, new employees at Boeing must familiarize themselves with a distinct vocabulary of acronyms such as "BOLD" (Boeing online data) and "CATIA" (computer graphics-aided three-dimensional interactive application). Organizations frequently generate unique terminology to refer to their equipment, offices, important personnel, suppliers, customers, or products that are linked to their activities [24]. Initially, new employees may feel overwhelmed by the acronyms and jargon, but after around 6 months on the job, these terms become an integrated part of their language. Once learned, this specialized terminology serves as a shared language for members of a particular culture or subculture within the organization.

4.2 The concept of organization culture

Organizational culture refers to "a system of shared issues and beliefs held by organizational members that determines how each individual acts towards one another". It can also be defined as an organization's shared values, attitudes, and practices. It is your company's personality, and it has a large impact on your employees' overall satisfaction, as well as the consistent organizational behaviors of employees and leaders [25]. From this definition, we can deduce that culture is description of a perception of a relationship between the organization and its persons, or glue that keeps organizations together. As a result, individuals within the organization end up influencing the culture just as much as the culture influences them. Hofstede's Multi-Focus Model consists of six separate variables or dimensions that offer understanding regarding the alignment between the existing culture and strategic direction. By considering different combinations of these dimensions, valuable insights can be gained regarding strategic compatibility, and the outcomes can be presented visually in an easily understandable manner according to Farinha [26] as follows:

Dimension 1: Means oriented vs. goal oriented: This dimension is strongly linked to the effectiveness of the organization. In a means-oriented culture, the primary focus lies on the methods and processes of work execution, with individuals identifying and aligning themselves with the "how" of accomplishing tasks. Employees in a goal-oriented culture are primarily motivated to achieve specific internal results or goals, even if these involve significant risks; people identify with the 'what' [27]. People in a means-oriented culture perceive themselves as avoiding risks and exerting minimal effort in their jobs, despite the fact that each workday is essentially the same. In contrast, in a highly goal-oriented culture, employees are primarily motivated to achieve specific internal results or goals, even if these involve significant risks;

Dimension 2: Internally driven vs. externally driven: Employees in a highly internally driven culture take may not take their responsibilities seriously, believing that business ethics and honesty just comes naturally. Such employees need to have a great understanding of what is beneficial for both the customer and the broader world. In contrast, in a very externally driven culture, the emphasis is on meeting the needs of the customer; the emphasis is primarily placed on achieving results, and a practical approach takes precedence over an ethical stance;

Dimension 3: Easy work vs. strict work discipline: Internal structuring, control, and discipline are introduced in this dimension. A relaxed culture is characterized by a flexible internal framework and a sense of unpredictability with a lack of discipline and control; there is an abundance of surprises and improvisation. A strict work discipline reveals the inverse. People are extremely cost-conscious, serious, and punctual;

Dimension 4: Local vs. professional: Employees within a local company tend to align themselves with either their supervisor or the specific department they belong to. In a professional organization, an employee's identity is determined by his profession and/or the nature of his job. In a highly localized culture, employees typically prioritize short-term goals, have a strong internal focus, and face significant social pressure to conform to the norms of the group. Conversely, in a highly professional culture, the situation is reversed;

Dimension 5: Employee oriented vs. work: Management philosophy has a strong connection to organizational culture. In employee-oriented organizations, there is a belief that personal matters are recognized and that the organization takes accountability for the welfare of its employees, even if it means compromising work goals. Conversely, in work-oriented organizations, there is considerable pressure to prioritize task completion, even if it means disregarding the welfare of employees; and,

Dimension 6: Close system vs. open system: This dimension focuses on the level of inclusivity within an organization. In a highly open culture, newcomers are warmly received, and the organization is open to both internal and external individuals. It is presumed that nearly anyone would be able to fit into the organization. On the other hand, in a highly closed organization, the situation is reversed.

4.3 Hofstede's cultural dimensions

According to Farinha (2018), Hofstede's cultural dimensions have the following strengths:

- Comprehensive study of how national culture influences organization values: sample of over 116,000 employees from over 70 countries
- This seminal work emphasizes the importance of understanding national cultural differences and the implications for multinational corporations.
- Updated on a regular basis.
- Qualitative studies support the findings by validating and clarifying them.
- Capability to account for other variables, such as organizational culture.
- Objections to Hofstede's Cultural Dimensions
- A survey is a "blank instrument" for illuminating the complexities of national culture.
- Describes but does not explain what is happening, relying heavily on qualitative studies to 'validate' and elucidate findings.
- Organizational culture may not be constant, and there are other non-national cultural sources.
- Generalizes organization findings and other selective samples such as students to societies.
- Failure to account for differences between countries, such as strong regional subcultures.
- Some differences between countries are omitted, for example, the United States and Australia have similar scores for cultural dimensions, but there are differences in work motivation: (responsibility and recognition vs. job security and monetary rewards).
- D'Iribarne suggests that survey questions and interpretations may be invalid.

- Power disparities are very high in France, but D'Iribane argues that power is not the same as hierarchies. While France has extensive organization hierarchies, managers have little power.

- Questions may be ambiguous, for example, high work stress is not a proxy for Uncertainty Avoidance.

- D'Iribane's research includes interviews and observations.

Acknowledging that organizational culture possesses shared characteristics does not negate the presence of subcultures within a given culture. In most large organizations, there is a dominant culture that reflects the core values embraced by the majority of its members. Additionally, a diverse range of subcultures coexist within the organization. When we talk about an organization's culture, we are talking about its dominant culture. The macro perspective of culture is what gives an organization its unique personality. In large organizations, subcultures form to reflect common situations, experiences, or problems members are faced with. These subcultures are usually defined by department; for example, a department may have a subculture that is shared only by members of that department. It will include the dominant culture's core values as well as values specific to members of the purchasing department. Similarly, an organizational unit or office that is when a unit or department is physically isolated from the main operations of an organization, it can develop its own unique identity. While the core values are generally maintained, they are adapted to suit the specific circumstances and challenges faced by the separated unit.

A strong ethical standard is more likely to be established in an organizational culture that demonstrates a high level of risk tolerance, moderate aggressiveness, and a focus on both means and outcomes. Managers in such a culture are encouraged to take risks and innovate; they are encouraged to avoid excessive or unrestricted competition; and they will pay attention to how and what goals are achieved [20]. A strong organizational culture exerts a more pronounced influence on employees compared to a weak culture. When the culture is robust and promotes high ethical standards, it is likely to have a substantial and positive effect on employee behavior. A notable example of a company with a strong culture is Johnson & Johnson, which has long emphasized its organization responsibilities towards customers, employees, the community, and shareholders.

4.4 How organization culture determines employee's actions

Organizational culture is depicted as the manner in which members of an organization establish connections and interactions with each other and their work. The perception of relationships with the external world, in comparison to other organizations, can either hinder or enhance an organization's strategy. Organizational culture plays a significant role in shaping these relationships. The Hofstede Insights on organizational culture is a strategic tool aimed at assisting companies in becoming more functional using a comprehensive representation of the following:

- How employees truly relate to their organization's culture which ensures a consistent representation across employee recruitment messages and the practical working environment.

- The readiness of an organization to accept change; for example, are employees experiencing a lot of nervousness; is there enough trust; and are the relevant experts prepared for the change?
- How have the existing practices and desired practices within an organization align with the ideal culture to support the implementation of specific strategies, with the available resources and time?
- How proficiently can management utilize their behavior to establish a standard or example (lead by example)?
- How indirect change initiatives can help ensure a better fit between the current and optimal ways of working.

4.5 Importance of organization culture

Organizational culture makes it easier to achieve an organization's strategic goals. The culture portrays the organization's core values and gives a reflection of the leadership of the organization. A strong company culture will attract the best candidates and keep them engaged as employees. Research shows that up to 77% of adults would take into account a company's culture prior to applying for a job opportunity [28]. Perhaps more importantly, 56 percent consider organizational culture to be more important than compensation. It takes time and effort to develop a winning organizational culture; Ensuring that your culture accurately represents your values and is in line with your overarching mission is a significant undertaking, but do not give up: your efforts will be rewarded in the end.

The organizational culture becomes apparent in how decisions are made, whether through a top-down or bottom-up approach, and in the level of comfort employees feel in expressing their thoughts and opinions without the fear of negative consequences. It is reflected in the organization's benefit plans and in how employees are acknowledged and rewarded for surpassing expectations in their work. The Competing Values Framework is the most well-known classification of organizational culture types. At the University of Michigan, Kim Cameron and Robert Quinn identified four distinct types of organizational culture. Every organization possesses a distinctive combination of the four types of organizational culture, with one usually prevailing over the others. As the organization grows in size, the likelihood of having multiple cultures increases. While this can bring advantages, it may also present challenges in maintaining a unified culture, especially in geographically dispersed or globally operating organizations.

4.6 Types of organization culture

According to Cameron and Quinn, organizational cultures may be categorized into four types as follows:

- *Adhocracy culture*: This type of culture is characterized by a dynamic and entrepreneurial environment.
- *Clan culture*: This culture focuses on fostering collaboration and maintaining a friendly atmosphere.

- *Control culture*: This culture emphasizes structure, processes, and hierarchy.
- *Market culture*: This culture is driven by competition and a strong focus on achieving results.

It is critical to understand the type of culture change we are attempting to effect with the appropriate technology tools, as well as how this tool will enable the desired culture. Information Technology will drive significant change not only in technology but also in processes, team reorganization, and so on during a digital transformation or organizational culture change. The company is expected to assess its own processes to see what can be streamlined or automated to improve efficiency and the employee experience. As the rate of technological innovation accelerates and competition for faster delivery in the shortest time becomes more important in determining winners and losers in the software industry, it is essential that organizations adopt approaches that are research-driven.

DORA's 2018 Accelerate: State of DevOps report adds to the tech community's current understanding of what drives performance by introducing many new findings, but the following are a few highlights:

SDO performance unlocks benefits such as increased profitability, productivity, market share, customer satisfaction, and the ability to achieve organizational goals. High performance is driven by mastering key technical practices such as monitoring and observability, continuous testing, database change management, incident response and management, and integrating security earlier in the software development process. Forbes Daily features our best stories, exclusive reporting, and Forbes perspectives on the day's top news, as well as insider information on the world's most influential entrepreneurs [29]. When aiming to attain exceptional performance as a technology-focused organization, industry makes no difference.

4.7 Implications for non-technologists

The ability of technology companies to create, test, and deploy software updates is becoming increasingly important for all of us. Just imagine if every time you tried to log into your preferred online shopping platform, your purchases were consistently unable to process. This would not only jeopardize the provider's revenue potential, but it would also greatly degrade the customer experience which is not acceptable in an age when consumer purchasing habits are becoming increasingly reliant on technology and convenience. Based on the latest research from DORA, organizations that fall under the category of elite performers (referring to the highest performing organizations) can deploy code updates 46 times faster than others. They are also 7 times less likely to experience change failures, but are 2604 times faster at recovering from incidents than their peers. There is no doubt that such levels of performance can have tangible and measurable impacts on the market.

While many conversations about improving deployment velocity acknowledge the influence of organizational culture, it is often treated as a secondary consideration. This tendency is not unexpected, as technology-focused discussions tend to prioritize topics such as continuous delivery, cloud infrastructure, availability, continuous testing, and deployment automation. People are still struggling to wrap their heads around the topic of culture [30]. Unfortunately, this does not diminish its significance in terms of long-term success. The DORA study explored the impact of culture on performance within the technology sector, confirming the importance of this topic as discussed in recent years. The study utilized Ron Westrum's model of organizational culture as a measure of culture.

This study has identified several key cultural realities that aid in the elicitation of best practice behaviors among technology teams that should be highlighted. The findings indicate that team dynamics are far more important to performance than individual skills of team members. Researchers at Google conducted a comprehensive study on more than 180 engineering teams, revealing that psychological safety emerged as the primary predictor of high performance. The study also highlighted the significance of other factors such as dependability, structure, clarity of work, and the sense of meaning and impact. Psychological safety fosters a culture where team members feel secure in taking actions that contribute to performance, such as cooperation, openly addressing issues without fear of reprisal, breaking down barriers between departments, conducting thorough reviews of past projects, and continually experimenting to drive progress.

The insights from DORA's study are highly significant as they shed light on the transformative impact of reevaluating notions of responsibility, accountability, and the traditional blame game within prestigious software development and operations companies. According to J. Paul Reed, a consultant in the field of DevOps and a human factors researcher, this paradigm shift holds profound implications for these organizations' ability to execute effectively in the market. In this year's DORA study, there was a novel focus on the role of leaders in influencing culture. The research findings indicate that leaders who empower their teams by granting them autonomy in performing their jobs foster a sense of trust and provide a platform for employees to express their opinions. These factors, trust and voice, play a crucial role in shaping the organization's culture. As for leaders, what specific behaviors can they adopt to facilitate the exercise of autonomy by their teams?

Several intriguing research findings from DORA stand out: Clearly establish and communicate goals, while granting employees the autonomy to determine the best approach to achieve them.

- Simplify rules to eliminate obstacles and streamline processes.
- Enable teams to modify rules that hinder progress towards goals.
- Encourage the team to prioritize positive customer outcomes, even if it means deviating from established rules.

DORA's research findings also validated the significance of conducting postmortems or retrospectives in influencing performance and fostering a culture that appreciates the value of such activities for overall success. Retrospectives create a secure environment where teams can thoroughly analyze their work, identify effective practices, and make necessary adjustments to improve future outcomes. Their objective is to enhance their understanding of intricate systems and foster a culture of continuous learning throughout the organization, involving individuals at all levels, from code developers to top executives. This shift to continuous learning in a psychologically safe environment aids in shifting the organizational culture to support future efforts, resulting in a generative cycle aimed at improving performance.

Culture, being a complex and profound concept, exerts a multifaceted influence on the performance of technology organizations, a depth that we are only just beginning to grasp. Despite the challenges associated with measuring and comprehending culture, it is crucial not to undermine its significance in driving velocity within the technology sector. Rather than merely acknowledging its importance and swiftly moving on to more tangible aspects of technology, it is imperative to prioritize the understanding and evolution of tech firms' cultures to foster the necessary behaviors for driving velocity. Neglecting culture poses a clear and imminent threat to organizations seeking to undergo technological transformation [31].

4.8 Organization culture as a driver of employee satisfaction

Employee satisfaction refers to whether or not employees are happy and content, and whether or not their desires and needs are met at work. When employees are willing to adapt to the organizational culture, they are highly satisfied. They are less or completely dissatisfied when they are unwilling to adapt to the organizational culture [32]. Organizational culture is manifested in how an organization conducts business, treats its employees, customers, and the larger community. It is the degree to which decision-making autonomy and freedom are allowed, as well as the development of new ideas and personal expression. Finally, organizational culture determines how power and information flow throughout the organization hierarchy and the level of employee commitment to collective goals. A strong organizational culture can help drive business results, but determining which elements of the culture can lead to superior performance requires a cultural audit (**Figure 1**).

When employees embrace a strong organizational culture, it can lead to high employee performance. For example, if the organizational culture is innovative and employees enjoy improving and trying new things, this can lead to high performance. However, if the organization's culture is opaque and unaccepted by its employees, it can lead to poor performance. For example, if the organizational culture is team-oriented and the employee is individualistic, low performance may result. Strong organization cultures lead to social control, social glue, and frequently aid in decision making. Strong organization culture content, on the other hand, may be incompatible with the organization's environment, may focus attention on one mental model, and frequently suppress dissenting values from subcultures.

Figure 1.
Dimensions of organizational culture profile (OCP). Source: Adapted from information in O'Reilly et al. [33].

4.9 Technology: emerging technology or appropriate technology

Technology can be described as the practical utilization of scientific knowledge to meet human needs and goals. It involves the manipulation and alteration of the human environment for various purposes. There are a number of terms used in relation to technology as follows:

4.10 Emerging technology

The term "emerging technology" typically refers to a new technology that is in its early stages of development. However, it can also encompass the continuous advancement and evolution of an existing technology. The specific interpretation of this term may vary depending on the field in which it is used, such as media, business, science, or education [34]. The term is commonly used to describe technologies that are in the process of being developed or are anticipated to become available in the next 5–10 years. These technologies are often characterized by their potential to have substantial social or economic impacts.

Emerging digital technologies have created new opportunities while also posing new legal challenges, particularly in the areas of intellectual property, trademarks, patents, royalties, and licensing. The emergence of new digital communication technologies and media has presented new challenges related to the reproduction and distribution of copyrighted works [35]. In response, various stakeholders, including the government, affected industries, and public interest groups, have been actively addressing these issues. Their actions aim to establish appropriate measures and legal frameworks that protect the rights of copyright holders, provide clarity to digital technology companies, and serve the interests of the public and other involved parties.

4.11 Appropriate technology

Appropriate technology refers to a movement that promotes the use of small-scale and locally accessible technological solutions. These solutions are characterized by decentralization, reliance on labor rather than capital, energy efficiency, environmental sustainability, and local autonomy. The concept was initially described by economist Ernst Friedrich "Fritz" Schumacher as "intermediate technology" in his book "Small Is Beautiful" [36]. Both Schumacher and present-day advocates of appropriate technology emphasize the significance of technology being centered around people's needs and well-being.

Appropriate technology has been applied across various domains to address different challenges. Examples of such applications include water pumps and other equipment powered by bicycles or hand-operated mechanisms, the invention of bicycles themselves, the universal nut sheller, self-contained solar lamps and streetlights, and the design of passive solar buildings [37]. These well-known instances demonstrate the practical implementation of appropriate technology in solving specific problems. Today, appropriate technology is frequently developed using open source principles, which has resulted in open-source appropriate technology (OSAT). The open-source appropriate technology (OSAT) movement has made numerous technology plans readily accessible through the Internet, allowing for widespread availability and adoption [38]. This approach to technology has been suggested as a viable model to foster innovation in sustainable development.

Appropriate technology is most commonly discussed in relation to economic development and as an alternative to more capital-intensive technology transfer from developed to developing countries. However, both developing and developed countries have appropriate technology movements. The appropriate technology movement in developed countries arose from the energy crisis of the 1970s and is primarily concerned with environmental and sustainability issues. Today, the concept is multifaceted; in some contexts, appropriate technology can be defined as the most basic level of technology capable of achieving the intended goal, whereas in some contexts, appropriate technology refers to engineering practices that consider the social and environmental implications in a comprehensive manner. The facets are linked by toughness and sustainable living.

Appropriate Technology is a concept that pertains to sustainable community advancements and initiatives characterized by long-term considerations regarding components, maintenance, investment, and operation. This concept emerged as a response to the failures observed in large-scale, high-cost development approaches that proved unworkable due to issues such as inadequate infrastructure, lack of parts, or insufficient technical expertise following their initial implementation. These failures often occurred when solutions successful in one region were indiscriminately applied to different areas without considering the specific contextual differences.

The concept of Appropriate Technology emerged as a response to the inappropriate introduction of High Technology solutions into communities and economies that were unable to sustain them in the long term. Dr. Eric Schumacher established the 'Intermediate Technology Development Group' (ITDG) in 1966 with a focus on addressing the needs of some of the world's poorest communities. Schumacher recognized that large, costly, and advanced technological solutions that might be successful in wealthier regions often proved ineffective when implemented in areas with inadequate infrastructure or significant environmental differences. According to the ITDG, the essence of this alternative development approach lies in adopting a local and small-scale perspective rather than a national and large-scale one. It emphasizes the creation of numerous low-cost workspaces where people reside, particularly in rural areas, and utilizes appropriate technologies suited to their specific needs that can be created and controlled by the people who use them, allowing them to be more productive and earn money."

4.12 Technology and innovation

Technology is a key driver of innovation, and innovation plays a vital role in the success of small and medium-sized enterprises (SMEs). The effective utilization of technology and the ability to innovate act as significant facilitators for SMEs, offering them opportunities for growth and development at the individual enterprise level and the broader level of the industry. These factors contribute to understanding the variations in growth rates observed at the firm, regional, and national levels. Therefore, technological innovation holds a central position in driving economic change, serving as the ultimate source of productivity and long-term growth. According to Stiglitz [39], it is through technological innovation that economies consistently achieve superior performance. The adoption of technology among small and medium-size enterprises is a subject of increasing importance, particularly in developing countries. While there are established theories on technology adoption that have been extensively studied in Western contexts, their application to the specific context of developing countries has been limited. Technology adoption is also critical for private-sector business growth.

4.13 Technology as a change agent

Companies of all sizes are using technology to support their cultures. However, it is not only the technology itself that is important, but also the opportunities that technology provides. A new ERP implementation or change, for example, may necessitate a complete reengineering of business processes, how people interact internally and externally (Customers), and how the business is perceived in the market. All of these outcomes will undoubtedly have an impact on profit. Another example is how technology is influencing new modes of communication. Solutions such as Microsoft Teams, Slack, and others have brought new ways of meeting and sharing in the organization, and this is undoubtedly the new normal.

Having said that, it is critical to understand that every technology decision cannot be made solely based on the acquisition of technology, but must also take into account the impact of people adoption and engagement, such as training approach, how friendly the adoption curve will be, and so on. Wrong technological decisions made without these considerations will slow the cultural change and cause it to lose momentum. Employee engagement is required for a positive employee experience, but measuring the health of a company's culture is difficult. The percentage of employees who participate in the programs and the feedback they provide, as well as other statistics such as changes in turnover and absenteeism, or in the achievement of business objectives, indicate whether a company is making progress. According to Rhonda Gardner's article "Leading a Successful Cultural Transformation at Your Organization," cultural transformation will occur on multiple fronts, including how people behave and work. When done correctly, this has a positive impact on business outcomes (**Figure 2**).

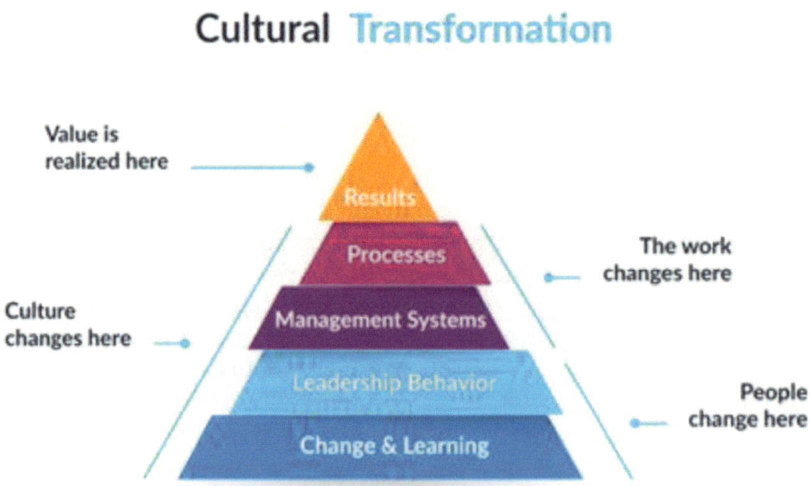

Figure 2.
Cultural transformation. Adopted from Rhonda Gardner [40].

4.14 Important considerations when driving change through technology

- There is no "one-size-fits-all" strategy or recipe, but the following points must be included in the Cultural Change from Tech agenda:
- As with any strategy, full top-level engagement and sponsorship are required. Nothing will happen unless it is present. "Change" will not occur unless all key stakeholders agree to it.
- As an IT leader, you must be a change agent. You will need to be an evangelist for how technology will drive change, empower those who use it, and propel the business to new heights. On the other hand, being a leader entails the obligation to "deliver."
- Maintain clear and consistent communication about what is going on and how things are progressing. The two most important factors in achieving results are clear project management and lean communications.
- Ensure adequate funding and resource allocation. Any major endeavor will necessitate cultural change.
- We will not discuss cost, but rather investment. Cost is sometimes necessary for business operations, but the difference is that when you invest rather than spend, you are focusing on and delivering profit!
- Make a road! Cultural change is laying the groundwork for the company's future, so you must pave the way. This must be done through persuasion, engagement, and delivery.
- Rule and set a good example! You will not achieve the above if you and your team are not ready for the challenge and the significant effort that change entails. You and your IT organization must be the first to buy-in and believe in the path that must be taken before others will.
- When driving engagement, keep the standard distribution gauss bell approach in mind. It is critical who you bring over first in order for others to follow! (See my article "Another Cultural Transformation Talk!" for more information.)
- Always set the bar as high as possible while remaining realistic! Setting reasonable goals rarely yields high results. However, if you raise the bar, you will be able to accomplish more.
- Encourage, encourage, encourage... Gain momentum as you go. When people are motivated, they are much more productive. Sometimes a price is given, and other times only recognition is given. You will be astounded at how a simple gesture of recognition can affect people and teams. Make success as public as possible, and keep corrections to a minimum!
- Continue to evolve while also delivering. When the company believes that cultural change has occurred, do not stop there. Begin working in the new or

next phase. Because culture is inextricably linked to time and chronology, it is a living thing. Markets change, and businesses must adapt to meet new demands, new ways of doing things, and technological advancements. As a result, we must consider that culture will need to go through a period of change in the future, or at the very least suffer and adapt over time. Prepare for it by planning ahead of time and anticipating the requirements. Culture will need to evolve, so we must plan for cultural change evolution.

- The only constant in life is change! Once again, cultural change will occur through persuasion rather than mandate.

- Construct safe heavens. Always be honest when it comes to setting expectations.

- Deliver only what you can commit to. Underperformance or poor performance is a cultural killer. Over delivering can sometimes mean that you did not set the bar high enough.

- Implement internal marketing and branding. Using project names and mojos to drive engagement and identification across the organization during the adoption and team identification process. It will also facilitate communication.

- Put the leadership to the test. As an IT leader in the midst of a technological cultural shift, you will need to challenge your colleagues. Some will be simple, but others will require you to kick some doors and desks.

- Be a pragmatic leader when it comes to dealing with problems and constraints. To avoid losing momentum, do not take too long. This is especially true when working on high-impact projects.

- Have fun on the ride. Take the cultural transformation seriously, but enjoy the journey because it will become part of your DNA.

4.15 Using technological innovation to drive cultural change

According to Bryan Walker and Sarah A. Soule "Culture is a breeze. It is imperceptible, but its impact can be seen and felt. Smooth sailing when the wind is blowing in your direction. Everything is more difficult when the wind is blowing against you." From IoT to block chains, data lakes, and AI, the raw potential of new technology is astounding. While the usability of many technologies is improving, comprehending the specific ways in which a technology can bring about transformative opportunities remains highly challenging. It is especially difficult to adapt technology to specific needs of the company and integrate it with current processes. To make matters worse, most businesses have deeply embedded legacy systems that are difficult to change. Solving these problems requires individuals with a strong technical background, a broad understanding of the subject matter, and the capacity to collaborate effectively within the larger organization. The reality is that most data in many industries today is not up to basic standards, and the rigors of change necessitate far better data quality and analytics.

Data presents an intriguing paradox; transformation entails understanding emerging types of unstructured data, massive amounts of data from outside the business, leveraging and incorporating proprietary data. Today's technology can assist businesses by allowing them to collect data on the environment, health, and safety. Predefined requirements are now being assessed through leading indicators using straightforward online and offline protocols, which have become more significant than lagging indicators. This facilitates the collection of compliant information and, more importantly, encourages ongoing improvement in environmental, health, and safety practices, as well as cultural transformation. It is critical to act on the data once it has been obtained. Businesses can respond to such cases within predefined parameters and bring them to a satisfactory conclusion using technology. Furthermore, comprehensive EHS and compliance software systems give organizations a centralized location for consistently logging events, assigning corrective actions, analyzing root causes, and reporting on incident rates. Numerous organizations are utilizing specialized and integrated mobile applications for incident management on iOS and Android platforms to enhance EHS management and reporting. These apps enable employees to conveniently document findings or report incidents while on the go. Use of Apps can also provide offline support if the user is not connected to the internet; tasks and activities can be added and completed on the go, and data can be synchronized to the cloud later.

4.16 Interplay between technology innovation and competitiveness

People created the language so they could communicate with elders and learn from their stories. They created tools for agriculture, homes, and weapons for hunting and protection. As the population grows, more technology is developed. Technology has not only extended human life spans but has also changed the way we live [41]. The invention of the printing press revolutionized access to information, enabling widespread dissemination of news, increased literacy rates, and the establishment of communities within cities to preserve and support diverse cultures. Every nation and community have their own unique coherence, culture, tradition, and social norms and values. The living standards have greatly improved and become more sophisticated as a result of technological advancements [42].

Kacker explains that the term "innovation" originates from the Latin word "innovare," which conveys the concept of creating something novel. Innovations entail fresh approaches to tasks and are linked to elements such as risk, potential failure, unconventional management perspectives, and the need to abandon outdated practices. Drucker defines innovation as the process of introducing enhanced capabilities or improving utility. Another perspective describes innovation capability as the organization's capacity to create innovative solutions in response to changing contexts and opportunities, without causing significant disruptions, excessive time and costs, or compromising performance. The advancement of technology innovation has led to various benefits such as improved precision in business planning, enhanced marketing efficiency, increased global sales, streamlined management practices, real-time monitoring capabilities, and prompt customer support. Entrepreneurs acknowledge that innovation not only enhances the quality of products or processes but also contributes positively to the economic outcomes of small businesses.

According to Oslo, there are four primary types of innovation. These are process, product, service, and marketing innovation. Process innovation involves implementing new or significantly improved production or delivery methods that causes substantial changes in production techniques in an organization. Product and service innovation entail introducing new or significantly improved goods or services in terms of their intended use or characteristics. Marketing innovations involve implementing new marketing methods that include changes to product design, promotion, pricing, and placement. Organizational innovation, also known as strategic innovation, refers to the adoption of new organizational methods in a company's business practices, organization, organization, or external relations. Technology plays a vital role in driving business innovation, which, in turn, increases value, improves quality, and enhances productivity. For SMEs aiming to increase profits, innovation is the most rapid and effective pathway to achieve that goal.

4.17 Technological impact on culture

The culture of a society can be seen its values and practices. It can be observed through the people through their perceptions, values, practices, and technological transfers. Technological changes have exerted significant influence in various essential elements of cultures, such as art, language, education, mobility, and religion. These aspects form the bedrock of our cultural identity and play a crucial role in shaping our perceptions, judgments, and evaluations of technology. The culture of a community serves as a framework or benchmark through which technology is understood and assessed. Technology plays a pivotal role in shaping the trajectory of cultural development as it permeates all aspects of culture. For technology to become an integral part of a broader cultural dimension, it must align with the social and cultural context of a community. Failure to achieve this alignment can lead to conflicts between technological progress and the preservation of cultural values. In essence, the compatibility between technology and cultural values is essential to ensure harmonious coexistence and balanced cultural evolution. Striking a balance enables individuals, irrespective of their ethnicity, age, or educational background, to freely express themselves within the realm of technology. It helps people to fulfill their aspirations and desires, but the absence of proper restrictions, regulation, and accountability may lead to potential cultural deterioration.

4.18 Technological impact on tradition

In any community, there is always a struggle between technology and tradition. Globalization has reduced the world to the size of a village due to technological advancements [43]. Imagining modern life without electricity, transportation, communication, and so on takes us back in time. Technological advancements have been instrumental in driving progress in various disciplines such as medical science, engineering, economics, and more. Because of the positive impact of technology, industrialization, urbanization, modernization, transportation and communication development are all possible. It has aided networking of society's culture, tradition, and coherence leading to technological advancements, the twenty-first century has moved so far ahead.

In her TED talks, Sherry Turkle highlights the phenomenon of expecting more from technology while expecting less from human interactions. She emphasizes that our reliance on technology can hinder the development of meaningful relationships with others, as we treat technology as if it were a genuine substitute for human connection. The constant influx of electronic communication, such as texts, tweets, and emails, can also contribute to feelings of isolation and detract from the ability to engage in deep thinking and active listening. Another negative impact of technology, according to Turkle, is the dominance of Western culture over less prominent cultures, resulting in a disregard for social values which leads to loss of coherent traditional practices. Traditional style thrives when it has a recognized value. Rather than killing tradition, technology aids in the modification of production methods or industrialization. Thus, if the beneficiary part is considered, technology allows for the preservation of tradition.

4.19 Technological impact on social values

Technology has provided a wide range of topics for discussion. People gain extensive knowledge about any subject, and more information is effectively shared. Technology aids in the transformation of the economy as well as the evolution of new social classes [44]. It can help to strengthen interpersonal connections. It has contributed to all demographic factors of society, for instance, modern farming methods have supplanted traditional agricultural practices, leading to higher crop yields, reduced time requirements, and other benefits.

People spend more time on technology and less time on social activities. Technology has been criticized for the decline of traditional media platforms like television and newspapers. Its widespread adoption has been limited to educated individuals on the fringes of society. The more technology advances, the more human beings regress. The invention of robots and machines has rendered humans lazy and reliant. Technology has led to creation of bombs, nuclear weapons, and missiles. The implementation of technology has an impact on societal values by changing expectations and realities. People have lost trust as a result of overemphasis on technology.

5. Conclusion

Despite the advantages and disadvantages, technology has significantly enhanced our lives. It has effectively conserved valuable resources like time and money, while also promoting global connectivity by turning the world into a closely-knit community. This transformation has facilitated the bridging of cultural, racial, and geographical gaps, enabling people to overcome barriers more effortlessly. The increasing preference for online communication over in-person interactions has a significant influence on culture at both local and global levels, owing to the ease and convenience of connecting through technology and engaging in online communication.

6. Recommendations

The study recommends that organizations be helped to buy and implement Appropriate Technologies in form of digital computers and Information Communication Technologies, which will help to enhance innovative processes in the organizations. Organizations are also urged to train their employees on how to use these technologies as means of connecting individuals, fostering promotion of values, mutual respect, and innovation. Once trained, employees will be able to use the technologies to tell their stories for culture impact and social values, and so as to foster loyalty, cohesiveness, and organizational commitment for economic change, productivity and long term growth. Consequently, the employees will help in their organizational productivity, profitability growth and customer satisfaction.

Expected learning outcomes

1. Description of culture.
2. Role of organizational culture in driving employee's actions.
3. How organizations drive cultural change through technological innovation.
4. Interplay between technology and culture in driving change for employee satisfaction.

Author details

Peter Paul Kithae
Management University of Africa, Nairobi, Kenya

*Address all correspondence to: pkithae@mua.ac.ke

References

[1] Griswold W. Cultures and Societies in a Changing World. Sage; 2012

[2] Sarantuya J, Altanchimeg Z, Tsolmon J, Buyankhishig S. Relationship Between Organizational Culture Employee Satisfaction and Organizational Commitment. 2023. Available from: https://www.researchgate.net/publication/348301327 [Accessed: June 28, 2023]

[3] Samovar LA, Porter RE, McDaniel ER, Roy CS. Intercultural Communication: A Reader. Cengage learning; 2014

[4] Peters J, Waterman R. In Search of Excellence: Lessons from America's Best-Run Companies. Reprint ed. New York: Harper Business; 2006

[5] Rizwan RA, Munwar HP, Nadeem S, Faiz A. How and When Ethics Lead to Organizational Performance–Evidence from South Asian Firms. 2023. Available from: https://www.researchgate.net/profile/Rizwan-Ahmed-7 [Accessed: June 28, 2023]

[6] Bushiri C. The Impact of Working Environment on Employees' Performance, the Case of Institute of Finance Management in Dar es Salaam. [Masters thesis]. The Open University of Tanzania; 2014

[7] Kyungyul J, Yoon BY, Seungsuk L, Dong-Soo L. Factors influencing customer decisions to use online food delivery service during the COVID-19 pandemic. Food. 2022;**11**(1):64. DOI: 10.3390/foods11010064

[8] Bagozzi RP, Davis FD, Warshaw PR. Development and test of a theory of technological learning and usage. Human Relations. 1992;**45**(7):660-686. DOI: 10.1177/001872679204500702

[9] Davis F. Perceived usefulness, perceived ease of use, and user acceptance of information technology. MIS Quarterly. 1989;**13**(3):319-340. DOI: 10.2307/249008

[10] Venkatesh V. Determinants of perceived ease of use: Integrating control, intrinsic motivation, and emotion into the technology acceptance model. Information Systems Research. 2000;**11**:342-365

[11] Hofstede G. Dimensionalizing cultures: The Hofstede model in context. Online Readings in Psychology and Culture. 2011;**2**(1):2307-0919

[12] Nardon L, Steers RM. The culture theory jungle: Divergence and convergence in models of national culture. In: Cambridge Handbook of Culture, Organizations, and Work. 2009. pp. 3-22

[13] Oishi S, Diener E, Lucas RE, Suh EM. Cross-cultural variations in predictors of life satisfaction: Perspectives from needs and values. In: Culture and Well-Being: The Collected Works of Ed Diener. 2009. pp. 109-127

[14] Ahmed T, Mouratidis H, Preston D. Website design guidelines: High power distance and high context culture. International Journal of Cyber Society and Education. 2009;**2**(1):47-60

[15] Wierzbicka A. Cross-cultural pragmatics. In: Cross-Cultural Pragmatics. De Gruyter Mouton; 2009

[16] Eringa K, Caudron LN, Rieck K, Xie F, Gerhardt T. How relevant are

Hofstede's dimensions for inter-cultural studies? A replication of Hofstede's research among current international business students. Research in Hospitality Management. 2015;**5**(2):187-198

[17] Heskett JL. Service Breakthroughs. Simon and Schuster; 1990

[18] Gustavo. Culture: Weak VS. Strong. 2015. Available from: http://drgustavo.com/culture-weak-vs-strong/

[19] Sveiby KE. The New Organizational Wealth: Managing & Measuring Knowledge-Based Assets. Berrett-Koehler Publishers; 1997

[20] Robbins SP. Organizational Behaviour. Pearson Prentice Hall; 2005

[21] Ind N. Living the Brand: How to Transform every Member of your Organization into a Brand Champion. Kogan Page Publishers; 2007

[22] Smith AC, Smith AC. Consequences. Palgrave Macmillan UK; 2016. pp. 217-240

[23] Hoffman AJ. Carbon Strategies: How Leading Companies Are Reducing their Climate Change Footprint. University of Michigan Press; 2007

[24] Homburg C, Workman JP, Jensen O. Fundamental changes in marketing organization: The movement toward a customer-focused organizational structure. Journal of the Academy of Marketing Science. 2000;**28**:459-478

[25] Sageer A, Rafat S, Agarwal P. Identification of variables affecting employee satisfaction and their impact on the organization. IOSR Journal of Business and Management. 2012;**5**(1):32-39

[26] Farinha J. Cultural dimensions-the different impacts on leadership behaviors. Theory and Applications in the Knowledge Economy. 2018;**425**

[27] Singh K. Study of achievement motivation in relation to academic achievement of students. International Journal of Educational Planning & Administration. 2011;**1**(2):161-171

[28] Schmiedel T, Müller O, Vom Brocke J. Topic modeling as a strategy of inquiry in organizational research: A tutorial with an application example on organizational culture. Organizational Research Methods. 2019;**22**(4):941-968

[29] Forbes DP, BorchertPS,Zellmer-BruhnME,SapienzaHJ. Entrepreneurial team formation: An exploration of new member addition. Entrepreneurship Theory and Practice. 2006;**30**(2):225-248

[30] Hendry J. Wrapping Culture: Politeness, Presentation, and Power in Japan and Other Societies. Oxford University Press; 1993

[31] Ostrom AL, Bitner MJ, Brown SW, Burkhard KA, Goul M, Smith-Daniels V, et al. Moving forward and making a difference: Research priorities for the science of service. Journal of Service Research. 2010;**13**(1):4-36

[32] Kotter JP. Organisation Culture and Performance. Simon and Schuster; 2008

[33] O'Reilly CA III, Chatman JA, Caldwell DF. People and organizational culture: A profile comparison approach to assessing person-organization fit. Academy of Management Journal. 1991;**34**:487-516

[34] Cozzens S, Gatchair S, Kang J, Kim KS, Lee HJ, Ordóñez G, et al. Emerging technologies: Quantitative

identification and measurement. Technology Analysis & Strategic Management. 2010;**22**(3):361-376

[35] De Filippi P, Hassan S. Blockchain technology as a regulatory technology: From code is law to law is code. arXiv:1801.02507; 2018

[36] Akubue A. Appropriate Technology for Socioeconomic Development in third world countries. The Journal of Technology Studies. 2000;**26**(1):33-43. DOI: 10.21061/jots.v26i1.a.6

[37] Mokyr J. The Lever of Riches: Technological Creativity and Economic Progress. Oxford University Press; 1992

[38] Pearce JM, Mushtaq U. Overcoming technical constraints for obtaining sustainable development with open source appropriate technology. In: 2009 IEEE Toronto International Conference Science and Technology for Humanity (TIC-STH). IEEE; 2009. pp. 814-820

[39] Stiglitz JE. Learning to learn, localized learning and technological progress. Economic Policy and Technological Performance. 1987:125-153

[40] Rhonda Gardner. Leading a Successful Cultural Transformation at Your Organization. 2023. Available from: https://www.aihr.com/blog/cultural-transformation/ [Accessed: June 4, 2023]

[41] Barbara Bray. Technology and its Impact on Society and Culture; 2007

[42] Alekseeva L, Azar J, Giné M, Samila S, Taska B. The demand for AI skills in the labor market. Labour Economics. 2021;**71**(Aug):1-60

[43] African Hydrogen Trade Partnership. AHP. 2022. Available from: https://www.afr-h2-p.com [Accessed: December 9, 2022]

[44] Abraham A, Rodrigues JJPC, Pani SK, Dash S, Acharya B, editor. AI, Edge, and IoT-Based Smart Agriculture. Academic Press; 2021

Chapter 9

The Influence of Employer Brand Dimensions on the Affective Organizational Commitment of Employees in Small and Medium-Sized Enterprises

Matea Cvjetković and Tihana Babić

Abstract

Employer branding is becoming a crucial talent management and communications strategy in many organizations today, given the importance of human resources as the most significant intangible asset of the company. In order to attract, recruit, and retain skilled employees, many companies systematically and proactively implement employer branding programs aimed at their existing and potential future employees. This can be challenging for small and medium-sized enterprises (SMEs) since their HR and marketing departments lack well-established processes, which can affect the commitment of employees. Thus, the aim of this research was to investigate the impact of five employer brand dimensions on affective organizational commitment, as the strongest type of organizational commitment. Data for the study was collected from 104 respondents employed in SMEs in Croatia and was empirically analyzed by applying the PLS-SEM method. The findings of the study showed that application and interest values positively influence affective organizational commitment, outlying the importance of knowledge transfer, workplace creativity, and innovation in a customer and humanitarian-oriented environment, as crucial elements for achieving affective organizational commitment. The research contributes to the existing literature on employer branding for SMEs operating in developing countries and provides guidance to owners and managers when building successful employer brands within their organizations.

Keywords: employer branding, affective organizational commitment, talent management, small and medium-sized enterprises, Croatia

1. Introduction

Today's business world is characterized by fierce competition among organizations that are in search of the most talented employees [1]. This is a consequence of numerous demographic changes (population aging, migration, etc.), as well as the development of new trends in which the importance of work-life balance is strongly emphasized. Additionally, in today's globalized world with many possibilities for remote work, employees can switch between careers and job positions within different companies across the globe. At the same time, many industries are going through extremely rapid technological changes that require new technical and professional skills [2]. As a result, 7 out of 10 organizations struggle with finding and hiring competent and qualified employees [3]. For this reason, many organizations systematically create, integrate, and proactively implement programs for attracting and retaining talented employees [4].

This new approach to managing talent through internal and external promotional activities is defined as employer branding [5]. Building a successful employer brand combines elements of human resources management and marketing and is increasingly considered an effective organizational strategy that can differentiate a company from its competition [6]. Given that it focuses on the uniqueness and exceptionality of the work environment, it has recently become an important strategy for building the company's reputation and image as a credible and reliable employer [7]. A successfully built employer brand brings multiple benefits to the company. Employer branding activities positively affect the intention of potential candidates to apply for a job position [6], but also increase the motivation and retention of existing employees within the organization [7]. Additional benefits of employer branding include: building a positive image of the company in the eyes of customers, strengthening the financial performance of the organization, establishing a competitive advantage in the market, and creating a favorable organizational culture and work climate [8], which ultimately results in greater employee engagement and commitment [9].

This is particularly important for small and medium-sized enterprises (SMEs), which play a major role in creating new jobs [10]. However, SMEs today operate in a challenging environment, while simultaneously facing limited financial and human resources that can sometimes constrain them from successfully managing all their business operations, including talent management. That can lead to putting higher pressure on the employees who may work in conditions of overtime work, high expectations, and unattainable plans, which can have a negative impact on their job satisfaction and loyalty [10]. For that reason, creating a favorable place to work for their employees has become a focus of many SMEs, who try to differentiate themselves from other companies and become the desirable employer, that is the "employer of choice" [1]. The main focus of the employer branding process is to design a healthy workplace by identifying and including the elements that are important to the company's current and future employees [7], so as to fulfill their needs and encourage their commitment to the organization. This way employees will stay longer within the company and be motivated to perform at their best, which will reflect on the organizational success as well [9].

Considering the above, the main goal of this study is to realize what elements of the employer brand influence organizational commitment in small and medium-sized enterprises, with a focus on affective organizational commitment (AOC). Affective organizational commitment is considered the most effective approach to measuring loyalty to an organization [11] and is often categorized as the "core essence", that is, as a permanent, irreplaceable, and central component of organizational commitment [12]. Previous research that has studied employer branding and organizational commitment has focused on large organizations, most of which already have well-established processes and procedures at the level of the human resources department with the intention of providing a stimulating work environment to their employees

[13–17]. Due to the differences between large, small, and medium-sized enterprises, the conclusions of the mentioned studies cannot be directly applied to small and medium-sized enterprises [18]. SMEs are characterized by an informal structure that lacks systemic processes on the organizational level [19], which can affect the comprehensive management of human resources. Thus, the aim of this research is to deepen the conceptualization of previous studies made on employer branding and organizational commitment and to expand the theoretical framework for SMEs operating in developing countries, by understanding which elements of employer brand influence affective organizational commitment for employees working in small and medium-sized enterprises.

The research follows the establishment of employer brand dimensions defined by Berthon, Ewing, and Hah, who observed employer branding through the concept of "employer attractiveness" and defined five elements that form "the best employer": (1) *interest value*, which focuses on the exciting and creative work environment, (2) *social value*, whose focus is on collegial connections and team spirit, (3) *economic value*, which places importance on salary and other compensational packages, (4) *development value,* that puts imperative on work recognition, self-esteem, and career development, and (5) *application value,* that appreciates the possibility of knowledge transfer, in the work settings that are customer oriented and humanitarian [20]. By examining the mentioned dimensions, this research aims to shed light on the elements that are important for employees for developing an affective organizational commitment in SMEs. It is estimated that in emerging markets, SMEs generate 7 out of 10 jobs [21], but despite the fact that SMEs employ the majority of workers, little attention and research have been devoted to investigating the impact of employer brand dimensions on affective organizational commitment [22], especially in the European context. Thus, this research aims to fill the identified gap.

The paper is systematized as follows: the introduction is followed by a literature review that briefly presents the concepts of employer branding and affective organizational commitment. The third section focuses on the development of hypotheses, while the fourth section specifies the research methodology. The fifth section presents the empirical analysis and the results of hypotheses testing, which is followed by a discussion of the results together with the limitations and recommendations for future research. In the end, a conclusion systematizes the key findings of the research and describes the theoretical and practical contributions.

2. Literature review

The theoretical basis for this study is found in the resource-based view, the social exchange theory, and the psychological contract theory. According to the resource-based view (RBV), all the investments in employees (material and immaterial) affect the progress, growth, and development of their skills, which are key to establishing the organization's competitive advantage [6]. The competitive advantage comes from the company's internal resources that provide added value, are unique or rare, are difficult to imitate, and are not substitutable [23]. As a result, they increase the intellectual capital of the organization [24] through the complex interaction of people, skills, and technologies that affect the efficiency and productivity of the company [23]. The focus of RBV is on the long-term approach to creating a bond between the employer and the employee [25]. In return for the tangible and intangible investments of the company, employees are more likely to develop feelings of loyalty and commitment toward the organization and work on developing firm-specific resources that help organizations attain their goals.

A similar relationship can be observed through the theory of social exchange, in which organizational commitment appears in the form of the employee's psychological reactions to the benefits provided by the company and is demonstrated with the investment of time and effort to participate in the success of the organization [26]. Correspondingly, the theory of the psychological contract considers that organizational commitment is formed based on mutually fulfilled promises and is also grounded on the emotional connection between the organization and its employees [27]. As the name suggests, a psychological contract refers to an unspoken agreement that states shared expectations and obligations between two parties; in this case between an employee and an organization [28]. The psychological contract represents a dynamic process that gradually unfolds through the time before employment and throughout various phases of employment [29]. It is precisely the employer branding activities that unify those processes and phases, creating a systematical approach toward the existing and potential employees.

2.1 Employer branding

Building a brand, or "branding," is a very researched concept in marketing literature, and at its most basic level, it serves differentiation [30]. Differentiation in marketing brings numerous benefits and is observed as a competitive advantage, but in recent years the concept became important in talent management as well. The term "employer branding" was shaped by Ambler and Barrow in 1996 as a set of "functional, economic, and psychological" substances that result from working in a certain company ([7], p. 4). Building an employer brand refers to building a company's positive reputation as an employer, meaning its potential (future) and current employees perceive it as a great place to work [31].

Building an employer brand is a long-term process that should ensure a constant flow of potential candidates, while simultaneously developing and positioning a positive image of the organization in the eyes of future and current employees [32]. Due to the "global war for talent" and the fact that organizations around the world are struggling to fill their vacant positions with qualified employees, many companies have opened completely new departments dedicated exclusively to strengthening their employer brand [33]. Establishing procedures within the HR department is an important dimension in the way employees are managed, which is often lacking in many small and medium-sized enterprises [34]. Most often, in SMEs, HR processes are managed by the owner-manager [19]. For that reason, creating and establishing an employer brand is a challenge for small and medium-sized enterprises and can affect the motivation and commitment of the employees [35].

Although research related to employer branding in some instances is still in its early stages, it is being recognized as a long-term approach in the future, as organizations increasingly start to realize that the loyalty of employees cannot be taken for granted [36]. Employees are no longer tied to one organization and can freely decide who they will work for, and where they will stay in the long term. Employer branding thus builds upon the discipline that has already proven its value; "branding" assesses the uniqueness of the brand and focuses on its differentiation [36]. It also encourages people's loyalty and commitment, which is one of the most effective approaches to attracting and retaining employees. For that reason, it is important for organizations to strategically plan the implementation of employer branding strategies, in order to reap all the benefits that come from successfully managing an employer brand, with the ultimate goal of providing their employees with a stimulating working environment, where they will develop the deepest type of loyalty for their organizations—affective organizational commitment.

2.2 Affective organizational commitment

Organizational commitment is defined as a set of attitudes formed toward the organization, which is characterized by a permanent psychological connection that arises from embracing the organizational values and results in a desire to stay within the organization in the long run [23]. This research is based on the theoretical concept developed by Allen and Meyer [37], who observe organizational commitment through three perspectives: affective commitment, normative commitment, and continuance commitment. Affective organizational commitment develops as a result of loyalty and identification with the organization; continuance commitment arises when it is too costly for a person to leave the organization, while normative commitment evolves into a duty to stay within the company [37, 38]. In other words, employees who develop affective organizational commitment stay within the organization because they wish to, those who develop continuance commitment stay because they have to, while those employees whose connection to the organization is based on normative commitment stay in the organization because it is morally acceptable [39].

Even though all three approaches to organizational commitment are often connected, the nature of their connections differs, meaning that the most importance is given to affective organizational commitment [40] since it is considered a crucial element of the organization's success [35]. Employees with strongly expressed affective organizational commitment invest more effort in their work and demonstrate better results than those employees who have a low level of affective organizational commitment [41]. The intensity of the employee's commitment to the organization is based on the organizational characteristics, and not the characteristics of the employees. Organizational commitment arises at higher levels in small enterprises than in large ones [42], which is why SMEs need to pay careful attention to developing and maintaining the organizational commitment of their employees. Well-aligned talent management practices incorporated into the thought-out employer brand should help in reaching this goal.

2.3 Employer branding practices in SMEs in developing countries

Small and medium-sized enterprises in developing countries play a major role in contributing to economic growth, but their business operations are constrained by different market conditions and obstacles such as difficult access to finance, high taxations, frequent employee fluctuations, etc. [43], which is why implementing strategies in building an employer brand can become especially challenging for key people in SMEs. Croatia, as one of the ex-transition countries in Central and Eastern Europe, but also a member state of the European Union, is going through several changes in its talent management practices [44], while simultaneously encountering different challenges with regard to demographic trends (older population, migrations), high cost of labor, vastly present forms of informal work (getting paid under the counter), and high unemployment rates [45]. Moreover, society as a whole is lagging behind the EU standard in its digital transition, and there is a growing need to support the development of digital skills of many employees, promote the development of new, digital jobs and create conditions in which individuals can progress in their careers, with the goal of accelerating the digital transition of society and the economy as a whole [46].

A total of 153,477 SMEs were operating in Croatia in 2021, representing a share of 99.7% of all businesses [47]. They also accounted for a 67.4% share in employment and 63.7% in added value, thus contributing significantly to the country's economic growth. Many SMEs were severely affected by the COVID-19 crisis, which was especially manifested in liquidity and employment issues [47]. Through various governmental measures, until mid-2021, around 1 billion Euros has been paid to support SMEs' business functions and save their employees' jobs [47]. These problems were just added to the existing challenges that SMEs need to cope with, while at the same time struggling to be competitive in the labor market [48]. Due to the limited financial resources, lots of SMEs find it difficult to keep pace with larger organizations, especially in terms of offering attractive compensational packages and benefits. This scarcity of organizational resources affects the application of best human resource management practices due to the high costs of their adoption [49]. The strategies for attracting talented employees can be particularly demanding because in transitional societies small companies are not perceived as the most desirable employers. In addition, job security and other benefits make large state-owned companies still more attractive as employers, compared to small companies that are mostly privately owned [48]. All the indicated reasons look for a more precise direction and understanding of the job elements that could be most appealing to employees of small and medium-sized enterprises in order to become "the employer of choice" [1].

3. Development of hypotheses

The research in this paper follows the goal of assessing the influence of employer brand dimensions on affective organizational commitment. The analysis of the literature has shown that research on this topic is still very fragmented since it either tests a part of the variables of employer branding [16] or explores different and isolated work elements and conditions that affect organizational commitment [50]. Several studies observed a relationship between employer branding as one, comprehensive construct, and organizational commitment, also as one, comprehensive construct [4, 14]. There is a need to define precisely which dimensions of employer branding affect different types of organizational commitment. This research focuses on affective organizational commitment, as the strongest type of organizational commitment. The hypotheses were formed based on previous research [11, 15, 16, 51], but they were placed in the context of small and medium-sized enterprises operating in a developing country. For a better understanding of the research background, the next sections will provide an overview of the employer brand elements and empirically investigate their influence on the development of affective organizational commitment.

3.1 Dimensions of employer brand and affective organizational commitment

In the last three decades, psychologists, scientists, and the academic and business community studying employer branding have been trying to define and group the factors that constitute a successful employer brand. A well-known approach in the literature is the one defined in 2005 by Berthon, Ewing, and Hah, who developed the

"Employer Attractiveness ("EmpAt") Scale" to test employer attractiveness, observing it through five dimensions: (1) application value (the possibility of applying the existing knowledge in different business situations), (2) interest value (exciting work environment, new work challenges, focus on creativity and innovation), (3) social value (importance of teamwork and collegial relationships), (4) economic value (above-average salary, job security, and other benefits), and (5) development value (the possibility to grow within the organization and build new skills) [20]. The "EmpAt" scale is built upon the definition set by Ambler and Barrow in 1996, where dimensions of interest and social value refer to psychological dimensions, economic value refers to economic benefits, and dimensions of development and application value refer to functional benefits [20].

The studies conducted so far on SMEs have shown that there is a connection between corporate social responsibility and employer branding, and the above has had an additional positive effect on the long-term retention of employees in the company [52]. It was also demonstrated that socially responsible behavior and internal marketing activities were positively related to job satisfaction and commitment to the organization [53]. Another study on SME employees showed that certain dimensions of employer brand, such as application value, economic value, and social value positively influence their decision to stay in the company within the next 6 months [54]. Likewise, a study on small and medium-sized enterprises operating in Switzerland proved that certain components of human resources management (organizational support, procedural justice, and organizational reputation) positively affect organizational commitment [55]. Following the indicated studies, this research aims to extend the understanding of the determinants of affective organizational commitment in small and medium-sized enterprises operating in a developing country, by observing them within the defined dimensions of employer branding.

If an organization fosters a harmonious relationship with its employees, they will, in turn, perform better at the workplace [56]. A well-developed and defined employer brand can influence the behavior of employees [57], and increase their satisfaction [51], work engagement [58, 59], and job involvement [56]. Also, building a successful employer brand can influence the development of trust in the organization and thus increase identification with the organization [60]. Employees who are committed to the organization show a higher level of motivation and stay longer in their organizations [56]. Considering the above, the following hypotheses were formed:

H1: The application value of the employer brand positively influences employees' affective organizational commitment.

H2: The interest value of the employer brand positively influences employees' affective organizational commitment.

H3: The social value of the employer brand positively influences employees' affective organizational commitment.

H4: The economic value of the employer brand positively influences employees' affective organizational commitment.

H5: The development value of the employer brand positively influences employees' affective organizational commitment.

4. Methodology

To test the proposed hypotheses, a survey questionnaire was chosen as a method in a quantitative approach. The questionnaire as a research method was chosen due to its numerous advantages, such as the simplicity of use and the broad availability of respondents [61]. It is also easy to create and distribute. The survey was conducted through an online questionnaire created in Google Forms, and it consisted of closed-ended questions. All the details of the research were presented to the respondents, at the same time informing them that their answers were anonymous to avoid bias development.

The questionnaire consisted of three parts. The first part comprised questions concerning the respondents' demographics (gender, age, education, position in the company, and the company's core activity). The second part of the questionnaire measured independent variables—employer brand dimensions, while in the third part, the respondents had to answer questions that measured the dependent variable—affective organizational commitment.

4.1 Sampling

The sampling frame was chosen from the financial portal Finiinfo, which provides financial and operational information for Croatian companies [62]. A random sample of small and medium-sized enterprises was chosen from the data, taking into account their representation in the activity sector [63]. Every company was double-checked to make sure it fits the definition of SME [64]. The questionnaire was distributed in September 2022, to around 900 e-mail addresses, which were provided by the database. Given that all questions in the questionnaire were marked as mandatory, 100% of all completed questionnaires were considered valid. It took around 3 weeks to collect the answers, which resulted in 104 completed questionnaires, representing a response rate of 11.5%. The demographics of the sample, presented in **Table 1**, reveal that out of 104 respondents, 59.6% are women and 40.4% are men. The majority of respondents are aged between 31 and 51 (72.1%) and have a higher education level (73.1%). The respondents hold different positions in the organization and are employed in companies of various business activities, ranging from service industries to production, construction, and trade indicating that the sample is representative of the observed population [63].

Construct	Characteristic	Frequency	Percentage
Gender	Women	62	59.6
	Men	42	40.4
Age	<25	1	0.9
	25–30	9	8.7
	31–40	44	42.3
	41–50	31	29.8
	51–60	14	13.5
	61+	5	4.8
Education	Elementary school	0	0
	High school	28	26.9
	Higher education	63	60.6
	Postgraduate studies	13	12.5

Construct	Characteristic	Frequency	Percentage
Position in the company	Owner	25	24
	Director	15	14.4
	Manager	29	27.9
	Administration	35	33.7
Industry	Production	19	18.3
	Construction	15	14.4
	Trade (retail/wholesale)	22	21.2
	Communication services	9	8.7
	Hospitality	4	3.8
	Transport	0	0
	Financial services	4	3.8
	Other service industries	31	29.8

Table 1.
Characteristics of the respondents.

4.2 Operationalization of the observed variables

All observed variables, dependent and independent ones, were measured with a five-point Likert-type scale, whereby employees of small and medium-sized enterprises had to express their agreement or disagreement with given statements ranging from 1 (strongly disagree) to 5 (strongly agree). Cronbach's alpha coefficients of all observed variables are above 0.7, which indicate a high internal consistency of the instrument [65]. As a dependent variable, *affective organizational commitment* was measured with items from Allen and Meyer's Organizational Commitment Scale [37]. It is the multiitem scale that measures three different types of organizational commitment: affective commitment, continuance commitment, and normative commitment. Since this study observes affective organizational commitment, 5 out of 8 questions from the indicated subscale were used in the questionnaire. Certain questions were changed from a negative form to a positive one, mostly to avoid later mistakes when coding the answers [66]. An example of the question included is: "*I would be very happy to spend the rest of my career with this organization*". Cronbach's alpha reliability coefficient is 0.935.

The dimensions of employer branding, as independent variables, were measured with the "Employee Attractiveness ("EmpAt") Scale" [20]. This multiitem scale consists of 25 items measuring employer attractiveness through 5 dimensions: application value, interest value, social value, economic value, and development value. Each of the dimensions was measured with four items. Examples of the questions included are: "*The organization both values and makes use of my creativity*", or "*How important is it for you to have a good relationship with your colleagues?*". Cronbach's alpha reliability coefficients of the scales are social value ($\alpha = 0.892$), interest value ($\alpha = 0.798$), economic value ($\alpha = 0.780$), application value ($\alpha = 0.731$), and development value ($\alpha = 0.785$).

5. Results

For the analysis and interpretation of the results and the testing of the proposed hypotheses, the method of partial least squares structural equation modeling (PLS-SEM) was applied, since it has already been used in a large number of similar studies [16, 35, 56, 67]. The method was performed using the SmartPLS 3 software [68]. There are several reasons for choosing PLS-SEM as an analysis method: it works effectively with small samples as well as with complex models and can be applied in a large number of different research situations [69]. The advantage of the PLS approach compared to multiple regression analysis is that the PLS approach considers the entire conceptual model and shows the effects of all related constructs that can be influenced by the regression [35]. Another advantage is that with the PLS-SEM method, there are no assumptions about data distribution [70].

5.1 Results of multivariate statistical analysis

The results obtained by the PLS-SEM method were processed in two phases: (1) the assessment of the measurement model and (2) the assessment of the structural model [71], which are described in detail in the next sections. Given that the conceptual model was determined to be of a reflective type, the research follows the predetermined steps set for its analysis [69].

5.1.1 Assessing the measurement model

The assessment of the measurement model includes the evaluation of reliability and validity [72]. Cronbach's alpha and the composite reliability (CR) are used in the reliability analysis, with acceptable values over 0.70 [71]. To evaluate the validity, the measures of indicator reliability, convergent validity, and discriminant validity are used. Indicator reliability is confirmed if the values of standardized outer loading are above 0.7, while the convergent validity is presented with average variance extracted (AVE), whose acceptable values are higher than 0.5. The results of indicator reliability and convergent validity are presented in **Table 2**.

Construct	Variable	Outer loadings	CA	CR	AVE
Social value	SOC1	0.903	0.892	0.921	0.744
	SOC2	0.788			
	SOC3 SOC4	0.856 0.898			
	ECON1	0.798			
Economic value	ECON2	0.691	0.780	0.851	0.590
	ECON3	0.862			
	ECON4	0.708			
Interest value	INT1 INT2	0.749 0.860	0.798	0.868	0.623
	INT3	0.692			
	INT4	0.845			

Construct	Variable	Outer loadings	CA	CR	AVE
Application value	APP1	0.744	0.731	0.828	0.547
	APP2	0.810			
	APP3	0.720			
	APP4	0.679			
	DEV1	0.894			
Development value	DEV2	0.894	0.785	0.824	0.533
	DEV3	0.610			
	DEV4	0.493			
	AOC1	0.888			
Affective org. Comm.	AOC2	0.876	0.935	0.951	0.794
	AOC3	0.897			
	AOC4	0.906			
	AOC5	0.888			

Notes: CA = Cronbach alpha, CR = composite reliability, AVE = average variance extracted.

Table 2.
Model evaluation measurements.

As visible from the table, the measures of Cronbach's alpha and composite reliability (CR) are within acceptable ranges, and so are the measures for average variance extracted. On the other hand, standardized outer loadings for several items (ECON2, INT3, APP4, DEV3, DEV4) are below their acceptable value of 0.7, so further analysis was conducted to see if the indicator deletion would have an impact on AVE and composite reliability [69]. As this was not the case, the loadings were retained in the model.

In order to assess discriminant validity, the Fornell-Larcker criterion and the heterotrait-monotrait (HTMT) ratio of correlations were observed [69]. **Table 3** shows the Fornell-Larcker criterion. From the table it is visible that the AVE of each latent variable is higher than the squared correlations of the other latent variables, so the criterion is satisfied as well [71].

Another measure of discriminant validity is the HTMT ratio, shown in **Table 4**. For the model to be valid, the interval of the HTMT data should not include the value of one for all the combinations of constructs, which is also present in this case [69].

	1	2	3	4	5	6
1. AOC	0.891					
2. Social value	0.215	0.863				
3. Economic value	0.128	0.646	0.768			
4. Interest value	0.594	0.278	0.221	0.789		
5. Application value	0.445	0.414	0.548	0.317	0.740	
6. Development value	0.250	0.535	0.695	0.223	0.566	0.744

Note: AOC = affective organizational commitment.

Table 3.
Discriminant validity: Fornell–Larcker criterion.

	1	2	3	4	5	6
1. AOC						
2. Social value	0.206					
3. Economic value	0.131	0.791				
4. Interest value	0.671	0.308	0.261			
5. Application value	0.511	0.537	0.758	0.382		
6. Development value	0.214	0.648	0.943	0.247	0.737	

Note: AOC = affective organizational commitment.

Table 4.
Discriminant validity: HTMT ratio.

The indicated results demonstrate that model is appropriate for further analysis of the structural model assessment and hypothesis testing.

5.1.2 Assessing the structural model

Before analyzing the structural model, the variance inflation factor (VIF) was calculated in order to check for multicollinearity issues [72]. **Table 5** reports such results, which are all within acceptable values of below 5.

The absence of multicollinearity allows the valuation of the structural model, which was derived from the bootstrapping method with 5000 samples [69]. The results are presented in **Table 6**, which also indicates the outcomes of hypothesis testing.

The table shows that the application value positively influences affective organizational commitment ($\beta = 0.361$; $p < 0.05$), which confirms hypothesis H1. The interest value also has a positive influence on affective organizational commitment ($\beta = 0.504$; $p < 0.01$), thus confirming the second hypothesis. Other independent variables did not show a statistically significant or positive influence on affective organizational commitment, so hypotheses H3, H4, and H5 cannot be confirmed.

The coefficient of determination, R^2, is used as a measure of the predictive accuracy of the model [69]. The R^2 for affective organizational commitment in this study is 0.462, which can be interpreted as moderate [71], and reveals that 46.2% of the variation in developing affective organizational commitment occurred under the influence of employer branding dimensions [73]. Additionally, predictive validity was calculated through a cross-validated redundancy measure, which is based on Stone-

Construct	Affective organizational commitment
Affective org. Commitment	
Social value	1.812
Economic value	2.547
Interest value	1.147
Application value	1.661
Development value	2.176

Table 5.
Multicollinearity—Variance inflation factor (VIF).

		Structural relations	Path Coef.	SD	t-value	p-value	Result
H1	Application	- > AOC	0.361**	0.123	2.942	0.003	**Confirmed**
H2	Interest	- > AOC	0.504***	0.100	5.044	0.000	**Confirmed**
H3	Social	- > AOC	0.058	0.115	0.503	0.615	Not confirmed
H4	Economic	- > AOC	−0.292	0.152	1.923	0.055	Not confirmed
H5	Development	- > AOC	0.105	0.133	0.788	0.431	Not confirmed

Note: AOC = affective organizational commitment.
$^{*}p < 0.10$.
$^{**}p < 0.05$.
$^{***}p < 0.01$.

Table 6.
Hypothesis testing.

Geisser's Q^2 value [70]. The Q^2 value for affective organizational commitment is $Q^2 = 0.353$, which is interpreted as acceptable predictive relevance, meaning that the model has predictive validity for the endogenous construct [71]. The effect size coefficient is obtained by calculating Cohen's f^2 [72]. The effect size is interpreted according to reference values, where 0.02 represents a small, 0.15 is a medium, and 0.35 is a large effect of an individual exogenous construct on an endogenous construct [74]. From the above, it follows that interest value has a large effect on affective organizational commitment ($f^2 = 0.412$), application value has a medium effect on affective organizational commitment ($f^2 = 0.146$), while other values have a weak effect on affective organizational commitment (f^2 economic value = 0.062, f^2 development value = 0.009, f^2 social value = 0.003).

6. Discussion

The main objective of this research was to measure and understand the influence of employer brand dimensions on affective organizational commitment. To achieve the indicated goal, the research was placed within the framework of already established studies in the domain of employer branding, by testing five elements of the employer brand to identify the factors that are significant for the development of affective organizational commitment, as the strongest type of organizational commitment.

The study showed that the application value ($\beta = 0.361$; $p = 0.003 < 0.05$) has a positive and significant effect on the affective organizational commitment among employees of Croatian small and medium-sized enterprises, thus confirming hypothesis H1. This means that employees develop an emotional connection and identification with the organization when the company provides the opportunity to apply the previously gained knowledge, so they understand that the effort invested in training and education pays off through activities at the workplace. Given that no research was found that measured the impact of the same independent variable, the results can be linked to the research conducted on employees of medium-sized and large public and private organizations in Portugal, which showed that career development and communication in the organization positively affect the AOC [11]. Another study on IT employees in India proved a significant relationship between employer branding (as a comprehensive construct) and organizational commitment (also as a comprehensive construct) [75]. Similarly, a study conducted on employees of two banks in India, showed that all five dimensions of employer brand have a positive influence on organizational commitment, with the mediating influence of employee engagement [56]. The results indicate that it is important for SME employees to know that their knowledge and skills are used in a valuable way that contributes to the success of the company. They want to learn and grow at their workplaces but also encourage the growth of their colleagues. The importance of information sharing at all organizational levels indicates the significance of an inclusive, open environment where no employee is left behind. By sharing knowledge and ideas, employees together provide valuable products or services to their customers while giving back to their community. They want to make a difference. The importance of a humanitarian work environment was also demonstrated in a study on 347 executives in India whose results indicated corporate social responsibility influenced the perception of the entire employer brand [76]. On the other hand, research on small and medium-sized enterprises in Switzerland showed that employee skills management does not affect the development of affective organizational commitment [55]. The lack of research on application value, and the varying results in the published literature ask for additional studies in order to gain better insights into the effect of application value on AOC. The differences between developing and developed countries also demonstrate that employees in developing countries are in need of further training to upgrade their skills to be competitive in the labor market, which could be one of the explanations for why this element of employer branding is valuable for SME employees in Croatia.

This research has also shown that interest value ($\beta = 0.504$; $p = 0.000 < 0.01$) has a positive and significant effect on the affective organizational commitment of employees in SMEs, meaning that hypothesis H2 was also supported. In other words, when a company provides an exciting work atmosphere in which employees are presented with numerous work challenges where they can use their creativity, they will develop a psychological and emotional connection with that company. The results can be connected with research conducted on managers of multinational companies in Belgium, which showed that the lived employment experience, which is manifested by a sense of personal achievement obtained through challenging and creative tasks, is positively related to the development of AOC [75]. This is important for SMEs since they are known for their innovativeness and creativity, which often influences their success [77]. Knowing that an organization fosters out-of-the-box thinking and encourages employees' originality can do a great deal for the development of AOC and long-term connection to the organization. This was also proven in a study conducted on small and medium-sized ICT enterprises in China, which showed that AOC mediated the influence of interpersonal trust on employee innovation. The mentioned study also tested gender differences and showed that the direct impact of interpersonal trust on innovative behavior was significantly larger for women, however for men, the affective organizational commitment increased their knowledge-sharing intentions [78].

Future studies are also encouraged to test the gender differences to understand if there are differences between the man and women in their perception of EB dimension importance and to see whether these differences have an effect on affective organizational commitment. The results of H1 and H2 hypothesis testing point to the fact that employees look for interesting and challenging organizational culture in which their work is meaningful and appreciated. Through their skills, open communication, and knowledge sharing, they can contribute to the success of their company, while at the same time working in an environment that takes care of its customers and society.

Although the literature points out that economic value, in terms of salaries, compensation, bonuses, and other rewards, positively affects the development of organizational commitment [4, 11], in this case, it turned out to be exactly the opposite; that is, it has a negative impact on affective organizational commitment ($\beta = -0.292$; $p = 0.055 < 0.10$), thus rejecting hypothesis H4. It can be concluded that above-average compensation packages or above-average salaries for SME employees do not play a significant role in the development of emotional attachment to the organization. This is important for small and medium-sized enterprises that lack financial resources and cannot compete with large organizations in offering stimulating compensation packages. Results could be partially compared to the study conducted on the employees working in government agencies in UAE, which showed that salary was not significantly related to affective organizational commitment [79]. On the contrary, a study conducted on the universities' academic and administration staff in Central and Eastern Europe, showed that rewards and salaries significantly influence employees' attitudes related to the increase in organizational performance, and this effect was mediated by affective organizational commitment, meaning that economic benefits have a direct effect on AOC, which in turn also influences the performance of employees [80]. Another study conducted on SME employees in Pakistan showed that salary package increases the organizational commitment of employees [81]. Future studies on SMEs in the European context are encouraged, to get a precise answer on the influence of economic value on the AOC, due to the large differences in cultural, economic, political, and other environmental factors between the mentioned countries, and because people in particular Eastern, Asian, economies tend to place greater importance on extrinsic factors due to the lower living standards [82].

Social ($\beta = 0.058$; $p = 0.615 < 0.10$) and development values ($\beta = 0.105$; $p = 0.431 < 0.10$) in this study did not show a significant impact on affective organizational commitment, meaning that hypotheses H3 and H5 could not be supported. However, several studies have shown that they play a large role in building the overall commitment of employees [4, 11, 15, 56], therefore they should not be neglected when creating a positive and stimulating work environment. A partial comparison of the results could be found in a study on Chinese SMEs that discovered that co-worker support did not influence organizational commitment [82]. On the contrary, a study conducted on U.S. Army personnel demonstrated that interpersonal conflict was negatively related to affective organizational commitment, while support from the supervisors positively influenced affective organizational commitment [83]. Another research conducted on employees of government districts showed that social networks among employees predict affective organizational commitment [84]. In spite of the results of this study on Croatian SMEs, it is still recommended to keep a friendly atmosphere within the company and encourage positive bonds and collegial support among co-workers, since many studies showed it influenced organizational commitment as a whole, making employees feel as part of a bigger family and contributing to their sense of belonging [35]. The same applies to the development value as some studies have shown that support practices that influence the self-esteem, fulfillment, and development of employees help in achieving AOC [55]. The above can result in higher productivity, loyalty, and better performance of employees [4]. The company can then affirm itself as a good and desirable employer, allowing its employees to build their identity as the important and valuable human capital of the organization.

6.1 Research limitations and recommendations for future studies

The main limitation of the study is the sample size. A small percentage of completed questionnaires indicates insufficient motivation of employees of small and medium-sized enterprises to participate in the research. The recommendation for future studies goes in the direction of collecting a larger number of responses. Also, the questionnaire as a data collection method has certain weaknesses that are most often manifested in misunderstanding the questions or not reading the statements carefully [85]. The study is cross-sectional in nature, thus providing only a snapshot of the employee's current opinions and beliefs at the moment they were fulfilling the questionnaire. Future studies should observe the longitudinal impact of the EB dimension on affective organizational commitment to gain better and more accurate insights.

Another limitation relates to the number of dimensions through which the employer brand was observed. Since some authors used a larger number of employer brand dimensions in their research [11, 86], there is a possibility that the results would be different if more elements were included. Future studies are encouraged to include more EB dimensions to get a comprehensive picture of all the elements that influence affective organizational commitment in SMEs in developing countries. This research measured the influence of the employer brand on affective organizational commitment as one of the three types of organizational commitment. It would be advisable to include normative and continuance commitment in future studies in order to get a complete picture of the influence of the employer branding dimensions on the organizational commitment of small and medium-sized enterprises in the Republic of Croatia, while additional research could include a larger number of moderating and mediating variables, such as organizational support, internal communication, work-life balance, etc.

7. Conclusion

This research aimed to investigate the influence of employer branding dimensions on the affective organizational commitment of employees working in small and medium-sized enterprises operating in Croatia. Previous research that studied the indicated connection is scarce and fragmented, taking into consideration just a few elements of the employer brand, or the organizational commitment as a comprehensive construct, not observing its individual dimensions. In order to fill the identified research gap, the model was developed to test the link between 5 employer brand dimensions and affective organizational commitment. The results proved that for SME employees two dimensions have a significant influence: application value and interest value.

The development of affective organizational commitment is one of the most valuable feelings that an employer can gain from their workers because it translates into employee loyalty, increased motivation, and a desire to stay in the long run within the company. This is important for small and medium-sized enterprises that display informal organizational structure and approach to human resources management, and due to the lack of financial resources cannot compete with large organizations in offering stimulating compensation packages. The challenges that SMEs face are even bigger when operating in developing countries. Considering the turbulent and changing environment in which companies today operate, employees need to feel secure in their organizations in order to give their best and outperform their competition. Employer branding serves as an important link that connects human resources, internal communications, and marketing, therefore creating a synergy through which a unified message is sent to all the stakeholders while promoting an organization as a desirable place to work. Important theoretical and practical contributions arise from this study and are elaborated on in detail in the following section.

7.1 Theoretical and practical contributions

Several contributions emerge from the research. On the theoretical side, this is one of the first studies that aims to confirm the connection between the dimensions of employer brand and affective organizational commitment, at the same time placing the constructs in the context of small and medium-sized enterprises operating in Croatia, as a developing country. This research has shown that in small and medium-sized enterprises, two dimensions of the employer's brand are extremely important for the development of AOC: application value and interest value. The findings additionally support the theoretical basis of the study grounded on the resource-based view, social exchange theory, and psychological contract theory. The results of the study demonstrate that when an organization fosters an environment that enables employees to learn and express themselves in a creative way, at the same time feeling useful to the company and other stakeholders, psychological bonds will develop between them and their company. This research additionally improves the understanding of the employer branding concept from the standpoint of small and medium-sized enterprises and allows for a better understanding of which dimensions are most important to their employees. Another theoretical contribution that builds on the previous studies is in confirming that HR procedures and policies are needed at the organizational level, as to ensure the high satisfaction and loyalty of employees, and that includes SMEs as well, which often lack such practices [55].

On the practical side, the research can help human resources managers and key people in small and medium-sized enterprises by pointing out those elements that are important in creating a stimulating work environment in which employees want to stay in the long term. By understanding the concept of employer branding and the influence of its dimensions on affective organizational commitment, key people in SMEs can effectively manage talent within their organizations, despite the many constraints they face. This can also result in the development of a positive reputation and public image as a desirable employer. The research has demonstrated that by focusing on intangible benefits, primarily by allowing employees to apply their knowledge in different business situations and offering exciting, challenging, and creative work environments, SMEs can be competitive in the labor market and create positive employer brands. Knowing what employees look for in an organization is the key to fulfilling their needs, which could result in developing strong affective organizational commitment. Companies need to be aware that it is extremely important to put employees in the first place and give them a reason to stay within the organization—before someone else does.

Appendix A: Assessment of the measurement model

Table A.1. Outer loadings

	Aff. comm.	SOC.	ECON	INT	APP	DEV
AF_COMM1	0,888					
AF_COMM2	0,876					
AF_COMM3	0,897					
AF_COMM4	0,906					
AF_COMM5	0,888					
SOC1		0,903				
SOC2		0,788				
SOC3		0,856				
SOC4		0,898				
ECON1			0,798			
ECON2			0,691			
ECON3			0,862			
ECON4			0,708			
INT1				0,749		
INT2				0,860		
INT3				0,692		
INT4				0,845		
APP1					0,744	
APP2					0,810	
APP3					0,720	
APP4					0,679	
DEV1						0,894
DEV2						0,894
DEV3						0,610
DEV4						0,493

Table A.2. Construct reliability and validity

	Cronbach's Alpha	rho_A	Composite reliability	Average variance extracted
Aff. comm.	0,935	0,936	0,951	0,794
Social	0,892	0,968	0,921	0,744
Economic	0,780	0,844	0,851	0,590

	Cronbach's Alpha	rho_A	Composite reliability	Average variance extracted
Interest	0,798	0,822	0,868	0,623
Application	0,731	0,756	0,828	0,547
Development	0,785	0,807	0,824	0,553

Table A.3. Discriminant validity—Fornell–Larcker criterion

	AFF.COM	SOC	ECON	INT	APP	DEV
Aff. comm.	0,891					
Social	0,215	0,863				
Economic	0,128	0,646	0,768			
Interest	0,594	0,278	0,221	0,789		
Application	0,445	0,414	0,548	0,317	0,740	
Development	0,250	0,535	0,695	0,223	0,566	0,744

Table A.4. Discriminant validity—heterotrait-monotrait ratio (HTMT)

	AFF. COMM	SOC	ECON	INT	APP	DEV
Aff. comm.						
Social	0,206					
Economic	0,131	0,791				
Interest	0,671	0,308	0,261			
Application	0,511	0,537	0,758	0,382		
Development	0,214	0,648	0,943	0,247	0,737	

Appendix B: Assessment of the structural model

Table B.1. VIF values

	Affective Commitment
AFFECTIVE COMMITMENT	
SOCIAL	1812
ECONOMIC	2547
INTEREST	1147
APPLICATION	1661
DEVELOPMENT	2176

Table B.2. Bootstrapping results – hypothesis testing

	Original Sample	Mean	St. Dev	T Stat.	P Value
SOCIAL - > AFF. COM.	0,058	0,032	0,115	0,503	0,615
ECONOMIC- > AFF. COM.	-0,292	-0,203	0,152	1923	0,055
INTEREST - > AFF. COM.	0,504	0,497	0,100	5044	0,000
APPLICATION - > AFF. COM.	0,361	0,350	0,123	2942	0,003
DEVELOPMENT - > AFF. COM.	0,105	0,050	0,133	0,788	0,431

Table B.3. Quality Criteria – R square

	Original Sample (O)	Sample Mean	Standard Deviation	T Stat	P Value
AFFECTIVE COMMITMENT	0,462	0,501	0,083	5536	0,000

Table B.4. Quality Criteria – Q value (Construct Crossvalidated Redundancy)

	SSO	SSE	Q^2 (=1-SSE/SSO)
AFFECTIVE COMMITMENT	520,000	336,476	0,353
SOCIAL	416,000	416,000	
ECONOMIC	416,000	416,000	
INTEREST	416,000	416,000	
APPLICATION	416,000	416,000	
DEVELOPMENT	416,000	416,000	

Table B.5. Quality Criteria – f square

	Original Sample	Mean	St. Dev	T Stats	P Values
SOCIAL - > AFF. COMM	0,003	0,017	0,027	0,126	0,900
ECONOMIC > AFF. COMM	0,062	0,051	0,054	1160	0,246
INTERES - > AFF. COMM	0,412	0,456	0,238	1733	0,083
APPLICATION - > AFF. COMM	0,146	0,167	0,114	1286	0,198
DEVELOPMENT - > AFF. COMM	0,009	0,020	0,026	0,367	0,714

Author details

Matea Cvjetković[1] and Tihana Babić[2]*

1 University North, Koprivnica, Croatia

2 Algebra University College, Zagreb, Croatia

*Address all correspondence to: tihana.babic@algebra.hr

References

[1] Poloski Vokic N, Mostarac V. Is there a need for a change in employer branding practices? – A shift in employer attractiveness attributes/dimensions during the last decade. EFZG working paper series. 2019;**5**:1-16

[2] Wiblen S, Marler JH. Digitalised talent management and automated talent decisions: The implications for HR professionals. The International Journal of Human Resource Management. 2021; **32**:2592-2621

[3] Manpower Group. Employment Outlook Survey Q3. Global Results [Internet]. 2021. Available from: https://go.manpowergroup.com/talent-shortage [Accessed: June 2, 2022]

[4] Rana G, Sharma R, Singh SP, Jain V. Impact of employer branding on job engagement and organizational commitment in Indian IT sector. International Journal of Risk and Contingency Management (IJRCM). 2019;**8**:1-17

[5] Theurer CP, Tumasjan A, Welpe IM, Lievens F. Employer branding: A brand equity-based literature review and research agenda. International Journal of Management Reviews. 2016;**20**:155-179. DOI: 10.1111/ijmr.12121

[6] Samoliuk N, Bilan Y, Mishchuk H, Mishchuk V. Employer brand: Key values influencing the intention to join a company, management & marketing. Challenges for the Knowledge Society. 2022;**17**:61-72

[7] Hadi NU, Ahmed S. Role of employer branding dimensions on employee retention: Evidence from educational sector. Administrative Sciences. 2018;**8**: 44. DOI: 10.3390/admsci8030044

[8] Aboul-Ela GMBE. Employer branding: What constitutes an employer of choice? Journal of Business and Retail Management Research. 2016;**1**:154-166

[9] Rana G, Sharma R. Assessing impact of employer branding on job engagement: A study of banking sector. Emerging Economy Studies. 2019;**5**:7-21. DOI: 10.1177/2394901519825543

[10] Anand A, Vohra V. The impact of organisation work environment on job satisfaction, affective organizational commitment, work-family conflict and intention to leave: A study of SMEs in India. International Journal of Entrepreneurship and Small Business. 2020;**4**:173-196. DOI: 10.1504/ijesb.2020.109931

[11] Alves P, Santos V, Reis I, Martinho F, Martinho D, Correia Sampaio M, et al. Strategic talent management: The impact of employer branding on employees' affective organizational commitment. Sustainability. 2020;**12**:9993

[12] Mercurio ZA. Affective organizational commitment as a Core essence of organizational commitment. Human Resource Development Review. 2015;**14**:389-414. DOI: 10.1177/1534484315603612

[13] Vaijayanthi P, Shreenivasan KA, Roy R. Employer branding as an antecedent to organisation commitment-an empirical study of manufacturing and service sector units. In: IEEE Colloquium on Humanities, Science and Engineering (CHUSER 2011); 5–6 December 2011; Penang. Malesia. Penang, Malayasia: IEEE; 2011. pp. 969-974

[14] Sharma R, Jain V, Singh PS. The impact of employer branding on

organizational commitment in Indian IT sector. IOSR Journal of Business and Management. 2018;**20**:49-54

[15] Sharma R, Rana G, Jain V, Sharma SR. Employer branding: Strategy for improving organizational commitment in Indian IT sector. Pal Arch's Journal of Archaeology of Egypt/ Egyptology. 2020;**17**:7283-7293

[16] Tanwar K. The effect of employer brand dimensions on organisational commitment: Evidence from Indian IT industry. Asia-Pacific Journal of Management Research and Innovation. 2016;**12**:282-290

[17] Tajpour M, Salamzadeh A, Hosseini E. Job satisfaction in IT department of Mellat Bank: Does employer brand matter. IPSI BgD Transactions on Internet Research. 2021; **17**:15-21

[18] Tansky JW, Heneman R. Guest editor's note: Introduction to the special issue on human resource management in SMEs: A call for more research. Human Resource Management. 2003;**42**:299

[19] Monteiro B, Santos V, Reis I, Sampaio MC, Sousa B, Martinho F, et al. Employer branding applied to SMEs: A pioneering model proposal for attracting and retaining talent. Information. 2020; **11**:574

[20] Berthon P, Ewing M, Hah L. Captivating company: Dimensions of attractiveness in employer branding. International Journal of Advertising. 2005;**24**:151-172. DOI: 10.1080/ 02650487.2005.11072912

[21] The World Bank. Small and Medium Enterprises (SMEs) Finance [Internet]. Available from: https://www.worldbank. org/en/topic/smefinance [Accessed: November 5, 2022]

[22] App S, Büttgen M. Lasting footprints of the employer brand: Can sustainable HRM lead to brand commitment? Employee Relations. 2016;**38**:703-723. DOI: 10.1108/er-06-2015-0122

[23] Dey T, Kumar A, Kumar YLN. A new look at the antecedents and consequences of organizational commitment: A conceptual study. International Journal of Humanities and Social Sciences. 2014;**4**:281-287

[24] Bulut C, Culha O. The effects of organizational training on organizational commitment. International Journal of Training and Development. 2010;**14**: 309-322. DOI: 10.1111/ j.1468-2419.2010.00360.x

[25] Collins CJ. Expanding the resource based view model of strategic human resource management. The International Journal of Human Resource Management. 2021;**32**:331-358. DOI: 10.1080/09585192.2019.1711442

[26] Liu X, Deng J. Development of organizational commitment based on the social exchange theory. In: Proceeding of the IEEE International Conference on Management and Service Science. 12–14 August 2011; Wuhan, China: IEEE; 2011

[27] Herrera J, De Las H-RC. The organizational commitment in the company and its relationship with the psychological contract. Frontiers in Psychology. 2011;**11**:609211

[28] Ruchika PA. Untapped relationship between employer branding, anticipatory psychological contract and intent to join. Global Business Review. 2019;**20**:194-213

[29] Backhaus K, Tikoo S. Conceptualizing and researching employer branding. Career Development International. 2004;**9**:501-517

[30] Tkalac VA. The impact of employee engagement, organisational support and employer branding on internal communication satisfaction. Public Relations Review. 2021;**47**:102009. DOI: 10.1016/j.pubrev.2021.102009

[31] Dabirian A, Kietzmann J, Diba H. A great place to work!? Understanding crowdsourced employer branding. Journal of Brand Management. 2017;**60**: 197-205

[32] Ivancevic S, Vlastelica T. Effective content for digital employer branding. CroDiM. 2022;**5**:77-88

[33] Küpper DM, Klein K, Völckner F. Gamifying employer branding: An integrating framework and research propositions for a new HRM approach in the digitized economy. Human Resource Management Review. 2021;**31**:100686. DOI: 10.1016/j.hrmr.2019.04.002

[34] Kok J, Uhlaner L. Organization context and human resource management in the small firm. Small Business Economics. 2001;**17**:273-291

[35] Valaei N, Rezaei S. Job satisfaction and organizational commitment. Management Research Review. 2016;**39**: 1663-1694. DOI: 10.1108/mrr-09-2015-0216

[36] Barrow S, Mosley R. The Employer Brand. Bringing the Best of Brand Management to People at Work. West Sussex, England: John Wiley & Sons Ltd; 2005 232p

[37] Allen NJ, Meyer JP. The measurement and antecedents of affective, continuance and normative commitment to the organization. Journal of Occupational Psychology. 1990;**63**:1-18

[38] Agostini L, Nosella A, Venturini K. Toward increasing affective organizational commitment in SME strategic networks. Business Process Management Journal. 2019;**25**: 1822-1840. DOI: 10.1108/bpmj-02-2018-0035

[39] Tvarog Malvic S, Sindik J, Sarac J. Percipirana organizacijska pravednost kao determinanta organizacijske odanosti. Ekonomska misao i praksa. 2014;**1**:43-62

[40] Low MP, Ong SF, Tan PM. Positioning ethics and social responsibility as a strategic tool in employees' affective organizational commitment. Annals in Social Responsibility. 2017;**3**:2-22. DOI: 10.1108/asr-12-2016-0013

[41] Ammari Alkurdi B, Alshurideh A, Alrowwad A. Investigating the impact of communication satisfaction on organizational commitment: A practical approach to increase employees' loyalty. International Journal of Marketing Studies. 2017;**9**:113-133

[42] Curado C, Vieira S. Trust, knowledge sharing and organizational commitment in SMEs. Personnel Review. 2019;**48**:1449-1468. DOI: 10.1108/pr-03-2018-0094

[43] Wang Y. What are the biggest obstacles to growth of SMEs in developing countries?–an empirical evidence from an enterprise survey. Borsa Istanbul Review. 2016;**16**:167-176

[44] Poloski VN. Competitiveness and sustainability of HRM activities in Croatia – CRANET survey results [conference presentation]. In: Via Futuri 2014 International Conference on Sustainability, Competitiveness Urban and Regional Development – On the Crossroads of Theory and Empirical Research; 27–28 November 2014; Pécs,

Hungary: EFZG working paper series; 2015. pp. 1-12

[45] Skjolstrup KA. Human Resource Development Country Analysis for Croatia, ETF Working Paper. European Training Foundation; 2008. p. 36

[46] Valentinova Misheva G. Croatia. National Development Strategy 2030 [Internet]. 2022. Available from: https://digital-skills-jobs.europa.eu/en/actions/national-initiatives/national-strategies/croatia-national-development-strategy-2030 [Accessed: November 12, 2022]

[47] European Commission. 2021 SME Country Fact Sheet – Croatia [Internet]. 2022. Available from: https://ec.europa.eu/docsroom/documents/46069/attachments/1/translations/en/renditions/pdf [Accessed: November 12, 2022]

[48] Nacinovic Braje I, Bosnic L. Nagradivanje zaposlenika u malim poduzecima: stanje i uloga iz perspektive menadzera. Zbornik radova Ekonomskog fakulteta Sveucilista u Mostaru. 2017;**23**:44-66

[49] Newman AN, Sheikh AZ. Determinants of best HR practices in Chinese SMEs. Journal of Small Business and Enterprise Development. 2014; **21**(3):414-430

[50] Moreira A, Sousa MJ, Cesário F. Competencies development: The role of organizational commitment and the perception of employability. Social Sciences. 2022;**11**:125

[51] Ognjanovic J, Slavkovic M. Impact of employer brand on Employees'satisfaction In Serbian hotel enterprises. Thematic Proceedings: Tourism International Scientific Conference Vrnjačka Banja (TISC). 2019;**4**(1):254-271 Vrnjačka Banja-TISC; 30 May – 1 June 2009; Vrnjacka Banja. Serbia; 2019. p. 254-27

[52] Okolocha CB. Influence of employee-focused corporate social responsibility and employer brand on turnover intention. European Journal of Business and Management. 2020;**12**: 55-61

[53] Shabnam S, Sarker AR. Impact of CSR and internal marketing on employee job satisfaction and Organisational commitment: A case study from export-oriented SMEs in Bangladesh. World Journal of Social Sciences. 2012;**2**:24-36

[54] Rozsa Z, Formánek I, Maňák R. Determining the factors of the employees' intention to stay or leave in the Slovak's SMEs. International Journal of Entrepreneurial Knowledge. 2019;**72**: 63-72. DOI: 10.12345-0011

[55] Giauque D, Resenterra F, Siggen M. The relationship between HRM practices and organizational commitment of knowledge workers. Facts obtained from Swiss SMEs. Human Resource Development International. 2010;**13**: 185-205. DOI: 10.1080/13678861003703716

[56] Yousf A, Khurshid S. Impact of employer branding on employee commitment: Employee engagement as a mediator. Vision: The Journal of Business Perspective. 2021:1-12. DOI: 10.1177/09722629211013608

[57] Angelopoulou M. Employer Branding Contextualised -a Qualitative Study in Greece during the Financial Crisis [Thesis]. Gothenburg, Sweden: University of Gothenburg; 2015

[58] Burawat P. The relationships among perceived employer branding, employee engagement and employee expectation

in service industry. International Business Management. 2015;**9**:554-559

[59] Chawla P. Impact of employer branding on employee engagement in business process outsourcing (BPO) sector in India: Mediating effect of person–organization fit. Industrial and Commercial Training. 2020;**52**: 35-49. DOI: 10.1108/ICT-06-2019-0063

[60] Kashyap V, Chaudhary R. Linking employer brand image and work engagement: Modelling organizational identification and trust in organization as mediators. South Asian Journal of Human Resources Management. 2019;**6**: 177-201

[61] Etikan I, Musa SA, Alkassim RS. Comparison of convenience sampling and purposive sampling. American Journal of Theoretical and Applied Statistics. 2016;**5**:1-4

[62] El koncept d.o.o. Finiinfo [Internet]. 2022. Available from: https://www.fininfo.hr/ [Accessed: August 22, 2022]

[63] Croatian Bureau of Statistics. Structural business indicators of enterprises, 2019 [Internet]. 2021. Available from: https://podaci.dzs.hr/2021/en/11125 [Accessed: August 22, 2022]

[64] Eurostat. Small and medium-sized enterprises (SMEs) [Internet]. Available from: https://ec.europa.eu/eurostat/web/structural-business-statistics/information-on-data/small-and-medium-sized-enterprises [Accessed: August 22, 2022]

[65] Taber KS. The use of Cronbach's alpha when developing and reporting research instruments in science education. Research in Science Education. 2018;**48**:1273-1296

[66] Sauro J, Lewis JR. When designing usability questionnaires, does it hurt to be positive? In: Proceedings of the 2011 Annual Conference on Human Factors in Computing Systems (CHI'11); 7–12 May 2011; Vancouver, Canada: ACM; 2011. pp. 1-9

[67] Pavlovic G, Zdravkovic S. The influence of employer brand on employees loyalty–the moderator effect of employees satisfaction. Balkans Journal of Emerging Trends in Social Sciences. 2019;**2**:140-149

[68] Ringle CM, Wende S, Becker JM. Smart PLS 3. Boenningstedt: SmartPLS [Internet]. 2022. Available from: https://www.smartpls.com

[69] Hair JF, Hult GTM, Ringle CM, Sarstedt M. A Primer on Partial Least Squares Structural Equation Modeling (PLS-SEM). 2nd ed. Thousand Oaks, California: SAGE Publications Ltd; 2017 350p

[70] Komsic J. Mjerenje reputacije turisticke destinacije na drustvenim medijima i zadovoljstva turista [thesis]. Opatija: University of Rijeka, The Faculty of Tourism and Hospitality Management; 2018

[71] Henseler J, Ringle CM, Sarstedt M. Using partial least squares path modeling in advertising research: Basic concepts and recent issues. In: Shintaro O, editor. Handbook of Research on International Advertising. Cheltenham, UK: Edward Elgar Publishing; 2012. pp. 252-276

[72] Hair JFJ, Sarstedt M, Hopkins L, Kuppelwieser V. Partial least squares structural equation modeling (PLS-SEM). European Business Review. 2014;**26**: 106-121. DOI: 10.1108/ebr-10-2013-0128

[73] Qalati SA, Yuan LW, Khan MAS, Anwar F. A mediated model on the

adoption of social media and SMEs' performance in developing countries. Technology in Society. 2021;**64**:101513

[74] Cohen J. A power primer. Psychological Bulletin. 1992;**112**:155-159

[75] Hanin D, Stinglhamber F, Delobbe N. The impact of employer branding on employees: The role of employment offering in the prediction of their affective organizational commitment. Psychologica Belgica. 2013;**53**:57-83

[76] Biswas M, Suar D. Antecedents and consequences of employer branding. Journal of Business Ethics. 2014;**136**: 57-72

[77] Zastempowski M, Cyfert S. Social responsibility of SMEs from the perspective of their innovativeness: Evidence from Poland. Journal of Cleaner Production. 2021;**317**:128400

[78] Yuan H, Ma D. Gender differences in the relationship between interpersonal trust and innovative behavior: The mediating effects of affective organizational commitment and knowledge-sharing. Behavioral Sciences. 2022;**12**:145

[79] Abdulla MH, Shaw JD. Personal factors and organizational commitment: Main and interactive effects in the United Arab Emirates. Journal of Managerial Issues. 1999;**11**:77-93

[80] Hadziahmetovic N, Dinç MS. The mediating role of affective commitment in the organizational rewards–organizational performance relationship. International Journal of Human Resource Studies. 2017;**7**:105-130

[81] Akhtar J. Impact of work environment, salary package and Employees' perception on organizational commitment: A study of Small & Medium Enterprises (SMEs) of Pakistan. International Journal of Academic Research in Business and Social Sciences. 2014;**4**:147-165

[82] Newman A, Sheikh AZ. Organizational commitment in Chinese small- and medium-sized enterprises: The role of extrinsic, intrinsic and social rewards. The International Journal of Human Resource Management. 2012;**23**: 349-367

[83] Thomas J, Bliese PD, Jex SM. Interpersonal conflict and organizational commitment: Examining two levels of supervisory support as multilevel moderators 1. Journal of Applied Social Psychology. 2005;**35**:2375-2398

[84] Lee J, Kim S. Exploring the role of social networks in affective organizational commitment: Network centrality, strength of ties, and structural holes. The American Review of Public Administration. 2010;**41**:205-223

[85] Rowley J. Designing and using research questionnaires. Management Research Review. 2014;**37**:308-330. DOI: 10.1108/mrr-02-2013-0027

[86] Alnıaçık E, Alnıaçık Ü. Identifying dimensions of attractiveness in employer branding: Effects of age, gender, and current employment status. Procedia-Social and Behavioral Sciences. 2012;**58**: 1336-1343